YOUR PERSONAL
HOROSCOPE
2025

LARS MELLIS

YOUR PERSONAL HOROSCOPE 2025

Month-by-month
forecast for every sign

Thorsons

Thorsons
An imprint of HarperCollins*Publishers*
1 London Bridge Street
London SE1 9GF

www.harpercollins.co.uk

HarperCollins*Publishers*
Macken House, 39/40 Mayor Street Upper
Dublin 1, D01 C9W8, Ireland

First published by Thorsons 2024

24 25 26 27 28 LBC 7 6 5 4 3

info@stardatamedia.com

Star ★ Data asserts the moral right to be
identified as the author of this work

A catalogue record of this book is
available from the British Library

ISBN 978-0-00-866751-1

Printed and bound in the United States

The author is grateful to the people of STAR ★ DATA, who truly fathered this book and without whom it could not have been written.

Contents

Introduction

Welcome to the fascinating and intricate world of astrology!

For thousands of years the movements of the planets and other heavenly bodies have intrigued the best minds of every generation. Life holds no greater challenge or joy than this: knowledge of ourselves and the universe we live in. Astrology is one of the keys to this knowledge.

Your Personal Horoscope 2025 gives you the fruits of astrological wisdom. In addition to general guidance on your character and the basic trends of your life, it shows you how to take advantage of planetary influences so you can make the most of the year ahead.

The section on each sign includes a Personality Profile, a look at general trends for 2025, and in-depth month-by-month forecasts. The Glossary (*page 5*) explains some of the astrological terms you may be unfamiliar with.

One of the many helpful features of this book is the 'Best' and 'Most Stressful' days listed at the beginning of each monthly forecast. Read these sections to learn which days in each month will be good overall, good for money, and good for love. Mark them on your calendar – these will be your best days. Similarly, make a note of the days that will be most stressful for you. It is best to avoid booking important meetings or taking major decisions on these days, as well as on those days when important planets in your horoscope are retrograde (moving backwards through the zodiac).

The Major Trends section for your sign lists those days when your vitality is strong or weak, or when relationships with your co-workers or loved ones may need a bit more effort on your part. If you are going through a difficult time, take a look at the colour, metal, gem and scent listed in the 'At a Glance' section of your Personality Profile. Wearing a piece of jewellery that contains your metal and/or gem will strengthen your vitality, just as wearing clothes or decorating your room or office in the colour ruled by your sign, drinking teas made from the herbs ruled by your sign or wearing the scents associated with your sign will sustain you.

Another important virtue of this book is that it will help you to know not only yourself but those around you: your friends, co-workers, partners and/or children. Reading the Personality Profile and forecasts for their signs will provide you with an insight into their behaviour that you won't get anywhere else. You will know when to be more tolerant of them and when they are liable to be difficult or irritable.

I consider you – the reader – my personal client. By studying your Solar Horoscope I gain an awareness of what is going on in your life – what you are feeling and striving for and the challenges you face. I then do my best to address these concerns. Consider this book the next best thing to having your own personal astrologer!

It is my sincere hope that *Your Personal Horoscope 2025* will enhance the quality of your life, make things easier, illuminate the way forward, banish obscurities and make you more aware of your personal connection to the universe. Understood properly and used wisely, astrology is a great guide to knowing yourself, the people around you and the events in your life – but remember that what you do with these insights – the final result – is up to you.

A Note on the 'New Zodiac'

Recently an article was published that postulated two things: the discovery of a new constellation – Ophiuchus – making a thirteenth constellation in the heavens and thus a thirteenth sign, and the statement that because the Earth has shifted relative to the constellations in the past few thousand years, all the signs have shifted backwards by one sign. This has caused much consternation, and I have received a stream of letters, emails and phone calls from people saying things like: 'I don't want to be a Taurus, I'm happy being a Gemini', 'What's my real sign?' or 'Now that I finally understand myself, I'm not who I think I am!'

All of this is 'much ado about nothing'. The article has some partial truth to it. Yes, in two thousand years the planets have shifted relative to the constellations in the heavens. This is old news. We know this and Hindu astrologers take this into account when casting charts. This shift doesn't affect Western astrologers in North America and Europe. We use what is called a 'tropical' zodiac. This zodiac has nothing to do with the constellations in the heavens. They have the same names, but that's about it. The tropical zodiac is based on the Earth's revolution around the Sun. Imagine the circle that this orbit makes, then divide this circle by twelve and you have our zodiac. The Spring Equinox is always 0 degrees (Aries), and the Autumn Equinox is always 0 degrees Libra (180 degrees from Aries). At one time a few thousand years ago, these tropical signs coincided with the actual constellations; they were pretty much interchangeable, and it didn't matter what zodiac you used. But in the course of thousands of years the planets have shifted relative to these constellations. Here in the West it doesn't affect our practice one iota. You are still the sign you always were.

In North America and Europe there is a clear distinction between an astrological sign and a constellation in the heavens. This issue is more of a problem for Hindu astrologers. Their zodiac is based on the actual constellations – this is called the 'sidereal' zodiac. And Hindu astrologers have been accounting for this shift all the time. They keep close tabs on it. In two thousand years there is a shift of 23 degrees, and they subtract this from the Western calculations. So in their system many a Gemini would be a Taurus and this is true for all the signs. This is nothing new – it is all known and accounted for, so there is no bombshell here.

The so-called thirteenth constellation, Ophiuchus, is also not a problem for the Western astrologer. As we mentioned, our zodiac has nothing to do with the constellations. It could be more of a problem for the Hindus, but my feeling is that it's not a problem for them either. What these astronomers are calling a new constellation was probably considered a part of one of the existing constellations. I don't know this as a fact, but I presume it is so intuitively. I'm sure we will soon be getting articles by Hindu astrologers explaining this.

Glossary of Astrological Terms

Ascendant

We experience day and night because the Earth rotates on its axis once every 24 hours. It is because of this rotation that the Sun, Moon and planets seem to rise and set. The zodiac is a fixed belt (imaginary, but very real in spiritual terms) around the Earth. As the Earth rotates, the different signs of the zodiac seem to the observer to rise on the horizon. During a 24-hour period every sign of the zodiac will pass this horizon point at some time or another. The sign that is at the horizon point at any given time is called the Ascendant, or rising sign. The Ascendant is the sign denoting a person's self-image, body and self-concept – the personal ego, as opposed to the spiritual ego indicated by a person's Sun sign.

Aspects

Aspects are the angular relationships between planets, the way in which one planet stimulates or influences another. If a planet makes a harmonious aspect (connection) to another, it tends to stimulate that planet in a positive and helpful way. If, however, it makes a stressful aspect to another planet, this disrupts that planet's normal influence.

Astrological Qualities

There are three astrological qualities: *cardinal*, *fixed* and *mutable*. Each of the 12 signs of the zodiac falls into one of these three categories.

Cardinal Signs
Aries, Cancer, Libra and Capricorn
The cardinal quality is the active, initiating principle. Those born under these four signs are good at starting new projects.

Fixed Signs
Taurus, Leo, Scorpio and Aquarius
Fixed qualities include stability, persistence, endurance and perfectionism. People born under these four signs are good at seeing things through.

Mutable Signs
Gemini, Virgo, Sagittarius and Pisces
Mutable qualities are adaptability, changeability and balance. Those born under these four signs are creative, if not always practical.

Direct Motion

When the planets move forward through the zodiac – as they normally do – they are said to be going 'direct'.

Grand Square

A Grand Square differs from a normal Square (usually two planets separated by 90 degrees) in that four or more planets are involved. When you look at the pattern in a chart you will see a whole and complete square. This, though stressful, usually denotes a new manifestation in the life. There is much work and balancing involved in the manifestation.

Grand Trine

A Grand Trine differs from a normal Trine (where two planets are 120 degrees apart) in that three or more planets are involved. When you look at this pattern in a chart, it takes the form of a complete triangle – a Grand Trine. Usually (but not always) it occurs in one of the four elements: Fire, Earth, Air or Water. Thus the particular element in which it occurs will be highlighted. A Grand Trine in Water is not the same as a Grand Trine in Air or Fire, etc. This is a very fortunate and happy aspect, and quite rare.

Houses

There are 12 signs of the zodiac and 12 houses of experience. The 12 signs are personality types and ways in which a given planet expresses itself; the 12 houses show 'where' in your life this expression takes place. Each house has a different area of interest. A house can become potent and important – a house of power – in different ways: if it contains the Sun, the Moon or the 'ruler' of your chart; if it contains more than one planet; or if the ruler of that house is receiving unusual stimulation from other planets.

1st House
Personal Image and Sensual Delights

2nd House
Money/Finance

3rd House
Communication and Intellectual Interests

4th House
Home and Family

5th House
Children, Fun, Games, Creativity, Pleasure and Love Affairs

6th House
Health and Work

7th House
Love, Marriage and Social Activities

8th House
Transformation, Regeneration, Fears and Anxieties

9th House
Foreign Travel, Higher Education and Spiritual Philosophy

10th House
Career and Legacy

11th House
Friends, Group Activities and Fondest Wishes

12th House
Spirituality and Mental Health and Wellness

Karma

Karma is the law of cause and effect which governs all phenomena. We are all where we find ourselves because of karma – because of actions we have performed in the past. The universe is such a balanced instrument that any act immediately sets corrective forces into motion – karma.

Long-term Planets

The planets that take a long time to move through a sign show the long-term trends in a given area of life. They are important for forecasting the prolonged view of things. Because these planets stay in one sign for so long, there are periods in the year when the faster-moving (short-term) planets will join them, further activating and enhancing the importance of a given house.

Jupiter
stays in a sign for about 1 year

Saturn
2½ years

Uranus
7 years

Neptune
14 years

Pluto
15 to 30 years

Lunar

Relating to the Moon. See also 'Phases of the Moon', below.

Natal

Literally means 'birth'. In astrology this term is used to distinguish between planetary positions that occurred at the time of a person's birth (natal) and those that are current (transiting). For example, Natal Sun refers to where the Sun was when you were born;

transiting Sun refers to where the Sun's position is currently at any given moment – which usually doesn't coincide with your birth, or Natal, Sun.

North and South Nodes

Points in the zodiac where the Moon's orbit intersects with the Earth's orbit (also known as the ecliptic). The signs the nodes occupy typically indicate which signs the eclipses will be in for that year. The north node is associated with increase and the south node with shedding.

Out of Bounds

The planets move through the zodiac at various angles relative to the celestial equator (if you were to draw an imaginary extension of the Earth's equator out into the universe, you would have an illustration of this celestial equator). The Sun – being the most dominant and powerful influence in the Solar system – is the measure astrologers use as a standard. The Sun never goes more than approximately 23 degrees north or south of the celestial equator. At the Winter Solstice the Sun reaches its maximum southern angle of orbit (declination); at the Summer Solstice it reaches its maximum northern angle. Any time a planet exceeds this Solar boundary – and occasionally planets do – it is said to be 'out of bounds'. This means that the planet exceeds or trespasses into strange territory – beyond the limits allowed by the Sun, the ruler of the Solar system. The planet in this condition becomes more emphasized and exceeds its authority, becoming an important influence in the forecast.

Phases of the Moon

After the full Moon, the Moon seems to shrink in size (as perceived from the Earth), gradually growing smaller until it is virtually invisible to the naked eye – at the time of the next new Moon. This is called the waning Moon phase, or the waning Moon.

After the new Moon, the Moon gradually gets bigger in size (as perceived from the Earth) until it reaches its maximum size at the time of the full Moon. This period is called the waxing Moon phase, or waxing Moon.

Planetary Rulers

Planets have dominion over specific signs which inform interpretation of the natal chart and astrological transits. Planets in a particular sign are influenced by that sign's planetary ruler. Houses of a natal chart are also influenced by the planetary ruler of the sign on the house's cusp. Traditional planetary rulers only include the first seven planetary bodies (the Sun to Saturn), while modern planetary rulers include all ten. The planetary rulers are as follows:

Aries
Mars

Taurus
Venus

Gemini
Mercury

Cancer
The Moon

Leo
The Sun

Virgo
Mercury

Libra
Venus

Scorpio
Mars (traditional); Pluto (modern)

Sagittarius
Jupiter

Capricorn
Saturn

Aquarius
Saturn (traditional); Uranus (modern)

Pisces
Jupiter (traditional); Neptune (modern)

Power Word

Similar to a 'Totem' (see definition below), but for each monthly horoscope. A power word is a single word that encapsulates the essence of the monthly horoscope.

Retrogrades

The planets move around the Sun at different speeds. Mercury and Venus move much faster than the Earth, while Mars, Jupiter, Saturn, Uranus, Neptune and Pluto move more slowly. Thus there are times when, relative to the Earth, the planets appear to be going backwards. In reality they are always going forward, but relative to our vantage point on Earth they seem to go backwards through the zodiac for a period of time. This is called 'retrograde' motion and tends to weaken the normal influence of a given planet.

Short-term Planets

The fast-moving planets move so quickly through a sign that their effects are generally of a short-term nature. They reflect the immediate, day-to-day trends in a horoscope.

Moon
stays in a sign for only 2½ days

Mercury
20 to 30 days

Sun
30 days

Venus
approximately 1 month

Mars
approximately 2 months

Totem

A literary device for this book; your totem for the year serves as an archetype to hold on to, providing an understanding of the thesis of the year for each sign.

T-square

A T-square differs from a Grand Square (see above) in that it is not a complete square. If you look at the pattern in a chart it appears as 'half a complete square', resembling the T-square tools used by architects and designers. If you cut a complete square in half, diagonally, you have a T-square. Many astrologers consider this more stressful than a Grand Square, as it creates tension that is difficult to resolve. T-squares bring learning experiences.

Transits

This term refers to the movements or motions of the planets at any given time. Astrologers use the word 'transit' to make the distinction between a birth, or Natal, planet (see 'Natal', above) and the planet's current movement in the heavens. For example, if at your birth Saturn was in the sign of Cancer in your 8th house, but is now moving through your 3rd house, it is said to be 'transiting' your 3rd house. Transits are one of the main tools with which astrologers forecast trends.

YOUR PERSONAL HOROSCOPE 2025

Aries

∀

THE RAM

Birthdays from
March 21 to
April 20

Personality Profile

ARIES AT A GLANCE

Element – Fire

Ruling Planet – Mars
  Career Planet – Saturn
  Love Planet – Venus
  Money Planet – Venus
  Planet of Fun, Entertainment, Creativity and Pleasure – Sun
  Planet of Health and Work – Mercury
  Planet of Home and Family Life – Moon
  Planet of Spirituality and Mental Health – Neptune
  Planet of Travel, Education, Religion and Philosophy – Jupiter

Totem – the Diamond

Colours – carmine, red, scarlet

Colours that promote love, romance and social harmony – green,
  jade green

Colour that promotes earning power – green

Gem – diamond

Metals – iron, steel

Scent – honeysuckle

Quality – cardinal (= activity)

Quality most needed for balance – caution

Strongest virtues – abundant physical energy, courage, honesty, independence, self-reliance

Deepest need – action

Characteristics to avoid – haste, impetuousness, over-aggression, rashness

Signs of greatest overall compatibility – Leo, Sagittarius

Signs of greatest overall incompatibility – Cancer, Libra, Capricorn

Sign most helpful to career – Capricorn

Sign most helpful for emotional support – Cancer

Sign most helpful financially – Taurus

Sign best for marriage and/or partnerships – Libra

Sign most helpful for creative projects – Leo

Best Sign to have fun with – Leo

Signs most helpful in spiritual matters – Sagittarius, Pisces

Best day of the week – Tuesday

Understanding an Aries

Aries is the activist *par excellence* of the zodiac. The Aries' need for action is almost an addiction, and those who do not really understand the Aries personality would probably use this hard word to describe it. In reality 'action' is the essence of the Aries psychology – the more direct, blunt and to-the-point the action, the better. When you think about it, this is the ideal psychological makeup for the warrior, the pioneer, the athlete or the manager.

Aries likes to get things done, and in their passion and zeal often lose sight of the consequences for themselves and others. Yes, they often try to be diplomatic and tactful, but it is hard for them. When they do so they feel that they are being dishonest and phoney. It is hard for them even to understand the mindset of the diplomat, the consensus builder, the front office executive. These people are involved in endless meetings, discussions, talks and negotiations – all of which seem a great waste of time when there is so much work to be done, so many real achievements to be gained. An Aries can understand, once it is explained, that talk and negotiations – the social graces – lead ultimately to better, more effective actions. The interesting thing is that an Aries is rarely malicious or spiteful – even when waging war. Aries people fight without hate for their opponents. To them it is all good-natured fun, a grand adventure, a game.

When confronted with a problem many people will say, 'Well, let's think about it, let's analyse the situation.' But not an Aries. An Aries will think, 'Something must be done. Let's get on with it.' Of course, neither response is the total answer. Sometimes action is called for, sometimes cool thought. But an Aries tends to err on the side of action.

Action and thought are radically different principles. Physical activity is the use of brute force. Thinking and deliberating require one not to use force – to be still. It is not good for the athlete to be deliberating the next move; this will only slow down his or her reaction time. The athlete must act instinctively and instantly. This is how Aries people tend to behave in life. They are quick, instinctive decision-makers and their decisions tend to be translated into action almost immediately. When their intuition is sharp and well tuned, their actions are powerful and successful. When their intuition is off, their actions can be disastrous.

Do not think this will scare an Aries. Just as a good warrior knows that in the course of combat he or she might acquire a few wounds, so too does an Aries realize – somewhere deep down – that in the course of being true to yourself you might get embroiled in a disaster or two. It is all part of the game. An Aries feels strong enough to weather any storm.

There are many Aries people who are intellectual. They make powerful and creative thinkers. But even in this realm they tend to be pioneers – outspoken and blunt. These types of Aries tend to elevate (or sublimate) their desire for physical combat in favour of intellectual, mental combat. And they are indeed powerful.

In general, Aries people have a faith in themselves that others could learn from. This basic, rock-solid faith carries them through the most tumultuous situations of life. Their courage and self-confidence make them natural leaders. Their leadership is more by way of example than by actually controlling others.

Finance

Aries people often excel as builders or estate agents. Money in and of itself is not as important as are other things – action, adventure, sport, etc. They are motivated by the need to support and be well-thought-of by their partners. Money as a way of attaining pleasure is another important motivation. Aries function best in their own businesses or as managers of their own departments within a large business or corporation. The fewer orders they have to take from higher up, the better. They also function better out in the field rather than behind a desk.

Aries people are hard workers with a lot of endurance; they can earn large sums of money due to the strength of their sheer physical energy.

Venus is their money planet, which means that Aries need to develop more of the social graces in order to realize their full earning potential. Just getting the job done – which is what an Aries excels at – is not enough to create financial success. The co-operation of others needs to be attained. Customers, clients and co-workers need to be made to feel comfortable; many people need to be treated properly in order for success to happen. When Aries people develop these abilities – or hire someone to do this for them – their financial potential is unlimited.

Career and Public Image

One would think that a pioneering type would want to break with the social and political conventions of society. But this is not so with the Aries-born. They are pioneers within conventional limits, in the sense that they like to start their own businesses within an established industry.

Capricorn is on the 10th house of career cusp of Aries' solar horoscope. Saturn is the planet that rules their life's work and professional aspirations. This tells us some interesting things about the Aries character. First off, it shows that, in order for Aries people to reach their full career potential, they need to develop some qualities that are a bit alien to their basic nature: they need to become better administrators and organizers; they need to be able to handle details better and to take a long-range view of their projects and their careers in general. No one can beat an Aries when it comes to achieving short-range objectives, but a career is long term, built over time. You cannot take a 'quickie' approach to it.

Some Aries people find it difficult to stick with a project until the end. Since they get bored quickly and are in constant pursuit of new adventures, they prefer to pass an old project or task on to somebody else in order to start something new. Those Aries who learn how to put off the search for something new until the old is completed will achieve great success in their careers and professional lives.

In general, Aries people like society to judge them on their own merits, on their real and actual achievements. A reputation acquired by 'hype' feels false to them.

Love and Relationships

In marriage and partnerships Aries like those who are more passive, gentle, tactful and diplomatic – people who have the social grace and skills they sometimes lack. Our partners always represent a hidden part of ourselves – a self that we cannot express personally.

An Aries tends to go after what he or she likes aggressively. The tendency is to jump into relationships and marriages. This is especially true if Venus is in Aries as well as the Sun. If an Aries likes you, he or she will have a hard time taking no for an answer; many attempts will be made to sweep you off your feet.

Though Aries can be exasperating in relationships – especially if they are not understood by their partners – they are never consciously or wilfully cruel or malicious. It is just that they are so independent and sure of themselves that they find it almost impossible to see somebody else's viewpoint or position. This is why an Aries needs as a partner someone with lots of social graces.

On the plus side, an Aries is honest, someone you can lean on, someone with whom you will always know where you stand. What he or she lacks in diplomacy is made up for in integrity.

Home and Domestic Life

An Aries is of course the ruler at home – the Boss. The male will tend to delegate domestic matters to the female. The female Aries will want to rule the roost. Both tend to be handy round the house. Both like large families and both believe in the sanctity and importance of the family. An Aries is a good family person, although he or she does not especially like being at home a lot, preferring instead to be roaming about.

Considering that they are by nature so combative and wilful, Aries people can be surprisingly soft, gentle and even vulnerable with their children and partners. The sign of Cancer, ruled by the Moon, is on the cusp of their solar 4th house of home and family. When the Moon is well aspected – under favourable influences – in the birth chart, an Aries will be tender towards the family and will want a family life that is nurturing and supportive. Aries likes to come home after a hard day on the battlefield of life to the understanding arms of their partner and the unconditional love and support of their family. An Aries feels that there is enough 'war' out in the world – and he or she enjoys participating in that. But when Aries comes home, comfort and nurturing are what's needed.

Horoscope for 2025

Do you know what HPHT stands for, Aries? High pressure, high temperature. HPHT is the process by which carbon is transformed into diamonds. This year starts off on the heels of a year that could be described as your very own carbon cycle. The north node was in your sign for the whole of 2024, and the push to holistically grow was profound, but this year starts off with the north node leaving your sign just 11 days into it. In doing so, the overarching theme for this year shifts from growth to refinement. Diamonds can be refined through cutting, grinding and polishing. The cosmic weather for 2025 will likely feel as if all three processes are taking place, but remember that the end result is you becoming a metaphorical diamond.

This is a special year because it features Saturn, Uranus and Neptune (all slow-moving planets) changing signs this year. These shifts have significant societal implications. More importantly for you, Aries, is that both Saturn and Neptune shift into your sign for part of the year. Saturn takes 28½ years to go around the zodiac, so this ushers in a new, approximately 29-year cycle centred around maturation and responsibility. Saturn spends about 2½ years in a sign, so this year represents the start of a 2½-year refinement period. Interestingly enough, Neptune is almost diametrically opposite to Saturn. While Saturn is concerned about structure and prestige, Neptune cares about interconnectedness and dreams. There's a beautiful juxtaposition you'll grow into this year, with both of these planets being co-present in your sign for a significant part of it.

One of the biggest areas of life you will focus on this year is physical and mental wellness. A big part of your refinement period over the next 2½ years will be disciplining the mind and body to support all the growth and expansion you've already undergone. Last year was a crucible, and the first part of this refinement period will be about healing and regenerating. The mind is inherently linked to the body, which is why one cannot be disciplined without the other. This will be discussed further in the health section of this horoscope.

Aside from physical and mental wellness, another major theme of this year will be home and family dynamics. Mars begins this year retrograde and, in early January, enters Aries' 4th house of home and family. Mars will be present in this sector of your chart from January 6 to April 18. Jupiter, the planet of expansion and conviction, enters your home and family sector midway through 2025 and stays for the remainder of the year. The combination of these energies is discussed in depth in the home and domestic life section of this horoscope.

For a quarterly view of the year, your first quarter centres primarily around family dynamics, dealing with the home and mental wellness. In the second quarter, the cosmic weather centres around healing, recharging and getting in touch with newfound dreams; the third quarter is dynamic and focuses on assuming responsibility and balancing that with your domestic life. The final quarter of the year centres around attaining a mind–body alignment.

Health

(Please note that this is an astrological perspective on health and not a medical one. Any health-related symptoms should be evaluated by a qualified healthcare professional.)

This year starts off with Mars, your planetary ruler, retrograde. While Mars won't be transiting a health house, its retrograde motion forces you to slow down. This transit occurs as the north node shifts into your 12th house of mental wellness, and the south node shifts into your 6th house of physical wellness and routines. One major call to action for you this year will be to refine your routines to be more amenable to your physical and mental well-being. While the north node brings with it increase to the area of one's chart that it's transiting, the south node brings the requirement to shed or declutter. For you, Aries, this is a major reason why this year is about redefining routines. The 6th house primarily relates to physical health, diet and exercise. Half of the eclipses occurring this year occur near the south node in this house. Eclipses are evolutionary transits that promote growth through scrutiny and shake-ups. Being focused on maintaining a healthy diet is always a good idea, but it's especially important in years where there's a lot of activity in this part of your chart. This is the year where you must attend all routine check-ups with medical professionals and not delay speaking with an expert if you have any type of concern.

Achieving greater mental wellness is also a major theme this year with Saturn wrapping up its 2½-year tenure in this part of your chart. One important adjustment to make this year to support your overall mental wellness will be striking a better balance between solo and social time. Both alone time and time with others are necessary for mental equilibrium. That being said, an over-abundance in either direction would be detrimental. Given that this is a year of refinement and there's so much focus on levelling up from the mental/emotional standpoint, beginning a collaboration with a life coach or therapist is very much in line with the plethora of 12th house transits occurring this year. In addition to the transits mentioned, there will be both a Mercury and Venus retrograde overlapping in your 12th house of mental wellness at the end of March and into the start of April.

Here are the specific areas of the body to focus on this year:

- Face and head: in medical astrology Aries rules the face and head, so these areas are a perennial focus for you. Given that this year features Saturn beginning to transit Aries' 1st house, the call to be especially focused on your face and head maintenance is made this year. Externally supportive behaviours like consistent skin care and craniosacral massages, plus internal support with diet, are paramount.

- Shoulders, arms and hands: with Uranus' shift into Gemini, it's important to be mindful of shoulder mobility and health this year. Integrating more mobility or muscle activation exercises prior to physical exercise will pay long-lasting dividends.
- Feet: the heavy concentration of 12th house transits for you means foot health is on the docket for this year. Integrating foot massages or reflexology into your schedule would be a high-minded way to honour the overarching astrological themes around your health and wellness this year.

Love and Social Life

The most notable season surrounding love this year is the spring, with your love planet, Venus, turning retrograde on March 1. This six-week retrograde features Venus oscillating between your sign and Pisces. Venus retrograde is always a time of profound re-evaluation of your value system and relationships. This retrograde asks the question, 'Are your emotional needs being met in your one-on-one relationships?' Of course, for those who have a partner, this specifically applies to your relationship with your significant other. However, regardless of your relationship status, this applies to all of your close or intimate one-on-one interpersonal relationships. Venus' retrograde occurs at the same time as the first eclipses happen, so don't be alarmed if there are shake-ups in the dynamic of your friend groups.

Saturn is the planet ruling the groups, organizations and communities you're immersed in, and it also oscillates between Pisces and Aries this year. This summer is noteworthy as Saturn transits your sign from May 24 to September 1. With this transit comes a call to assume additional responsibility in organizations or communities you're involved with. Saturn rules structure and maturity, so do your due diligence around investigating the specific role responsibilities of any new positions pitched to you. Moreover, remember that this year's primary goal is refining your routines, so ensure that your physical or mental wellness won't take too much of a hit by assuming a position of authority.

The Sun is your perennial romance and pleasure planet. This is a unique year for the Sun because it finds itself doing a tango with essentially all the outer planets at the same points of the year. That's because the outer planets all shift signs or reside in the first couple of degrees of a sign, so they actually stay closely connected to one another all year. For you, this means that there are noticeable peaks and troughs with romance and pleasure. Mercury's retrograde in Leo from July 18 to August 11 is a specifically noteworthy transit in this regard. The key is to not allow the troughs to destabilize you holistically. When you detect that you're in a trough period romantically, lean into creative self-expression as a means to uplift yourself.

Career and Finances

Becoming a diamond and embracing a refining process means there's a significant amount of cutting and buffing you'll be endeavouring to do when it comes to your career this year. That's because your career planet is Saturn. Saturn shows up in several sectors of your life because of the noteworthy shift it makes into your sign for the entire summer. The last time Saturn occupied your sign was just before it left it in 1999. Saturn in your sign promotes assuming additional responsibility in all the areas of your life that it rules. For you, Aries, that means career and organizations.

Saturn was deemed the 'Greater Malefic' in traditional astrology because of its associations with restriction, limitation and hard lessons. Essentially, Saturn rules the cold hard truth and raw reality of your situation. For you, this means that the summer of 2025 is likely to be met with grappling with some serious existential quandaries related to career and legacy. Confronting and making significant pivots to your career trajectory are likely and will be supportive if they're thought through and tethered to an action plan of some sort. Saturn is all about putting in the hard work and knowing that it may take months or years, but you will see results. Given that this is just the beginning of a 2½-year period during which Saturn will occupy your sign, expect for this to be a year of putting in the hard yards and not seeing much of an output from this work. Fear not! Through consistent hard work, Saturn will reward you later in its transit through your sign.

If you've been feeling unstable financially over the last few years, I'm happy to report that Uranus is finally leaving Taurus and entering Gemini this year. This is important as Uranus in Taurus transits Aries' 2nd house of finances. Uranus rules instability, innovation and individuality. Uranus' move into Gemini is especially important as it will lead to major innovations in technology around how communication and learning are approached. This has major implications for the ways you have been making money and can make money moving forward.

Your finance planet is Venus, and it's especially wise to keep a tighter budget during its retrograde period from March 1 to April 18. Unless you're born in the last couple of days of Aries' season, Venus retrograde will be interwoven into your solar return (birthday) chart for the year, meaning that there's a subtle lingering of the retrograde throughout the year. From a finance standpoint, Venus retrograde is about getting your bearings around all the money in your account and *not* losing sight of this. That means investing in accounting software and scheduling monthly routine financial check-ins with yourself.

Home and Domestic Life

This section of your life has two very different energies affecting it at different points in the year. As mentioned earlier in this horoscope, Mars will be present in your 4th house of home and family dynamics from January 6 to April 18. Mars will be retrograde from the start of the year until February 23. Mars rules drive, assertion and confrontation, among many other significations. When Mars is retrograde, these energies are directed inwards instead of outwards. Essentially, this period of time is commonly associated with anger powder kegs, meaning that if frustration isn't expressed directly it boils under the surface until something minor triggers a major reaction. The key to navigating this period is to consistently choose to respond instead of to react. Mars rules the home, so Mars retrograde is an ideal time to circle back to home-improvement projects that are long overdue.

Thankfully, abundant Jupiter will also be transiting your 4th house for the second half of the year (June 9 to December 31). This transit is associated with expansion, which could very well materialize as a move. Given that Jupiter will be in Cancer during this time, it's extra important that you address the feng shui of your living situation regardless of whether or not you move. Jupiter moving into Cancer provides ample opportunity to revitalize the energy of your space and also to set it up to support you as you navigate this refining year.

Self-improvement

Neptune moves into your sign for the first time in your lifetime. For context, it takes Neptune 160 years to go around the zodiac, meaning it was last in Aries in 1875. Neptune transits your sign from March 30 to October 22, before entering its stay in Aries next year. This transit focuses on spiritual enlightenment above all else. A big key to unlocking the balance you'll be striving to achieve between work and play or mind and body is through your spiritual practices. Your spirit should be the bridge connecting and uplifting your body and mind. Taking time to refine your spiritual value system through exploring philosophers' works you haven't read is one way to honour this transit. Spiritual practices that tether you to the present moment, such as meditation, yoga and mindfulness, will be vital to supporting your mental wellness this year during this transit. Neptune rules both metaphorical and literal fog, so when feelings of being daunted or lost come up this year, having these kinds of spiritual practices in your toolkit will be beneficial.

Communication is another area of self-improvement you'll be called upon to refine as both Jupiter and Uranus transit your 3rd house of communication. Jupiter stays in your 3rd house for the first five months of the year and audits if your communication style aligns with your beliefs and convictions. More authenticity around communication is the overarching theme, especially when Uranus transits Gemini from July 7 to November 7.

Month-by-month Forecasts

January

Best Days Overall: 26-31
Most Stressful Days Overall: 14-19
Best Days for Love: 20-23
Best Days for Money: 1-2
Best Days for Career: 8-11
Power Word: Pace

Happy New Year, Aries! You may be known for getting stuff done and moving quickly, but this month's astrology urges you to go at a slow and steady pace. The cosmic weather begins on January 2 with Venus moving into Pisces. This transit supports adopting practices or behaviours that connect your spirit to your mind. Meditation, mindfulness, journaling or spending time by bodies of water are all examples. It's very important that you lean into routines that provide balance for you, because Mars, your planetary ruler, is retrograde.

On January 6 Mars retrograde re-enters Cancer. This transit probes family dynamics and sheds light on how you navigate life as a result of these existing dynamics. Spending quality time with family and focusing on the home is the name of the Mars retrograde in Cancer game. If you've been feeling like the energy of your living space is stale, take this transit as a strong suggestion to do some good old-fashioned feng shui. On January 11 the north node leaves your sign after 18 months and enters Pisces. This transit indicates that a big focus of this year is on your health and wellness routines. Your planetary ruler forms a harmonious aspect with Neptune on the 12th, further promoting rest and recovery over the need for extreme output. This transit is built into the full Moon in Cancer on the 13th. Honour this astrology by taking it easy!

Aquarius' season begins on the 19th and centres on the groups and organizations you're involved with. Which of these help stabilize you in the hustle and bustle of daily life? Make a concerted effort this week to express gratitude for those people or organizations that do this day in, day out. Aquarius' season can also spotlight organizations that take more from you than they give. Slow down in these spaces to protect your energy. The new Moon on the 29th in Aquarius is a great time to immerse yourself in whichever communities make your heart flutter. The last day of the month features a glorious Sun trine to Jupiter, which is a beautiful day to express yourself creatively.

February

Best Days Overall: 23–27
Most Stressful Days Overall: 10–14
Best Days for Love: 6–9
Best Days for Money: 1–3
Best Days for Career: 9–10
Power Word: Unique

Happy February, Aries! I'm happy to report that this is the month where Mars, your planetary ruler, finally goes direct. Mars will go direct on the 23rd, so more on that later. Let's start off on the 4th with Venus entering your sign. Traditionally, Venus was defined as the 'lesser benefit' because of its associations with love, splendour and beauty. Venus transiting your sign is a joyous transit centred around those associations. Schedule time this month for self-love, and remind yourself how beautiful you are. Venus in Aries is a great time to work up a sweat too.

The most noteworthy piece of cosmic weather to highlight is the bombastic full Moon in Leo occurring on February 12. This full Moon in Leo is a little spicier than normal because it's tensely aspecting Uranus. Uranus has dominion over innovation, instability and individuality, among many other significations. Ubiquitously this is a lunation that shakes things up. For you, dear ram, this transit centres on your 5th house of creativity and romance. This lunation wants you to creatively self-express what makes you uniquely you, because that makes you awesome. With romance, this full Moon provides the energy to approach romance in new or spontaneous ways. It's important to note that this transit is likely to be a bit of a powder keg, so it's also important to think through confrontation with partners or creative collaborators.

Pisces' season begins on the 18th. As you know, one of the big themes for this year is mental health. The Sun is bright, and when it joins the north node in Pisces it only provides stadium-level spotlighting to this theme. If you haven't made much of an effort to regulate your mind, the cosmic weather will likely spur you to do so. There's no need to make radical adjustments, just small incremental ones that can become habitual. The new Moon on the 27th is a great time to begin these practices.

Mars goes direct in Cancer on the 23rd. This is like a blockage being cleared, and a pathway forward begins to be freed up for you. With eclipse season around the corner, kinetic energy will mount fast.

March

Best Days Overall: 8-10, 20-22
Most Stressful Days Overall: 14-18, 28-29
Best Days for Love: 20-22
Best Days for Money: 8-12
Best Days for Career: 23-24
Power Word: Self

It's almost Aries' season! March is one of the busiest months astrologically, with two retrogrades plus eclipse season. Venus turns retrograde on March 1 in your sign. This Venus retrograde revolves around your sense of self-worth and whether your individual relationships uplift and support your self-esteem. This absolutely also includes your relationship with yourself. More specifically, this retrograde is focused on your perception of beauty and how that point of view affects your self-worth. This is your body for this lifetime, so give it the respect and TLC it deserves.

Eclipse season starts off on March 14 with a full Moon total lunar eclipse in Virgo. Eclipses catalyse major changes, typically through encouraging parting with 'the old' in order to welcome 'the new'. This eclipse is likely to be felt in the body, so prioritize rest and recovery for the next two weeks. Virgo rules the intestines, so focusing on nourishing your body is of the utmost importance at this time. This eclipse may also stir up feelings of frustration around not being recognized for your hard work. If you feel like this theme is applicable during March, do your best to maintain composure when confronting the issue. Definitely do not ignore these feelings, as eclipses are wily and this buried frustration will eventually boil over. Mercury retrograde begins the next day (March 15) in your sign as well. Mercury retrogrades force us to reflect on patterns of thought and communication. Remember, communication is a two-way street, with active listening being just as important as actively expressing yourself.

Your solar season begins on the 20th, with a new Moon solar eclipse in your sign occurring on the 29th. These transits only spotlight the retrograde themes of the month. Solar returns (birthdays) and new Moons both represent new cycles because they literally are new astronomical cycles. Identify three adjectives you seek to embody this year and integrate them into your meditation or mindfulness practices. Describe in your journal why you seek to embody these words or discuss this with a confidant. This exercise will help orient and channel all of this Aries energy in a productive way.

April

Best Days Overall: 4-8, 18-20
Most Stressful Days Overall: 13-14, 27-29
Best Days for Love: 4-8
Best Days for Money: 16-19
Best Days for Career: 20-22
Power Word: Plan

Happy Birthday! April's cosmic weather begins with a confluence of supportive transits occurring in the first week of the month. Mars, your planetary ruler, is harmoniously aligned with both Saturn and Uranus on the 5th. This is productive energy to lean into! If you have a to-do list, this is your time to check off several items. If not, this is the time to get organized and use this energy to set yourself up for success and get to work.

Mercury ends its retrograde on the 7th. This Mercury retrograde was heavy for Aries because Mercury was in your sign for most of its retrograde period. On the 12th there's the annual full Moon in Libra. This lunation is heavily relationship-focused for you, Aries. If you have a partner, this is the ideal transit to spend quality time with your special someone. If you're single, this is the ideal transit to put yourself out there or treat yourself to a self-date. Venus ends its retrograde on this date too, which is super-helpful for relationship work. The harmonious transits from the first week of April are still active at this time. However, this full Moon is at odds with Mars. This full Moon is the perfect time for you to expend all that mounting kinetic energy building inside you: go for a run, do some exercise, play a sport, practise tae kwon do, etc.

Taurus' season begins on the 19th. Taurus is a fixed-earth sign focused on security in all senses of the word. For Aries, Taurus evokes the need for financial security. With both retrogrades now behind you, you have the green light to move forward with any plans to accrue greater wealth. Taurus' season is your annual prompt to put pen to paper and plan out action steps towards tackling the year's major goals. The end of the month is tenser than how the month started, with Mars facing off with Pluto. This transit can unearth buried rage or expose unequal power dynamics in your life. It's a good idea to prioritize nesting and resting during the last weekend of the month.

May

Best Days Overall: 20–27
Most Stressful Days Overall: 12–18
Best Days for Love: 2–7
Best Days for Money: 22–26
Best Days for Career: 20–23
Power Word: Network

Spring has sprung, Aries! May's astrology begins on the 2nd, with Venus in Aries meeting up with Neptune in Aries for the first time in your lifetime. This glamorous transit inspires you to embody your individuality through your aesthetic, and is an ideal transit for anything beauty- or fashion-related. A few days later on the 5th, Mercury in Aries harmoniously aligns with Jupiter. This transit ramps up your communication prowess, so if you've got something to say – say it!

On May 12 the annual full Moon in Scorpio occurs. This full Moon features Mercury and Pluto significantly squaring off, and it has the potency to bring to light long-held secrets or frustrations that are inhibiting your personal transformation. Do not ignore what comes to light, but be mindful of addressing any situation with tact. The Sun is close to joining up with Uranus at this time as well. This conjunction is associated with liberation and sudden changes. Embrace flexibility at this time as plans are likely to change at the last minute. This full Moon is also financial in nature for Aries and can inspire hyper-vigilant behaviour around money. Do your best to temper this type of behaviour through sticking to your pre-planned budget and not making any major economic decisions at this time.

On May 20 the Sun enters Gemini. Gemini is the communicator and marketeer of the zodiac. Gemini's season is the ideal time for Aries to network and lean into their existing network for support or to form new connections. Venus cordially aspects Mars, your planetary ruler, on the 22nd. This is the perfect day for this time of networking. May 24 brings Saturn into Aries for the first time since leaving it 26 years ago. This transit ushers in a three-year period of maturation for you, Aries. Lots of responsibility is headed your way! On May 26 the new Moon in Gemini occurs. This lunation features an alignment with Pluto that supports confronting fears head on. Harmony with Jupiter means this lunation also supports speaking your truth.

June

Best Days Overall: 23-27
Most Stressful Days Overall: 10-14
Best Days for Love: 6-9
Best Days for Money: 1-3
Best Days for Career: 9-10
Power Word: Home

Summer is coming, Aries! On June 5 Mercury and Mars are supporting one another while Venus does the same with Jupiter. These two transits in isolation facilitate a very social and jovial environment. However, on the 9th, Venus will tensely square off with Pluto. This transit is associated with inflaming long-held struggles with self-esteem or worthiness. Though separated by four days, the three transits can overlap. As a result, it's best to still be social and surround yourself with friends, but make sure you're with those that lift you up or that you feel comfortable being your 100 per cent authentic self around. This is especially true for the weekend of the 7th.

June 9 also features Jupiter entering Cancer. Jupiter spent close to a year in Gemini and is now in the cardinal water sign associated with home and family. Jupiter is the great expander and magnifies the area of your chart he's transiting. For Aries, home and family dynamics are especially augmented. Jupiter can very well inspire a move or some form of upgrade to your living situation. The present relationships you have with family are also something that you can expect to grow during this time. It's important to note that by 'grow', I simply mean expand upon the existing dynamic. If there's a relationship you're seeking to work on, mend or develop, Jupiter in Cancer, plus the Sun entering Cancer on the 20th, will work with you to accomplish this.

The lunations for this month are a full Moon in Sagittarius on the 11th and a new Moon in Cancer on the 25th. The full Moon in Sagittarius is an adventurous lunation for Aries. This is the ideal lunation to go off travelling or to plan your next voyage. This is also a spiritual full Moon for you, so basking in the light of the Moon is recommended. The new Moon in Cancer is a tenser lunation, with the potency to inspire feelings of being overwhelmed around mounting responsibilities. The new Moon is harmoniously linked to Mars, so the best way to work with this energy is to break larger tasks down into small pieces and celebrate every step forward towards completing the task.

July

Best Days Overall: 6-10
Most Stressful Days Overall: 20-24
Best Days for Love: 3-7
Best Days for Money: 7-11
Best Days for Career: 8-12
Power Word: Busy

Happy July, Aries! July's cosmic weather starts off with Venus being the main character. On July 4 Venus conjoins with Uranus at the very last degree of Taurus and then subsequently enters a new sign, Gemini. Venus in Gemini is a very social energy, so definitely gather with friends or loved ones. That being said, Venus-Uranus transits can be spontaneous and jovial, with a touch of the unexpected. This energy is very kinetic, so do your best not to lose control in the midst of having lots of fun. On July 7 Uranus enters Gemini. This is a big deal because it takes Uranus 84 years to go around the zodiac. In fact, Uranus last left Gemini in 1949! Uranus in Gemini affects us on a collective level by revolutionizing innovations around communication and transportation. Uranus will stay in Gemini until November before a quick retrograde back to Taurus, and then will officially stay in Gemini from spring 2026.

July's full Moon brings a focus on career for you, Aries. The full Moon in Capricorn will occur on the 10th in Aries' house of career and legacy. This full Moon asks the question of you, 'What do you want your legacy to be and are you erecting the proper structure to achieve this?' Structure is a keyword when it comes to Capricorn. This question is food for thought because the end of the year features Mars bringing its fiery focus to career, so it's best to put some thought to this now. On the 18th Mercury turns retrograde for the second time this year. Mercury retrograde in Leo centres around romance and creative self-expression for you. If there's been a form of creativity you used to enjoy, this is the time to circle back and try your hand at it again.

Leo is known to be a loud sign, so it should come as no surprise that Leo's season starts off loud on the 22nd. The Sun forms aspects to five planets within the first three days of Leo's season! The new Moon on the 24th features all of these aspects, plus Venus and Mars tensely squaring off. When there is this much cosmic weather we tend to feel very busy. Fortunately, the Sun is forming primarily harmonious connections, with the exception of it opposing Pluto on the 25th. This Leo season is all about shedding those parts of your identity that are holding you back. This is especially true when it comes to living an authentic life instead of assuming identities others would prefer you to inhabit.

August

Best Days Overall: 12–16
Most Stressful Days Overall: 1–3, 6–10
Best Days for Love: 11–13
Best Days for Money: 22–25
Best Days for Career: 29–31
Power Word: Slow

I know Aries likes to go, go, go, but this month is all about taking it slow, slow, slow. The cosmic weather for August begins on the 1st with Venus squaring off with both Saturn and Neptune. This transit especially hits Aries because Saturn and Neptune are in your sign. Venus squaring off with Saturn is associated with grappling with doubts and insecurities around self-worth. Neptune's influence can either add an additional existential layer to this feeling or promote dissociative behaviour. The key with this transit is to be your own anchor and really make a concerted effort to internalize authentic self-love. Mars, your planetary ruler, enters Libra on the 6th. Libra is all about balance and integration, which confuses the fiery planet and results in the feeling of a slowdown. Mars in Libra scrutinizes your approach to conflict, so be mindful to reflect on the lessons it teaches you.

The slowdown continues and arguably reaches its peak on the 9th with the full Moon in Aquarius. This features Mercury barely moving, and Mars opposing Saturn and Neptune. The key with all this blockage is to pause. Pause to smell the roses. Pause to acknowledge your growth this year. Pause to catch up on actioning items you've been putting off. The full Moon in Aquarius is a social transit for Aries, and this lunation encourages fraternizing. Thankfully, Mercury turns direct two days later on the 11th. Mercury moving directly in Leo supports moving forwards with creative or romantic endeavours.

Virgo's season begins on the 22nd, and the first of two new Moons in the sign occurs the next day. This new Moon in Virgo ushers in a new cycle around caring for your body. Part of this slowdown has definitely been allowing yourself to feel into your body and what it needs. This new Moon squares off with Uranus, which intensifies this process. Virgo rules the digestive system, and this new Moon especially revolves around what you're putting in your body. The month concludes with Venus entering Leo on the 25th, then facing off with Pluto. This transit spotlights the strides you've taken this month – or need to begin to take – in order to cultivate self-compassion.

September

Best Days Overall: 11–16
Most Stressful Days Overall: 23–27
Best Days for Love: 14–16
Best Days for Money: 18–20
Best Days for Career: 2–6
Power Word: Equilibrium

Hi, Aries, it's that time of year again – eclipse season! Emotions are extra-heightened. This is especially true for Aries, given that Mars, your planetary ruler, squares off with Jupiter on the 5th. Jupiter is the great expander and Mars is all about kinetic – or frenetic – energy, so when the two don't see eye to eye you might feel overly energized or like you're juggling more balls than you can handle. This is important to note, because the first eclipse lights up Aries' spiritual and mental health sector on the 7th. This eclipse audits how routine self-care and alone time are for Aries. Last month's cosmic weather encouraged you to take things a little more 'slow, slow, slow'. If you haven't found a balance in your schedule, prepare for this eclipse to intervene. If you're making a concerted effort to harmonize the relationship between rest and work, this eclipse will only go towards supporting you in establishing this equilibrium. This eclipse occurs in Pisces and spurs you to carve out a sanctuary space to which you can retreat in order to recharge when necessary. This space can be a room, a bathtub or even a favourite nature trail nearby. Identifying this space is key to supporting all the growth the eclipses are prompting for you over the next six months.

The second eclipse occurs in Virgo on the 21st, but there's a heavy confluence of transits to note, starting four days prior to the eclipse and ending four days after it. Before the eclipse is formally exact, Mercury is responsible for most of the noteworthy weather in the lead-up to the lunation, with five transits between the 17th and 19th. These transits will force you to confront last month's theme around redefining your relationship to your body. Do you hold preconceived thoughts around your body's capabilities that limit you in some way? This eclipse seeks to liberate you from the beliefs you hold around what your body isn't capable of. In order to really tap into the transformative energy of this lunation, you'll have to dig deep to get to the root cause of these self-limiting beliefs. Doing this will open you up to climbing to new heights over the next six months.

October

Best Days Overall: 26–31
Most Stressful Days Overall: 7–11
Best Days for Love: 13–16, 21–22
Best Days for Money: 22–25
Best Days for Career: 1–3
Power Word: Key

Happy October, Aries! This month's cosmic weather begins with a full Moon in your sign on the 6th. The full Moon in Aries spotlights your personality and temperament, as well as how this changes between the various interpersonal dynamics you hold dear. This lunation occurs on the day that Mercury enters probing Scorpio, so be prepared for this Moon to hold a mirror to yourself. This full Moon is an opportune time to advocate for your needs in those relationships in which you feel like you may censor yourself or soften yourself too much. Moreover, given Aries' association with 'the self', this lunation serves as an invitation to pause and do something kind for yourself.

The middle of the month is heavily relationship-oriented for Aries, as Venus enters Libra on the 13th, and aspects Saturn, Uranus, Neptune and Pluto between the 11th and the 15th. If you've got a partner, this week is replete with assessments around how grounded the 'keys' of your relationship are. Examples of these 'keys' include alignment around communication, understanding each other's conflict/conflict-resolution style, and intentionally catering to the ways in which you both uniquely express/receive love. If you're single, this week will spur you to get in touch with answering these questions for yourself, plus identifying what qualities you seek to embody when the right person is presented to you.

The new Moon in Libra occurs on the 21st and develops the themes of the previous week. This lunation can function as a 'chapter-turning' moment for you regardless of whether you're single or in a relationship. For those who are single, this new Moon will work with you to usher in new beginnings around approaching relationships or your general emotional availability for a relationship. If you've got a partner, this new Moon supports you by ushering in more intimacy and equity between you.

Scorpio's season begins on the 22nd, which changes the cosmic weather so that Aries should focus more on finances, specifically looking at the ways in which your money is wrapped up with or dependent upon other people. This solar season is the ideal time to audit your existing finances and also to identify sustainable ways in which your money can grow itself.

November

Best Days Overall: 17–22
Most Stressful Days Overall: 7–12
Best Days for Love: 21–24
Best Days for Money: 1–5
Best Days for Career: 20–23
Power Word: Dreams

It's November, Aries! This month's astrology begins with a few planets switching signs and the full Moon in Taurus. The full Moon occurs on the 5th. This full Moon is a financial transit for you and centres around security or insecurity in this domain. If you find you experience financial angst around this date, allow the bright light of this lunation to shine on the source of these shadows. On the 6th Venus moves into brooding Scorpio. This transit further develops the theme of the full Moon and supports making moves to acquire a feeling of greater security around finances. It's an ideal time to make steps towards discharging any debts you may owe. This is especially important as Venus immediately begins finding tension with Pluto, which has a tendency to bring to light skeletons long buried. Don't worry about acting on this immediately – work with the new Moon on the 20th to formally take steps with this if applicable.

On the 9th Mercury retrogrades for the last time this year. This Mercury retrograde occurs in Sagittarius and centres around education and spirituality for you, Aries. If you ever paused or halted getting any sort of education, whether it be a certification or just vital independent research, now is the time to circle back to this. This Mercury retrograde also strongly encourages utilizing your spiritual practices as a means to quiet your mind. Meditation, mindfulness, immersing yourself in nature – these all apply.

One of the most harmonious transits of the year – a grand water trine – is closest to being exact on the 17th. This transit involves the Sun, Jupiter and Saturn all metaphorically holding hands, and it strongly supports embracing your individuality and forming/experiencing heart-to-heart connections.

The Sun joins Mars in Sagittarius on the 21st, inspiring you to dream big! This solar season absolutely is the time where you'll really be getting in touch with your 2026 goals. The Sun finds harmony with Neptune on the 21st and with Pluto two days later. These transits further support carving out time to analyse which of your long-term dreams have changed and how you can get the ball rolling this season to best maximize achieving them next year.

December

Best Days Overall: 1–4
Most Stressful Days Overall: 8–13
Best Days for Love: 19–21
Best Days for Money: 21–23
Best Days for Career: 24–27
Power Word: Declare

Hi, Aries! December starts off with the prompt to say what you need to say and recognize the gravity of your message. That's because there's a noteworthy full Moon in Gemini occurring on the

4th. This full Moon is significant for every sign because of how it interacts with the north node and the south node. Essentially, this aspect amplifies the effect of the lunation. For Aries, this full Moon is all about communication and how you craft your message. There are obviously some necessary conversations you need to have or that are brewing in the next couple of weeks. When confronted with these scenarios, take special care to choose your words wisely. This doesn't mean censoring yourself! In fact, I'd argue this lunation supports honest authentic communication. Just don't be unfiltered.

Another reason the stakes are a little higher than normal is because Mars, your planetary ruler, squares off with Saturn on the 9th. As with every tense transit, there's a light and a shadowy side to this astro-weather. On one hand, this transit is very much associated with taking stock of everything you've got going on in the present moment and being able to tackle outstanding deliverables you've lost sight of. However, this transit is significantly associated with restlessness, a feeling of unproductivity and frustration. Lean into the higher vibration of this transit and take care of to-do items within your locus of control. Moreover, as Mars and Saturn angrily square dance, Mercury forms several aspects of its own with other planets from the 10th to the 13th. These Mercury transits only compound the themes illuminated by the full Moon.

Thankfully, after the tense Mars transit dissipates, you get a productive jolt from the fiery planet, given that it enters Capricorn on the 15th. Mars in Capricorn is your biannual world domination transit! For the next six weeks your planetary ruler occupies the sign that's all about summiting metaphorical mountains. Basically, this is a heavily goal-oriented transit coming at the ideal time of year to focus on future achievements. Capricorn season begins on the 21st. What do you want to be remembered for, Aries? Break out the climbing gear because it's time to scale the mountain known as your dreams.

Taurus

THE BULL

Birthdays from
April 21 to
May 20

Personality Profile

TAURUS AT A GLANCE

Element – Earth

Ruling Planet – Venus
   Career Planet – Uranus
   Love Planet – Pluto
   Money Planet – Mercury
   Planet of Health and Work – Venus
   Planet of Home and Family Life – Sun
   Planet of Spirituality and Mental Health – Mars
   Planet of Travel, Education, Religion and Philosophy – Saturn

Totem – the Gymnast

Colours – earth tones, orange

Colours that promote love, romance and social harmony – red-violet,
violet

Colours that promote earning power – yellow, yellow-orange

Gems – coral, emerald

Metal – copper

Scents – bitter almond, rose, vanilla, violet

Quality – fixed (= stability)

Quality most needed for balance – flexibility

Strongest virtues – endurance, loyalty, patience, stability, a harmonious disposition

Deepest needs – comfort, material ease, wealth

Characteristics to avoid – rigidity, stubbornness, a tendency to be overly possessive and materialistic

Signs of greatest overall compatibility – Virgo, Capricorn

Signs of greatest overall incompatibility – Leo, Scorpio, Aquarius

Sign most helpful to career – Aquarius

Sign most helpful for emotional support – Leo

Sign most helpful financially – Gemini

Sign best for marriage and/or partnerships – Scorpio

Sign most helpful for creative projects – Virgo

Best Sign to have fun with – Virgo

Signs most helpful in spiritual matters – Aries, Capricorn

Best day of the week – Friday

Understanding a Taurus

Taurus is the most earthy of all the Earth signs. If you understand that Earth is more than just a physical element, that it is a psychological attitude as well, you will get a better understanding of the Taurus personality.

A Taurus has all the power of action that an Aries has. But Taurus is not satisfied with action for its own sake. Their actions must be productive, practical and wealth-producing. If Taurus cannot see a practical value in an action they will not bother taking it.

Taurus' forte lies in their power to make real their own or other people's ideas. They are generally not very inventive but they can take another's invention and perfect it, making it more practical and useful. The same is true for all projects. Taurus is not especially keen on starting new projects, but once they get involved they bring things to completion. Taurus carries everything through. They are finishers and will go the distance, so long as no unavoidable calamity intervenes.

Many people find Taurus too stubborn, conservative, fixed and immovable. This is understandable, because Taurus dislikes change – in the environment or in their routine. They even dislike changing their minds! On the other hand, this is their virtue. It is not good for a wheel's axle to waver. The axle must be fixed, stable and unmovable. Taurus is the axle of society and the heavens. Without their stability and so-called stubbornness, the wheels of the world (and especially the wheels of commerce) would not turn.

Taurus loves routine. A routine, if it is good, has many virtues. It is a fixed – and, ideally, perfect – way of taking care of things. Mistakes can happen when spontaneity comes into the equation, and mistakes cause discomfort and uneasiness – something almost unacceptable to a Taurus. Meddling with Taurus' comfort and security is a sure way to irritate and anger them.

While an Aries loves speed, a Taurus likes things slow. They are slow thinkers – but do not make the mistake of assuming they lack intelligence. On the contrary, Taurus people are very intelligent. It is just that they like to chew on ideas, to deliberate and weigh them up. Only after due deliberation is an idea accepted or a decision taken. Taurus is slow to anger – but once aroused, take care!

Finance

Taurus is very money-conscious. Wealth is more important to them than to many other signs. Wealth to a Taurus means comfort and security. Wealth means stability. Where some zodiac signs feel that they are spiritually rich if they have ideas, talents or skills, Taurus only feels wealth when they can see and touch it. Taurus' way of thinking is, 'What good is a talent if it has not been translated into a home, furniture, car and holidays?'

These are all reasons why Taurus excels in estate agency and agricultural industries. Usually a Taurus will end up owning land. They love to feel their connection to the Earth. Material wealth began with agriculture, the tilling of the soil. Owning a piece of land was humanity's earliest form of wealth: Taurus still feels that primeval connection.

It is in the pursuit of wealth that Taurus develops intellectual and communication ability. Also, in this pursuit Taurus is forced to develop some flexibility. It is in the quest for wealth that they learn the practical value of the intellect and come to admire it. If it were not for the search for wealth and material things, Taurus people might not try to reach a higher intellect.

Some Taurus people are 'born lucky' – the type who win any gamble or speculation. This luck is due to other factors in their horoscope; it is not part of their essential nature. By nature they are not gamblers. They are hard workers and like to earn what they get. Taurus' innate conservatism makes them abhor unnecessary risks in finance and in other areas of their lives.

Career and Public Image

Being essentially down-to-earth people, simple and uncomplicated, Taurus tends to look up to those who are original, unconventional and inventive. Taurus people like their bosses to be creative and original – since they themselves are content to perfect their superiors' brainwaves. They admire people who have a wider social or political consciousness and they feel that someday (when they have all the comfort and security they need) they too would like to be involved in these big issues.

In business affairs Taurus can be very shrewd – and that makes them valuable to their employers. They are never lazy; they enjoy working and getting good results. Taurus does not like taking unnecessary risks and they do well in positions of authority, which makes them good managers and supervisors. Their managerial skills are reinforced by their natural talents for organization and handling details, their patience and thoroughness. As mentioned, through their connection with the earth, Taurus people also do well in farming and agriculture.

In general a Taurus will choose money and earning power over public esteem and prestige. A position that pays more – though it has less prestige – is preferred to a position with a lot of prestige but lower earnings. Many other signs do not feel this way, but a Taurus does, especially if there is nothing in his or her personal birth chart that modifies this. Taurus will pursue glory and prestige only if it can be shown that these things have a direct and immediate impact on their wallet.

Love and Relationships

In love, the Taurus-born likes to have and to hold. They are the marrying kind. They like commitment and they like the terms of a relationship to be clearly defined. More importantly, Taurus likes to be faithful to one lover, and they expect that lover to reciprocate this fidelity. When this doesn't happen, their whole world comes crashing down. When they are in love Taurus people are loyal, but they are also very possessive. They are capable of great fits of jealousy if they are hurt in love.

Taurus is satisfied with the simple things in a relationship. If you are involved romantically with a Taurus there is no need for lavish entertainments and constant courtship. Give them enough love, food and comfortable shelter and they will be quite content to stay home and enjoy your company. They will be loyal to you for life.

Make a Taurus feel comfortable and – above all – secure in the relationship, and you will rarely have a problem.

In love, Taurus can sometimes make the mistake of trying to control their partners, which can cause great pain on both sides. The reasoning behind their actions is basically simple: Taurus people feel a sense of ownership over their partners and will want to make changes that will increase their own general comfort and security. This attitude is OK when it comes to inanimate, material things – but is dangerous when applied to people. Taurus needs to be careful and attentive to this possible trait within themselves.

Home and Domestic Life

Home and family are vitally important to Taurus. They like children. They also like a comfortable and perhaps glamorous home – something they can show off. They tend to buy heavy, ponderous furniture – usually of the best quality. This is because Taurus likes a feeling of substance in their environment. Their house is not only their home but their place of creativity and entertainment. The Taurus' home tends to be truly their castle. If they could choose, Taurus people would prefer living in the countryside to being city-dwellers. If they cannot do so during their working lives, many Taurus individuals like to holiday in or even retire to the country, away from the city and closer to the land.

At home a Taurus is like a country squire – lord (or lady) of the manor. They love to entertain lavishly, to make others feel secure in their home and to encourage others to derive the same sense of satisfaction as they do from it. If you are invited for dinner at the home of a Taurus you can expect the best food and best entertainment. Be prepared for a tour of the house and expect to see your Taurus friend exhibit a lot of pride and satisfaction in his or her possessions.

Taurus people like children but they are usually strict with them. The reason for this is they tend to treat their children – as they do most things in life – as their possessions. The positive side to this is that their children will be well cared for and well supervised. They will get every material thing they need to grow up properly.

On the down side, Taurus can get too repressive with their children. If a child dares to upset the daily routine – which Taurus loves to follow – he or she will have a problem with a Taurus parent.

Horoscope for 2025

With all the astrological shifts occurring in 2025, this year will be a balancing act for you, Taurus. Starting in January, the north node shifts into Pisces, bringing expansion and eclipses to your social life. In addition to the nodes, this year will feature Saturn, Uranus and Neptune all switching signs. For context, Saturn hasn't changed signs since early 2023, Uranus hasn't changed signs since 2018 and Neptune hasn't changed signs since 2011. These shifts affect your macro-environment (the whole world) and you on a personal level.

Saturn, the planet that rules responsibility, discipline and hard work, begins to shift out of your social life sector and into your spirituality and mental wellness sector. This occurs for almost the whole summer, because Saturn shifts into Aries from Pisces, and it's noteworthy because there are actually four planets that undergo retrograde periods and oscillate between these two signs. This is where embodying 'the Gymnast' really comes into play for you in 2025, Taurus. This year will be about striving to achieve the proper balance between social time and solo time.

Mercury, Venus and Mars all undergo periods of retrograde motion this year, further compounding the necessity to strive for balance. Venus, your planetary ruler, will be retrograde in March during eclipse season. This retrograde is heavily relationship-focused and will be covered in the love and social life section below. March's astrology is covered in multiple sections of this yearly horoscope and the month-by-month forecasts section.

Your relationship to pleasure and creativity is strongly scrutinized this year by the eclipse cycles. Both eclipse cycles include eclipses in Virgo, which transit Taurus' 5th house of recreation and creative self-expression. Eclipses are evolutionary transits that stimulate growth through tension or shake-ups. This yearly horoscope will provide a multifaceted view on navigating these themes this year with the spring and autumn/fall eclipses.

Speaking of shake-ups, after seven long years in your sign, Uranus, the planet that rules instability and innovation, exits Taurus for close to half the year. The period of July to November, when Uranus is out of your sign, will be one of profound reflection centred around how your daily routines have developed to ground you during this extensive transit. Addressing which routines need to be updated in order to best serve your mental and physical well-being in this new phase of your life will be strongly encouraged during this period.

For a quarterly view of your year, the first quarter features the cosmic weather focusing on social standing and creative self-expression, the second features a shift towards mental health and work–life balance, the third fully leans into this theme and adds an additional focus on finances, while the final quarter returns the focus on to social standing and creativity.

Health

(Please note that this is an astrological perspective on health and not a medical one. Any health-related symptoms should be evaluated by a qualified healthcare professional.)

The astrology of 2025 poses the question, 'Have you been able to strike a balance between socializing and solo time in a way that supports your mental health?' This question will be investigated by the astro-weather this year. March is a big month surrounding this question as there are two planetary retrogrades, two eclipses and Neptune switches signs. Venus, your planetary ruler, will be retrograde from March 1 to April 12. In addition to love, Venus retrograde actually focuses on rethinking and re-evaluating our values. For you, Taurus, this transit begins in your 12th house of mental wellness. This retrograde compounds with some of the other transits this month to force you to confront dissociative behaviour that is not supportive of your holistic well-being.

Confronting dissociative behaviour starts in March, but it is a major focus topic in the realm of health and wellness for you this year. This month features two eclipses, the first of which lights up the pleasure sector of your chart on the 14th, with the second hitting your mental health sector on the 29th. As mentioned in the introduction to this horoscope, eclipses catalyse growth through scrutiny. Given that the astro-weather is especially frenetic during this month, expect to confront which stress-coping mechanisms are supportive and which are dissociative.

In addition to being your planetary ruler, Venus is also the planet that rules physical health and routines for you. Venus spends an extensive amount of time in your 11th house of communities, groups and organizations. Cultivating and bolstering your support systems around physical health are vital this year. Identifying workout buddies, friends you can meal-prep with, or taking group yoga or meditation classes are all examples of ways to leverage community to support your physical health.

The summer is where a lot of hard work around cultivating supportive routines for mental health takes place, given that Saturn enters your 12th house of mental well-being and spirituality. Saturn will be transiting this sector of your chart from May 24 to September 1. Saturn will force you to confront limiting patterns of thought and behaviour during this time as a means to encourage maturation. Working with mental health professionals, in addition to leaning on your support systems, is highly recommended during this transit.

Here are the specific areas of the body to focus on this year:

- Neck and throat: these parts of the body, including the tonsils and thyroid, are a perennial area of focus for you, given Taurus' rulerships in medical astrology. Avoid tension in the neck through being intentional about posture and stretching.
- Shoulders, arms, hands and fingers: Mars will be retrograde from January 6 to February 23 in Taurus' 3rd house, which in medical astrology correlates to these parts of the body. Shoulder massages or acupuncture are highly recommended, especially during this period given Mars' inflammatory quality.
- Breasts and lungs: Mars begins the first few days of the year retrograde in Taurus' 4th house and then re-enters this section

of the chart from April 19 to June 17. In medical astrology, the 4th house rules these parts of the body. Avoid behaviours such as smoking that irritate and pollute the lungs, especially during this period.

Love and Social Life

How you approach romance and pleasure undergoes an evolution this year, Taurus. With the north node entering Pisces at the start of the year, the south node enters Virgo at the same time and moves into the pleasure sector of your chart. The section of your chart transited by the south node goes through a period of shedding what no longer serves you or supports where you're headed. The forms of pleasure that you've outgrown or don't support your holistic development are on the chopping block.

This transit also brings with it two eclipses in this section of your chart. If you're single, the two eclipse cycles will spur you to address your emotional availability for a relationship and how you approach seeking one. Given this section of your chart's association with recreation, using your favourite forms of recreation as a means to meet others is recommended if you're seeking a relationship. For those who have a partner, the eclipse cycles will force you to confront or adjust how your relationship directly influences the social circles you reside in. Do these uplift you individually in addition to uplifting your relationship, or vice versa? Changes and evolution in social circles are strongly promoted by both eclipse cycles this year.

Both Venus and Mars rule over major themes in relationships and are both retrograde this year. Mars retrograde in the first two months of the year especially affects Taurus, as this planet rules Taurus' 7th house of partnership. Mars retrograde will scrutinize the sustainability of how you address conflict within your relationship. Is this a topic you need to realign on with your partner? If you're single, this applies to your closest interpersonal relationships as well. While frustrating, the purpose of this is for you to evolve individually and within the partnership by addressing this massively important dimension of any relationship.

Career and Finances

Your career planet is Saturn, which shifts into Aries after spending 2½ years in Pisces. Saturn will be in Aries from May until September before one final transit through Pisces. This is significant because a profound shift like this for your career planet influences your career trajectory. This summer will be a time of questioning your current career trajectory. Saturn in Aries inquires if your needs are being met within your current work situation. Moreover, Saturn in Aries is an ideal transit to identify ways you can be your own boss, whether through your primary career or through developing new income streams. Your career planet enters the mental wellness sector of your chart when it makes this transition in May, prompting you also to evaluate the cost-benefit of your current career and how it affects your mental health.

Pluto, the planet of transformation and power dynamics, finally stays in your career sector for the entire year, after oscillating to and fro for the past two years. Pluto in your career sector compounds the theme of contemplating your career trajectory and also spurs you to re-evaluate overarching career goals, taking into account the vastly changing world you live in. Pluto's shift into Aquarius occurs in tandem with Uranus' shift into Gemini. These transits will result in life-changing innovations as to how people in our society communicate and relate to one another. Given the rapidly changing world we're living in, the cosmic weather asks you to reframe your career goals through the understanding of this exciting future.

Uranus moves into Gemini after 7 years in your sign. Uranus is the planet of innovation, instability and individuality. By leaving your sign and entering Gemini, the planet will be transiting the finance sector of your chart (from July to November). Adopting a more frugal approach during this period is recommended, given the instability the planet provokes. Uranus' ultimate goal is liberation, and its transition of your financial sector means seeking long-lasting financial abundance. Educating yourself around the different types of retirement accounts or saving techniques you can employ is highly recommended, as Uranus will formally move into this sector of your chart next year. This is important to note because, until June, Jupiter brings growth and expansion to the finance sector of your chart. There's a noteworthy energetic transition that occurs in this area of life around finances. Adopting a frugal approach is less of a concern with Jupiter in this sector of your chart than with Uranus. Strive to anchor financial stability during the Jupiter transit in preparation for the unexpected, which Uranus is known to bring.

Home and Domestic Life

The Sun is your home and domestic life planet. This year features short bursts of activity within the home and longer periods of status quo. This is because most of the outer planets will stay within roughly the same degree of their signs for a considerable part of the year, meaning that when the Sun is activated by one of them, there will be a domino effect with the others. One noteworthy month where this occurs is September, which also features a solar eclipse mixed in with this confluence of transits. Anticipate some disruption or frenetic energy within your home and domestic life during this month. The summer would be a good time for home-improvement projects as a result. Late November is another example of a short period of several solar aspects that will be felt in the home. This unique astrological pattern present throughout this year further informs why this is your year to embody the Gymnast.

The most prominent transit through your home and domestic life sector is Mars retrograde. Mars will have spent almost all of December 2024 retrograde through this part of your chart, so you'll start the year with this transit. Mars retrograde in your home sector typically indicates a high level of tension at home. It's important to follow the cornerstone piece of Mars retrograde advice: 'respond instead of react'. Essentially, if engaged in confrontation during this period of time, take time to think through how you reply to whatever the provocation is instead of making a knee-jerk reaction.

Self-improvement

The first half of the year is a time of profound reflection as Venus, your planetary ruler, is not only retrograde for six weeks, but it also meets up with Saturn on three occasions. This is noteworthy because Saturn rules the higher education sector of your chart. Venus conjoining with Saturn indicates that this is a good year to study for an advanced degree or pursue additional education for self-improvement. March and April are two months that will catalyse changes across several areas of your life, and as a result are months during which you'll likely get in touch with the next steps around higher education. This also applies to teaching and coaching, in addition to becoming a student again. Spirituality and spiritual practices are a significant modality to help achieve the balance you'll be striving for this year as the Gymnast.

One of the biggest areas of self-improvement in 2025 is communication, with buoyant Jupiter moving into your communication sector for the first time in 12 years. Jupiter brings growth and expansion to the area of the chart it occupies. This astrology motivates you to embrace your authentic style of communication. Jupiter in this section of the chart is indicative of getting on soap boxes, so make sure the audience you're preaching to wants to listen. This transit begins in July and lasts to the end of the year. Identifying your convictions and your message is a major component of what makes this transit special – it influences all areas of your life, so be willing to take up space and not censor yourself.

If you are unaware of how to improve your approach to communication, Mars retrograde at the start of year will facilitate situations that show you areas of improvement. Mars will be retrograde in your communication sector from January 6 to February 23.

Month-by-month Forecasts

January

Best Days Overall: 27–31
Most Stressful Days Overall: 4–8
Best Days for Love: 12–17
Best Days for Money: 17–20
Best Days for Career: 27–29
Power Word: Truth

Happy New Year, Taurus! This month's astrology revolves around the truth, the whole truth and nothing but the truth. January's astrology kicks off on the 2nd with Venus, your planetary ruler, entering Pisces. Honour this transit by immersing yourself in the communities that uplift your spirit. January 6 is when the astrology of this month really starts to centre around the truth. Mars is currently retrograde and re-enters Cancer on this day. This transit functions as an audit of your communication. Do you feel comfortable speaking your truth or do you censor yourself to appease others? If it's the latter, Mars will spur you to address this head-on. I know this is tricky, though, because Mars retrograde is not an ideal time for confrontation. Direct, authentic communication doesn't need to be incendiary, just honest. If the dynamic is such that you frankly can't speak as directly or honestly as you'd like, honour these feelings through journaling or leaning into creative self-expression as outlets for them.

The full Moon in Cancer on the 13th only ramps up the focus on communication. Full Moons are usually emotional times, so schedule some TLC for this day or a day or so after to ground yourself. This full Moon also encourages spending time in your local community. Make it your intention to do something that gives back to your local community, like going to a farmers' market, volunteering or attending a local event.

Aquarius' season begins on January 19, which shifts the Sun's rays towards shining light on your career aspirations. With all this talk about being truthful, ask yourself if you feel like your current career aligns with your authenticity. The Sun meets up with Pluto two days later, challenging you to shed aspects of your personality that no longer serve you. The new Moon in Aquarius on the 29th also revolves around career. New Moons usher in new emotional cycles. This new Moon centres around the question posed above, regarding whether your work aligns with your authenticity. There's no need to make a drastic shift now, but allow yourself to plan out actionable steps towards feeling more fulfilled in the workplace at some point this year.

February

Best Days Overall: 1-3, 7-9
Most Stressful Days Overall: 10-14
Best Days for Love: 18-20
Best Days for Money: 6-9
Best Days for Career: 26-28
Power Word: Assert

Happy February, dear bull! February's astrology begins with a couple of harmonious alignments in the first three days of the month. Venus, your planetary ruler, meets up with Neptune on February 1, inspiring you to connect with the collective. This transit should be honoured through going out in nature or spending time in communities or organizations that nourish your spirit. The first weekend of the month also features Mercury and Jupiter getting close to their congenial formation, which is exact on the 3rd. Mercury and Jupiter working together absolutely supports all forms of communication for you. Mercury and Jupiter can inspire over-communicating, so be mindful to have a filter too.

February 12 features a noteworthy full Moon in Leo. This full Moon is metaphorically not seeing eye to eye with Uranus, so it's an emotional lunation. Uranus is a wildcard often associated with sudden shake-ups or creating an unstable dynamic to catalyse necessary changes. This full Moon revolves for you around home, real estate and family dynamics. If there has been tension in any of these departments brewing beneath the surface, expect this lunation to illuminate them. This lunation also supports planned changes to living situations, which could be something as simple as redecorating a room. Full Moons in Leo collectively are also creative and expressive in nature. Leverage the emotional energy the Moon affords by channelling it in creative pursuits. Leo rules the heart in medical astrology, so allow yourself to be guided by your heart at this time.

Pisces' season begins on the 18th, with a new Moon in the sign occurring on the 27th. These transits highlight the role you play in the organizations, groups and communities you belong to. The new Moon is an ideal transit to immerse yourself in a new group or to plan an event within an existing organization. A major theme for this year revolves around reciprocity in these communities, and the Sun moving into Pisces only highlights this. The new Moon in Pisces pushes you to surround yourself with people who recharge your battery.

March

Best Days Overall: 22–27
Most Stressful Days Overall: 1–4, 14–16
Best Days for Love: 20–23
Best Days for Money: 22–26
Best Days for Career: 8–10
Power Word: Limitless

March is one of the busiest months astrologically, Taurus, so let's jump right in! On March 1 Venus turns retrograde. This is super-important for you to know because Venus is your planetary ruler, so you feel Venus' retrogrades a little more profoundly. This Venus retrograde revolves around any self-effacing tendencies you have and the values that function as their root cause. Self-effacing tendencies are patterns of behaviour we act on that shrink us, limit us or prevent us from being seen. This will be a recurring theme for March because of the confluence of transits in Aries occurring through the month.

On March 14 the first eclipse of the year occurs. The full Moon total lunar eclipse in Virgo lights up your fifth house of creativity and romance. As mentioned in your yearly horoscope, 2025 features a shedding of sorts around the ways you creatively self-express and approach romance or pleasure. The eclipse is a major catalysing agent for this yearly theme. It's often hard for us to prioritize pleasure amid all the responsibilities we have. This eclipse will feel destabilizing if your work-life balance is askew or if you're actively denying yourself the opportunity to play or partake in recreation.

One day later Mercury turns retrograde in Aries. This Mercury retrograde builds on the themes of the Venus retrograde but adds an additional caveat regarding how you limit yourself both through not communicating your needs or censoring yourself. Aries' season begins on the 20th, with a new Moon solar eclipse occurring on the 29th in the same sign. Aries embodies the concept of 'I with myself'. This eclipse very likely will be taxing mentally or emotion-ally given that you are tackling some longstanding patterns of thought and behaviour. March's astrology asks you to identify your needs, prioritize them and readily assert them when necessary. The month concludes with Neptune finally entering Aries after being in Pisces since 2011. Neptune in Aries will be an extended transit revolving around dismantling how your ego influences the limiting behaviour highlighted by the previous transits in Aries.

April

> Best Days Overall: 4–6, 19–22
> Most Stressful Days Overall: 7–11, 26–28
> Best Days for Love: 5–8
> Best Days for Money: 2–5
> Best Days for Career: 21–23
> Power Word: Abundance

It's almost your season, Taurus! April's astrology begins with a cluster of harmonious transits occurring throughout the first week. Bookmark the 5th, which is the day that Venus, your planetary ruler, aligns with Mars. This is a great day to start getting super-productive. It's important to note that you'll also feel this transit on the 7th, when Mercury turns direct, which only adds to the productive vibes of the first week.

There's a full Moon in a fellow Venus-ruled sign, Libra, on the 12th. The annual full Moon in Libra is a relationship-oriented full Moon. For Taurus, this lunation also centres around physical health and wellness. If you're in a relationship, this is arguably the most potent lunation for doing something together that promotes physical wellness. Stocking your home with fresh produce, going on a run or getting massages are all examples of ways to honour this lunation. If you're single, all of these still apply, but ground yourself in the intention that this is an act of self-love. April 12 is also the day on which your planetary ruler finally turns direct. Yay! Now both Mercury and Venus are moving forwards. This is a universal unclogging of your gutters.

Before you know it, it's Taurus season on the 19th. Happy Birthday! Your sign has major associations with security and sensuality. Taurus' season is the time each year when you should surround yourself with those who make you feel safe. Moreover, given your solar season occurs in tandem with the heart of spring, it's time to cultivate abundance! Be focused on how you spend your time and with whom. The month concludes with a new Moon in your sign on the 27th, which is the transit associated with new beginnings for you. However, it's important to note that Mars faces off with Pluto on this day. It's a ubiquitously tense transit, so do your best to ground yourself around what is in your locus of control and what isn't. The focus for Taurus season is abundance, so don't lose sight of that.

May

Best Days Overall: 2-7
Most Stressful Days Overall: 9-13
Best Days for Love: 20-23
Best Days for Money: 24-27
Best Days for Career: 1-5
Power Word: Discover

Happy May, Taurus! This month's cosmic weather begins on the 2nd with Venus, your planetary ruler, meeting up with Neptune in Aries. This is the first time in your lifetime that Venus in Aries is conjoined with Neptune in Aries! This transit centres around mental health and private time for you. If you haven't already established a designated 'sanctuary space' where you can go to recharge alone in peace, this transit is the ideal time to do so. On the 6th Venus then moves to harmoniously align with Pluto. This soft aspect supports taking action that boosts your self-esteem. This could be a makeover, conquering a fear or being bold and putting yourself out there.

The full Moon this month is in your polar sign, Scorpio, on the 12th. This full Moon features a close connection between the Sun and Uranus. The vibe for this full Moon is about exploring the nooks and crannies of your relationships. However, given Uranus' involvement, you'll likely be surprised what you learn. This is the ideal lunation on which to dig deep and ask your partner or closest relationships thoughtful questions to bolster your relationship. This prompt can also be directed inwards if you're in a phase of personal self-discovery. Be mindful, though, that Mercury is squaring off with Pluto on this date. This transit supports investigation but can promote obsessive or compulsive thinking, so be curious but not hyper-vigilant.

Gemini's season begins on the 20th. This solar season is financial in nature for Taurus. Now is not the time for flagrant spending. Venus forms a lovely aspect with Mars on the 22nd, supporting you in cultivating prosperity at home or with loved ones. This is also an ideal transit for renovations or reorganization within the home. The month ends with a new Moon in Gemini on the 27th. This new Moon features a 'stellium' or cluster of four planets in Gemini and a stellium of three planets (plus Chiron) in Aries. Essentially, this new Moon is about addressing financial matters that may be weighing on your psyche so that you can alleviate the mental burden. Taking greater strides towards budgeting or managing finances will result in a significant boon to your mental wellness.

June

Best Days Overall: 3–8
Most Stressful Days Overall: 20–24
Best Days for Love: 1–6
Best Days for Money: 11–14
Best Days for Career: 26–28
Power Word: Worth

June starts off with multiple planets changing sign, Taurus. On June 6 Venus, your planetary ruler, enters your sign. This should be one of your favourite times of year, given that Venus loves being in your sign. Venus in Taurus orients the planet that rules pleasure towards sensuality and security. Saving money and creating splendour are the names of the game for this transit. When you treat yourself this week, also tuck some money away for a rainy day. Mercury and Jupiter enter Cancer on the 8th and 9th respectively. Transits in Cancer centre around communication for Taurus, especially within the home or with family. Jupiter in Cancer works with you to bolster your confidence around communicating your needs.

The 9th also features your planetary ruler harshly squaring off with Pluto. This transit can bring limiting thoughts to the surface around self-esteem or self-worth. For Taurus, this especially applies to career or career goals. Take stock of all your accomplishments this year and celebrate these achievements. The full Moon in Sagittarius occurs on the 11th. This lunation harmoniously aligns with Mars, promoting adventure or productivity. Sagittarius is associated with cheerleading, so work with the energy of this lunation by reaching out and hyping up friends or loved ones who support you day in, day out.

Mars enters fellow earth sign Virgo on the 17th. Mars in Virgo is creative and romantic for Taurus. Take the lead in planning dates or ramp up the amount of time you spend creatively expressing yourself. Cancer's season begins on the 20th, with the new Moon following on the 25th. This Cancer season starts off with the Sun harshly aspecting Saturn and Neptune. Being overwhelmed by the idea of accomplishing big goals – or simply managing responsibilities – is the most common signification for this alignment. Break up big tasks or goals into smaller pieces or checkpoints to sustain productivity around this date. The new Moon in Cancer promotes supporting your inner child through lovingly parenting yourself in the face of being overwhelmed or having feelings of uncertainty.

July

Best Days Overall: 3–8
Most Stressful Days Overall: 18–23
Best Days for Love: 1–5
Best Days for Money: 7–11
Best Days for Career: 22–26
Power Word: Authentic

Hi, Taurus! The cosmic weather for the start of the month centres around Venus, your planetary ruler. On the 4th Venus conjoins with Uranus at the very last degree of your sign, just before jumping into Gemini. This is a very social transit, with Uranus adding a bit of spontaneity and the unexpected into the mix. On the 6th Venus harmoniously aligns with Saturn and Neptune. These transits support keeping the good vibes going in your social life. Venus wraps up its confluence of aspects with a beneficial interrelation with Pluto. This transit is soft but has the potency to be transformative in cultivating self-compassion.

On July 10 the full Moon occurs in fellow earth sign Capricorn. This full Moon demands structure around themes of spirituality and education for Taurus. Spirituality can get very nebulous and lose its meaning without you structuring some routine around it and getting more specific about defining your spiritual values. This could include becoming increasingly focused on adopting a meditation practice, or you might like to do some explicit research to educate yourself on philosophical schools of thought that could flush out a sustainable supportive value system for your daily life. If you're involved in education or seeking to acquire a new certification, this lunation will promote dotting your i's and crossing your t's around this as well.

Mercury turns retrograde in Leo on the 18th. This retrograde will likely revolve around home and family dynamics for Taurus. Communication gets wonky, especially around its interpretation, so do your best to actively listen when communicating with family or members of your household. Leo's season begins on the 22nd and the Sun follows in Venus' footsteps by forming a confluence of aspects with other planets. The new Moon on the 24th contains all of these aspects and is a busy lunation. This new Moon is all about confronting or shedding aspects of your identity that you have assumed to appease family or loved ones. Authenticity is the ultimate goal of this new Moon – and this Leo season in general. Your planetary ruler enters Cancer on the 30th, which supports you in this journey as well as spurring you to spend quality time with family or loved ones.

August

Best Days Overall: 11–15
Most Stressful Days Overall: 1–5
Best Days for Love: 23–26
Best Days for Money: 12–15
Best Days for Career: 28–31
Power Word: Support

Your planetary ruler stirs up the cosmic weather again, Taurus. On August 1 Venus squares off with Saturn and Neptune, so it's vital to keep your regime around mental wellness intact as a result. When Venus and Saturn don't see eye to eye, self-worth, self-esteem and self-compassion tend to be the things we lose sight of. Moreover, Venus creating tension with Neptune can stir up old dissociative patterns of thought or behaviour. These transits encourage you to start this month off with the goal of doing things that support your mental health. This may mean taking things off your plate for the first few days.

The full Moon in Aquarius on the 9th centres around pausing to take stock of your current state of affairs. This full Moon features Mars picking up where Venus left off by opposing Saturn and Neptune. Essentially, this lunation demands that you focus on what is in your locus of control and don't allow uncontrollable variables to cause unnecessary blockages. Specifically, this request applies to your career, Taurus. This full Moon encourages you to circle back to complete tasks that you've put off, before endeavouring to take on new responsibilities at work. Mercury goes direct two days later, supporting you in resuming where you left off before taking the time to complete your existing to-do list. Saturn finds harmony with Uranus on the 12th, which is a great transit to support productivity in the wake of that full Moon. Moreover, Venus and Jupiter meet up on this day, reinforcing effective communication.

The Sun enters Virgo on the 22nd and meets up with the Moon on the 23rd. The new Moon in Virgo is all about carving out space for yourself to play. Stress can affect the physical body, and this lunation provides the opportunity to usher in a new cycle during which there is a greater balance between work, play and rest. The month ends with Venus opposing Pluto. This transit can provoke obsessive thinking or overthinking, further supporting the mission of the new Moon, which is to schedule in more time for pleasure.

September

Best Days Overall: 12–17
Most Stressful Days Overall: 5–8, 20–22
Best Days for Love: 1–4
Best Days for Money: 25–28
Best Days for Career: 18–20
Power Word: Reciprocity

Happy eclipse season, Taurus! The first eclipse of this month occurs on the 7th in Pisces. For Taurus, this lunation heavily revolves around how you fit into the groups, organizations and communities you're a part of. Eclipses are evolutionary transits that catalyse growth through shake-ups or scrutiny. Specifically, this eclipse highlights one of your major 2025 themes, which is reciprocity in the groups and communities you immerse yourself in. Eclipses support decisive action to precipitate growth, so push will come to shove as you make sure your needs are being met. Fortunately, if there is already reciprocity in these organizations, this eclipse will propel you to immerse yourself deeper within the community. Fortunately, Venus, your planetary ruler, harmoniously aspects Mars on the 16th, supporting quality time with said people.

The second eclipse of the month occurs in fellow earth sign Virgo on the 21st. There's a confluence of transits leading up to and in the wake of this lunation (a total of 15 transits!), so definitely don't overextend yourself at this time. The theme of this second eclipse is confronting the way you limit yourself in the realm of creativity and romance. Specifically, given Taurus' orientation towards security, this lunation will scrutinize whether you're unwilling to 'put yourself out there' in either arena. Getting to the bottom of whatever fear or insecurity promotes this limiting pattern of thinking is the end goal of this new Moon solar eclipse. As mentioned above, eclipses occur to facilitate evolution. This eclipse is calling on you to be brave, Taurus!

Libra's season begins on the 22nd, with the Sun then aspecting every planet between Saturn and Pluto over the following three

days. The Sun has everything to do with vitality, and these transformative aspects spur you to take steps towards transforming
your physical body. This month's eclipses shake things up to stimulate six months of exciting growth. In order for this growth to be
sustainable, Taurus, the cosmic weather demands you buckle
down in the realm of diet, exercise or holistic physical wellness.
Small digestible changes over the next six months with not only
become habitual, but will also pay long-lasting dividends for you.

October

Best Days Overall: 14–18
Most Stressful Days Overall: 7–11
Best Days for Love: 21–25
Best Days for Money: 28–31
Best Days for Career: 1–4
Power Word: Harmony

Happy October, Taurus! This month's cosmic weather begins with
a full Moon in Aries on the 6th. This lunation spotlights your
general mental health and also how your routine behaviours
support or detract from it. For Taurus, the start of October is the
ideal time to nest, rest and not rush to complete a million tasks. In
fact, this lunation also asks how much time you spend being social
as opposed to going solo – and whether this ratio is sustainable.
The goal of this full Moon is to encourage you to strike a balance
between socializing and recharging so that both are beneficial to
your overall mental wellness. On or around this date, be focused
on checking in with yourself on this.

The second week of the month is all about Venus, your planetary
ruler. Venus aspects Saturn, Uranus, Neptune and Pluto between
the 11th and the 14th, in addition to entering Libra on the 13th.
Given your association with this planet, you can bookmark the
second week of the month as feeling kinetic. These transits centre
around your relationship with your physical body and the steps
you're taking to nourish it. Check in with your body this week and
ask it what it needs to feel supported. The new Moon in Libra

occurs on the 21st and builds on this theme. If you've been meaning to make an appointment for your annual check-up or have been putting off seeing a specific type of doctor, now is the time to be your body's biggest ally by springing into action and doing it.

Scorpio's season begins on the 22nd with the Sun aspecting both Uranus and Pluto over the next two days. Scorpio season is relationship-oriented for Taurus. This solar season is about liberating yourself from getting in your own way when it comes to partnership (whether you're single or in a relationship already). Mercury finds harmony with Saturn on the 25th, supporting any important conversations you may seek out with partners or those with whom you seek to build meaningful connections. The month ends with Mars finding harmony with Jupiter. This transit is significantly productive and supports ticking long-overlooked items off your to-do list.

November

Best Days Overall: 15–18, 28–30
Most Stressful Days Overall: 6–12
Best Days for Love: 20–23
Best Days for Money: 18–21
Best Days for Career: 17–19
Power Word: Shadow

Happy November, Taurus! The astrology of November begins on the 5th with the full Moon in your sign. This transit spotlights your relationship with yourself and how you've evolved over the last six months. You've been through multiple retrogrades, eclipses and major planets shifting signs in that time frame! This full Moon promotes celebrating your growth in some way that is authentic to you. It may also bring to light some long-buried shadow work to resolve as your planetary ruler begins to find tension with Pluto (this will be perfected on the 8th). Plan on carving out time in your schedule on or around the 5th to nest and recharge.

Mercury turns retrograde one last time in 2025 on the 9th. This transit occurs in Sagittarius and is financial in nature for Taurus.

Mercury retrogrades are times to revisit, review and re-evaluate. As a result, it's time for you to audit your finances and review whether you should keep your long-term investments just as they are or make some changes. This retrograde will also have you revisiting or rethinking 'the dream' and analysing it through the lens of your finances. Whether that's reviewing how much money is required up-front or re-evaluating how much there's to be made from achieving this goal, the retrograde not only poses the question, 'Do you really want it?' but also whether the financial aspect will sway your decision.

The 17th features a grand water trine – one of the most harmonious aspects – between the Sun, Jupiter and Saturn. Occurring in these water signs, this transit provokes people to begin advocating for what they believe in and helps jump-start their personal development. If you're pursuing a promotion or trying to achieve some sort of levelling-up in your life, this transit is a staunch ally in getting you to your own personal next step.

The new Moon in Scorpio occurs on the 20th, the day before Sagittarius' season begins. This lunation centres on ushering in a new emotional cycle around relationships. If you're single, this is the ideal transit to put yourself out there or get in touch with what characteristics you seek to embody in your next relationship. If you're in a relationship, this new Moon will work with you to establish a new dynamic or facet between you and your partner if desired. It's also just a great opportunity to spend quality time with your special someone.

December

Best Days Overall: 19–23
Most Stressful Days Overall: 9–14
Best Days for Love: 15–17
Best Days for Money: 1–4
Best Days for Career: 21–25
Power Word: Propel

It's the last month of the year, Taurus! December's cosmic weather starts off with Venus, your planetary ruler, forming a soft harmonious aspect with transformative Pluto. The first half of this month is significantly financially focused for you. This transit is light compared with the full Moon coming in a couple of days and encourages a 'spend a little, save a little' mentality. The full Moon in Gemini occurs on the 4th and is extra special because the lunation squares off with the north node and the south node. When this happens, we feel the effects of the transit a little more profoundly. For Taurus, this lunation centres around growing your wealth in the coming year. Obviously, this time of year is notorious for spending, so be mindful not to go too overboard. Moreover, Gemini is the storyteller, and this lunation asks, 'How can you use your personal story to increase your wealth and abundance?'

The astro-weather slows things down in the second week of the month, with Mars squaring off with Saturn on the 9th. This transit strongly encourages focusing on your current circumstances and not obsessing over the future. Channel any restlessness you experience productively by ticking the items you've ignored up to this point off your to-do list. Thankfully, after this transit dissipates, Mars enters fellow earth sign Capricorn on the 15th. This is a major vibe change around productivity. For you, Taurus, this transit motivates you to travel as a means to gain perspective on your next steps or your goals for 2026.

The new Moon in Sagittarius occurs on the 19th and is also a financial lunation for you. Growing your wealth is a theme for the year and this lunation reminds you of the role others play in achieving this. One way to really make the most of this lunation would be to collaborate with a financial advisor on your portfolio or to fore-cast 2026. Capricorn's season begins on the 21st. This solar season encourages leaning into learning and education. If you've been meaning to go back to school, get a certification or even do an independent deep dive to gain expertise in a subject, the Sun in Capricorn supports you doing so and will propel you towards achieving the goals you've set for the following year.

Gemini

♊

THE TWINS

Birthdays from
May 21
to June 20

Personality Profile

GEMINI AT A GLANCE

Element – Air

Ruling Planet – Mercury
  Career Planet – Neptune
  Love Planet – Jupiter
  Money Planet – Moon
  Planet of Health and Work – Pluto
  Planet of Home and Family Life – Mercury

Totem – the Trendsetter

Colours – yellow, yellow-orange

Colour that promotes love, romance and social harmony – sky blue

Colours that promote earning power – grey, silver

Gems – agate

Metal – quicksilver

Scents – lavender, lilac, lily of the valley, storax

Quality – mutable (= flexibility)

Quality most needed for balance – thought that is deep rather than superficial

Strongest virtues – great communication skills, quickness and agility of thought, ability to learn quickly

Deepest need – communication

Characteristics to avoid – gossiping, hurting others with harsh speech, superficiality, using words to mislead or misinform

Signs of greatest overall compatibility – Libra, Aquarius

Signs of greatest overall incompatibility – Virgo, Sagittarius, Pisces

Sign most helpful to career – Pisces

Sign most helpful for emotional support – Virgo

Sign most helpful financially – Cancer

Sign best for marriage and/or partnerships – Sagittarius

Sign most helpful for creative projects – Libra

Best Sign to have fun with – Libra

Signs most helpful in spiritual matters – Taurus, Aquarius

Best day of the week – Wednesday

Understanding a Gemini

Gemini is to society what the nervous system is to the body. It does not introduce any new information but is a vital transmitter of impulses from the senses to the brain and vice versa. The nervous system does not judge or weigh these impulses – it only conveys information. And it does so perfectly.

This analogy should give you an indication of a Gemini's role in society. Geminis are the communicators and conveyors of information. To Geminis the truth or falsehood of information is irrelevant, they only transmit what they see, hear or read about. Thus they are capable of spreading the most outrageous rumours as well as conveying truth and light. Geminis sometimes tend to be unscrupulous in their communications and can do both great good or great evil with their power. This is why the sign of Gemini is symbolized by twins: Geminis have a dual nature.

Their ability to convey a message – to communicate with such ease – makes Geminis ideal teachers, writers and media and marketing people. This is helped by the fact that Mercury, the ruling planet of Gemini, also rules these activities.

Geminis have the gift of the gab. And what a gift this is! They can make conversation about anything, anywhere, at any time. There is almost nothing that is more fun to Geminis than a good conversation – especially if they can learn something new as well. They love to learn and they love to teach. To deprive a Gemini of conversation, or of books and magazines, is cruel and unusual punishment.

Geminis are almost always excellent students and take well to education. Their minds are generally stocked with all kinds of information, trivia, anecdotes, stories, news items, rarities, facts and statistics. Thus they can support any intellectual position that they care to take. They are awesome debaters and, if involved in politics, make good orators. Geminis are so verbally smooth that even if they do not know what they are talking about, they can make you think that they do. They will always dazzle you with their brilliance.

Finance

Geminis tend to be more concerned with the wealth of learning and ideas than with actual material wealth. As mentioned, they excel in professions that involve writing, teaching, sales and journalism – and not all of these professions pay very well. But to sacrifice intellectual needs merely for money is unthinkable to a Gemini. Geminis strive to combine the two. Cancer is on Gemini's solar 2nd house of money cusp, which indicates that Geminis can earn extra income (in a harmonious and natural way) from investments in residential property, restaurants and hotels. Given their verbal skills, Geminis love to bargain and negotiate in any situation, and especially when it has to do with money.

The Moon rules Gemini's 2nd solar house. The Moon is not only the fastest-moving planet in the zodiac but actually moves through every sign and house every 28 days. No other heavenly body matches the Moon for swiftness or the ability to change quickly. An analysis of the Moon – and lunar phenomena in general – describes Gemini's financial attitudes very well. Geminis are financially versatile and flexible; they can earn money in many different ways. Their financial attitudes and needs seem to change daily. Their feelings about money change also: sometimes they are very enthusiastic about it, at other times they could not care less.

For a Gemini, financial goals and money are often seen only as means of supporting a family; these things have little meaning otherwise.

The Moon, as Gemini's money planet, has another important message for Gemini financially: in order for Geminis to realize their financial potential they need to develop more of an understanding of the emotional side of life. They need to combine their awesome powers of logic with an understanding of human psychology. Feelings have their own logic; Geminis need to learn this and apply it to financial matters.

Career and Public Image

Geminis know that they have been given the gift of communication for a reason, that it is a power that can achieve great good or cause unthinkable distress. They long to put this power at the service of the highest and most transcendental truths. This is their primary goal, to communicate the eternal verities and prove them logically. They look up to people who can transcend the intellect – to poets, artists, musicians and mystics. They may be awed by stories of religious saints and martyrs. A Gemini's highest achievement is to teach the truth, whether it is scientific, inspirational or historical. Those who can transcend the intellect are Gemini's natural superiors – and a Gemini realizes this.

The sign of Pisces is in Gemini's solar 10th house of career. Neptune, the planet of spirituality and altruism, is Gemini's career planet. If Geminis are to realize their highest career potential they need to develop their transcendental – their spiritual and altruistic – side. They need to understand the larger cosmic picture, the vast flow of human evolution – where it came from and where it is heading. Only then can a Gemini's intellectual powers take their true position and he or she can become the 'messenger of the gods'. Geminis need to cultivate a facility for 'inspiration', which is something that does not originate in the intellect but which comes through the intellect. This will further enrich and empower a Gemini's mind.

Love and Relationships

Geminis bring their natural garrulousness and brilliance into their love life and social life as well. A good talk or a verbal joust is an interesting prelude to romance. Their only problem in love is that their intellect is too cool and passionless to incite ardour in others. Emotions sometimes disturb them, and their partners tend to complain about this. If you are in love with a Gemini you must understand why this is so. Geminis avoid deep passions because these would interfere with their ability to think and communicate. If they are cool towards you, understand that this is their nature.

Nevertheless, Geminis must understand that it is one thing to talk about love and another actually to love – to feel it and radiate it. Talking about love glibly will get them nowhere. They need to feel it and act on it. Love is not of the intellect but of the heart. If you want to know how a Gemini feels about love you should not listen to what he or she says, but rather, observe what he or she does. Geminis can be quite generous to those they love.

Geminis like their partners to be refined, well educated and well travelled. If their partners are more wealthy than they are, all the better. If you are in love with a Gemini you had better be a good listener as well.

The ideal relationship for the Gemini is a relationship of the mind. They enjoy the physical and emotional aspects, of course, but if the intellectual communion is not there they will suffer.

Home and Domestic Life

At home the Gemini can be uncharacteristically neat and meticulous. They tend to want their children and partner to live up to their idealistic standards. When these standards are not met they moan and criticize. However, Geminis are good family people and like to serve their families in practical and useful ways.

The Gemini home is comfortable and pleasant. They like to invite people over and they make great hosts. Geminis are also good at repairs and improvements around the house – all fuelled by their need to stay active and occupied with something they like to do. Geminis have many hobbies and interests that keep them busy when they are home alone.

Geminis understand and get along well with their children, mainly because they are very youthful people themselves. As great communicators, Geminis know how to explain things to children; in this way they gain their children's love and respect. Geminis also encourage children to be creative and talkative, just like they are.

Horoscope for 2025

This is the year you blaze trails and set trends, Gemini. The year starts off with a profound shift as the north node and south node move into Pisces and Virgo respectively. For you, this means the north node enters your 10th house of career and legacy. Not only does the north node bring increase to the area of life it's transiting, it also brings eclipses. 'What do you want to be remembered for?' This is a question you'll be answering this year as you work to cement your legacy.

This year is noteworthy astrologically because it features a confluence of slow-moving planets changing signs. These planets include Saturn, Uranus and Neptune. Saturn and Neptune will be buddies jutting between Pisces and Aries. For Gemini, this means the planet that rules discipline and responsibility (Saturn) and the planet that rules dreams and collective connections (Neptune) oscillate between the career sector of your chart and the part of your chart associated with social standing. This will be discussed further in the career section of this horoscope

Saturn and Neptune aren't the only two slow-moving planets that shift into or out of the same sign. Jupiter starts the year in your sign and moves into Cancer midway through, while Uranus waits until July to shift into Gemini. Having a substantial slow-moving planet in your sign for all 12 months means that from a self-improvement standpoint this is a big year for levelling up. Self-improvement is noteworthy as well, given the fact that most of the eclipses occur in Pisces and Virgo, signs that are grouped with Gemini by astrologers because the Sun occupies them during transition periods between seasons. Eclipses are evolutionary transits that stimulate growth through scrutiny and shake-ups.

Mercury, Venus and Mars all enter periods of retrograde motion this year. Both Mercury and Venus will follow the same pattern as Saturn and Neptune, and shift between Pisces and Aries. This occurs during eclipse season, and only adds to potency around career and social standing this year. Mars retrograde is heavily financial for you and will be discussed in that section of this horoscope. Mercury's other retrogrades primarily occur in fire signs, which add a significant relationship-oriented dimension to its retrograde periods for Gemini.

For a quarterly view of the year, your first quarter features a heavy emphasis on career pursuits and making moves to cement your legacy. This feeds into the second quarter, where the energy starts to shift towards your standing in the groups, organizations and communities of which you're a part. The third quarter follows suit, emphasizing social life and social standing to an even greater extent. The last quarter of the year circles back to a focus on career and adjustments to career trajectory.

Health

(Please note that this is an astrological perspective on health and not a medical one. Any health-related symptoms should be evaluated by a qualified healthcare professional.)

Health for this year can be divided up into physical wellness and mental wellness. Your physical wellness planet is Mars, which starts the year retrograde. When the planetary ruler of a section of your chart is retrograde, it's wise not to overexert yourself. Mars will be retrograde until February 23, so be mindful about overloading your schedule during this time. Retrogrades are times we embody 're-' words such as 'reflect', 'revise' and 'revisit'. The Mars retrograde at the start of the year is an opportune time to circle back for any overdue check-ups or wellness appointments that are outstanding. Mars rules inflammation, so it's especially important to avoid inflammatory foods and maintain as healthy a diet as possible during the first two months of the year.

Your mental health planet is Venus, which also undergoes a retrograde period, from March 1 to April 12. In addition, March features two eclipses that are felt all around the body. Based on this confluence of cosmic weather, it's apparent that March is a vital month to stay grounded. Scheduling routine nesting time or solo time to recharge is paramount to maintain emotional equilibrium at this time. Venus will be retrograde in Aries, which embodies the mantra 'I with myself'. Ensuring your emotional needs are met through enforcing boundaries will likely be testing during this month and, though not easy to do, will set you up for success with the kinetic astrology influencing you this summer.

Here are the specific areas of the body to focus on this year:

- Lungs or pulmonary system: this is a perennial area of focus for you as Gemini rules the lungs in medical astrology. With your health planet being retrograde at the start of this year, there's an added emphasis on supporting the Gemini-ruled parts of the body. Avoiding explicitly harmful behaviours such as smoking, especially at the start of this year, is strongly advised.
- The skull and brain: there's a cluster of planets either shifting into or in retrograde motion in Aries this year, including your spiritual and mental health planet. Aries rules the head in medical astrology, which means both internally and externally how you take care of this part of the body is up for review. Incorporating a diet that supports brain health, such as eating foods with omega-3s, and doing practices that promote emotional grounding, such as mindfulness, are strongly recommended.
- Neck, shoulders and arms: your physical health planet, Mars, spends about 25 per cent of this year in Gemini's 2nd house, which scrutinizes neck and shoulder health. Incorporating more shoulder mobility into your exercise routines is recommended. Gemini also rules the arms, so this is a perennial area of focus.

Love and Social Life

This is your year of embodying 'the Trendsetter', as your social life is heavily emphasized. It is noteworthy that both Saturn and Neptune shift into Gemini's 11th house of community, groups and organizations. To explain why this is significant, Saturn takes 28½ years to go around the zodiac and spends approximately 2½ years in each sign. Saturn just begins its stay in Aries in this sector of your chart for this summer (May 24 to September 1), before more firmly entering the sign next year. Saturn rules discipline, responsibility and even restriction. Saturn functions as an auditor and turns its gaze towards your social circles and groups of friends during the summer. This, combined with the fact that Mars is your ruling planet for your social life and is retrograde at the start of the year, means there will likely be some form of restriction or trimming within your social circles and organizations. Saturn is all about sustainable structure, so relationships that are predicated on mutual support will thrive during this time. Saturn rules responsibility and prestige, which contribute to the potency you have around blazing trails and setting trends.

Service- or stewardship-oriented groups and organizations are especially highlighted as holistically beneficial for Gemini as Neptune moves into this section of your chart from March 30 to October 22. This is the first time in your life that Neptune will be in Aries, as it takes 160 years for the blue planet to navigate the zodiac. Neptune rules compassion and the collective. Philanthropic work or work that supports the planet at large is also recommended, given the heavy astrological emphasis this year on your career and public-facing persona. The shadow side of Neptune involves illusion and disillusion, which includes the phenomenon of wearing 'rose-coloured glasses'. New social circles should be properly vetted as a result.

Jupiter is your love and relationship planet that spends the first half of the year in your sign. Jupiter in Gemini is a gregarious transit for Gemini, supporting frequent dating and networking for those who are single. Regardless of your partnership status, Jupiter in Gemini significantly emphasizes communication in partnerships. Making sure you and your partner are aligned on expressive and receptive communication styles is extra-important. Jupiter augments what is already present, so misaligned communication will only become a bigger issue if not addressed early in the year. Jupiter moves into its sign of exaltation, Cancer, on June 9. Jupiter in Cancer promotes nesting with loved ones. If single, you'll likely to feel the call to transition from more casual dating to long-term relationship-seeking. If you have a partner, this transit absolutely supports moving in with one another (just make sure you do your Jupiter in Gemini homework described above).

Career and Finances

A big component as to why this is the year of the Trendsetter for you is because of how the cosmic weather influences the career for Gemini. The north node takes 18 years to transit the zodiac and enters Pisces 11 days into 2025. The last time the north node occupied the career sector of your chart was in 2007. This transit is significant first and foremost because it ushers in a new 18-year cycle centred around career and cementing your legacy. Paired with this increase is the breath of fresh air that is Saturn leaving this sector of your chart during the summer.

Saturn has spent 2½ years turning this area of your life into a bit of a crucible in order to galvanize the exciting growth you're about to experience. However, it's important to note that there's also a transitional quality to the growth this year, as Saturn technically oscillates back into Pisces come the autumn/fall. Nonetheless, the combination of the north node occupying this area of your chart virtually all year and Saturn beginning its exit from it supports major jumps in your career. In addition to Saturn, Neptune also releases its grip on this area of life after many years of occupying the career sector of your chart. Neptune rules literal and metaphorical fog, so it exiting your career sector means that this year you can assess and make career decisions more objectively. The period during which Neptune is in Aries (March 30 to October 22) is the part of this year when major career transformation is most viable. The eclipse occurring in Gemini's 10th house in September is a time to bookmark, as it's likely associated with endings and beginnings.

Your career planet is Jupiter, which also goes through a significant transition mid-year from Gemini to Cancer. In fact, Jupiter and Saturn switch signs within 16 days of each other, meaning that the start of summer is ripe with career-expansion opportunities and/or a period of transition. Jupiter moving into Cancer signifies two additional layers to your career story this year. First, whereas in years past career decisions weren't primarily financially motivated, this year the role finances play in these decisions will be weighted much heavier. Cancer is the sign of the home, which means that career motivations have a higher likelihood of being influenced by family needs, wants or expectations.

Finances in 2025 are a mixed bag, with the astrology of the start of the year contributing to why financial implications play a more significant role in career decisions come the summer. This year begins with Mars, your finance planet, being retrograde and entering Gemini's 2nd house of personal finances. Drawing up a planned budget you can adhere to is paramount. This is because Mars transiting this sector of a chart is often associated with one's wallet metaphorically being on fire. Unnecessary spending is ill advised for the first two months of the year, given the planetary retrograde. The financial weather appears much sunnier after the spring, now that Mars is direct and functioning at full speed, with Jupiter making its ingress into Cancer. Jupiter moving into your 2nd house of finances brings with it growth and expansion. This transit is an opportune time to pursue new streams of income or investment. Jupiter enters Cancer on June 9 and stays in the sign for the remainder of the year.

Home and Domestic Life

The eclipses bring changes to home and domestic life, as half of 2025's eclipses occur in this sector for Gemini. Just as a reminder, eclipses are evolutionary transits that promote growth through scrutiny and shaking things up. Given this scrutiny, paying attention to the literal structure of your home and staying on top of necessary repairs is fundamental, especially during March and September, the two months during which these eclipses occur. Eclipses frequently function by spurring us to part with the old in order to usher in the new. Given eclipses occur in this sector of your chart both in the spring and autumn/fall, bookmark these two seasons as prime moving times.

Mercury is your planetary ruler and undergoes three retrograde periods during the year. The first retrograde period occurs from March 15 to April 7 with it beginning mere hours after the first eclipse in this section of your chart. The penchant for miscommunication and misinterpretation within the household is at an all-time high during this transit. Make an extra effort to clarify and not default to assumptions when communicating with family. Given the retrograde begins in a Mars-ruled sign, this is especially important because tensions are likely to ride high at this time. Mercury's other retrograde periods are in Leo from July 18 to August 11 and in Sagittarius and Scorpio from November 9 to November 29.

Self-improvement

Embracing your individuality is the major prompt in this area of life this year for you, Gemini. Uranus enters your sign for the first time in 76 years. Uranus rules innovation, breakthroughs and individuality, among many other significations. Uranus moving into your sign highlights your totem for this year as the Trendsetter. Remember, trends are only set by those who innovate them first, and they often go against the grain and the status quo. Uranus in Gemini will spur you to live a more authentic life. Relationships with others who prevent you from doing so will be under significant scrutiny after Uranus enters your sign in July. The big challenge for you will be how you balance the call to embrace your authenticity with financial concerns and influence from others. Being the Trendsetter means trusting that abundance will come when you're acting in accordance with your true self. Your most innovative and abundant ideas can only become a reality if you allow yourself to be authentic. One of the most noteworthy times of year centred around your individuality is Mercury's retrograde in Leo during July and August. Mercury will be transiting Gemini's 3rd house of communication in the sign that rules the heart. Leverage this retrograde as a time of meaningful reflection so that you're able to maximize the abundant energy of Uranus in Gemini.

Month-by-month Forecasts

January

Best Days Overall: 20–23
Most Stressful Days Overall: 5–9
Best Days for Love: 27–31
Best Days for Money: 11–13
Best Days for Career: 29–31
Power Word: Budget

Happy New Year, Gemini! January's astrology kicks off on the 2nd with Venus moving into sweet Pisces. This transit encourages you to focus on your current career and your overarching career goals. Pisces is the sign of dreams, so leverage the energy of this transit through journaling, creating a vision board or creatively expressing what you seek to achieve.

We enter 2025 with Mars, the planet that rules irritation and inflammation, already retrograde. On January 6 the fiery planet will re-enter Cancer. This transit holds a magnifying glass to your budget and spending habits. This applies generally, but it's especially potent with funds going towards home, real estate and family expenses. Themes around spending that were prominent during the autumn/fall of 2024 are very much at play right now. There's no need to be hyper-vigilant around finances; just be mindful of where your money is coming from and how much of it is being spent. The theme of monitoring your budget reaches fever pitch with the full Moon in Cancer on the 13th. Full Moons are always emotional, and ways to ground yourself amid this lunation could be investing in accounting software or a consultant who can provide you with clarity on financial matters. Also, this full Moon is the ideal time to start a college fund or some sort of long-term savings fund to financially support you or your loved ones later in life.

Aquarius' season begins on January 19. If you've been in college, there are transits happening this week that will likely feel scrutinizing. If you've been meaning to get some form of higher education, this is the season to really put pen to paper and properly start planning out the next steps. The cosmic weather also applies to travel. If you've been intending on planning a big trip, this is your time to do so, although you should be being mindful of the overarching energy around budgeting. The new Moon in Aquarius on the 29th is the perfect day on which to do either of these activities. Furthermore, this is a very spiritual new Moon, so regardless of your current situation, bookmark the 29th for doing something that honours your spirit.

February

Best Days Overall: 3-7
Most Stressful Days Overall: 10-14
Best Days for Love: 7-9
Best Days for Money: 24-28
Best Days for Career: 27-28
Power Word: Communication

Happy February, Gemini! Mercury, your planetary ruler, forms a harmonious alignment with Jupiter, which will be exact on the 3rd. This transit supports all forms of communication, whether it's writing, listening or talking. On the 4th Venus enters Aries. Venus in Aries is a positive transit for immersing yourself in the groups and organizations you love. Moreover, general socializing is supported when Venus is in your 11th house of large communities.

The most potent transit of the year is the full Moon in Leo, occurring on February 12. Fasten your seatbelt as this transit is bombastic, to say the least, because the full Moon is tensely aspecting Uranus. Uranus rules instability, liberation and breakthroughs, among many other significations. For you, Gemini, this transit is all about how you communicate. If necessary conversations have been avoided and are resulting in anger bubbling beneath the surface, consider this full Moon a powder keg ready to explode. Responding instead of reacting can be the difference between productive communication and destructive communication. This transit also relates to your neighbourhood and how you may or may not fit in. Take it upon yourself to immerse yourself in some facet of your local community, whether it be a farmers' market, local event or exploring a nearby nature spot.

Pisces' season begins on the 18th, with the new Moon following suit on the 27th. This means the Sun joins up with the north node and shines its light on all things career. Mars will go direct on the 23rd, which is opportune as the new Moon appears just a few days later. Mars moving directly equates to forward momentum, and the new Moon introduces new beginnings. Work with this lunation to plot out and take actionable steps towards long-term career goals. Mars moving directly in Cancer has a financial component for you, Gemini, so factor in financial metrics when doing your career forecasting. The eclipses coming next month will be the real catalysts of your career growth in 2025, with this month's new Moon and Mars' direct motion leading things off.

March

Best Days Overall: 23–27
Most Stressful Days Overall: 14–18
Best Days for Love: 27–30
Best Days for Money: 7–11
Best Days for Career: 20–22
Power Word: Symbiotic

Hey, Gemini! March has a ton of cosmic weather to discuss including Mercury, your planetary ruler, turning retrograde mid-month. Before that occurs, Venus turns retrograde on March 1. This transit revolves primarily around friends and reciprocity in those relationships. Two bio-indicators for sustainable friendships are whether you can be 100 per cent authentically yourself with friends, and if they support you to a similar degree to how you support them. However, it's important to note that support doesn't have to be the exact same actions. Some friendships are symbiotic and there's still mutual support – it's just provided in different ways. Keep this in mind as you navigate the astrology of this month.

The first eclipse of 2025 occurs on March 14. The full Moon total lunar eclipse in Virgo centres around themes of home, family and real estate. This is not the time to ignore physical issues within your home. If you know something needs to be replaced or is past the time it's due for inspection, please handle it accordingly. Eclipses are evolutionary transits that catalyse growth through shake-ups. Family dynamics are also stimulated by this eclipse. Make every effort to communicate methodically and directly with your family this month. This is especially true around the eclipse, because Mercury turns retrograde one day later. Your planetary ruler will also be retrograde in Aries, like Venus. Miscommunication and assumptions abound! Make sure to ask for clarity if conversations with friends or loved ones leave you scratching your head. An inference can only be made with the correct information, so don't make assumptions without having all the facts.

Aries' season begins on the 20th, with the new Moon solar eclipse in the fire sign occurring on the 29th. These transits catalyse growth or change in the groups and organizations you're involved with. If you've been meaning to join a new community, this is your astrological invitation to do so. Moreover, if you've been meaning to part ways or pull back from groups you're currently a part of, these transits function in the same way. Neptune moves into Aries for the first time in your lifetime at the end of the month. Neptune in Aries pushes you towards seeking greater spiritual fulfilment in the communities you're a part of.

April

Best Days Overall: 6-10
Most Stressful Days Overall: 14-17
Best Days for Love: 8-12
Best Days for Money: 4-6
Best Days for Career: 18-20
Power Word: Onward

It's April, Gemini! This month's cosmic weather begins with a clus-ter of supportive transits working in tandem with one another. Bookmark the 5th and 7th as two days in particular to pay atten-tion to. The 5th features a harmonious alignment between Venus and Mars. This is an ideal transit for spending time with loved ones or treating yourself to doing something that makes you feel special. Mars is wrapping up its extended tenure in Cancer, so it's probably best for this quality time to be spent at home. Mercury, your plan-etary ruler, ends its retrograde on the 7th and turns direct. Phew! Mercury direct puts some wind in your sails for forward momen-tum towards achieving your 2025 goals.

On April 12 there's a full Moon in Libra, your fellow air sign. This full Moon is romantic and creative for Gemini. Full Moons repre-sent culminations of emotional cycles. If you've been practising a creative art for some time, this lunation demands you put your talent on display. Creativity is also the medium you should lean into to ground yourself if you're feeling the heightened emotions of a full Moon. Romance is also definitely on the table. This is espe-cially true because Venus ends its retrograde and turns direct on this day too. If you've got a partner, mark on the calendar that you should spend some quality time with them. If you're single, this is an ideal night for a Moon bath - go out under the full Moon, bask in its light and soak up the nurturing vibes of this lunation.

Taurus' season begins on April 19, and centres around mental health and wellness for you. You're wrapping up another trip around the Sun, so it's best to brush up on your supportive mental health routines. There's a lot for you to accomplish this year, Gemini, so definitely make sure you have the mental bandwidth to accommodate all the exciting things coming your way. April ends with a little bit of turbulence, given that Mars then opposes Pluto. This transit occurs on the same day as the new Moon in Taurus, encouraging you to pay attention to potential imbalances of power in the groups and organizations of which you're a part.

May

Best Days Overall: 3-6, 25-27
Most Stressful Days Overall: 10-15
Best Days for Love: 20-25
Best Days for Money: 25-28
Best Days for Career: 20-22
Power Word: Balance

It's almost your birthday, Gemini! May's astrology starts off with Mercury, your planetary ruler, in a positive alignment with Jupiter on the 5th. Jupiter has been in your sign all year, and a harmonious aspect with Mercury is definitely noteworthy for you. You'll feel this transit a day or so before and after. Mercury–Jupiter heightens marketing, communication and networking for Gemini. This is definitely a week to flap your social butterfly wings. Mercury–Jupiter is helpful for writing as well, if that's something you need to accomplish or enjoy doing. Mercury then moves into Taurus on the 10th. Mercury joins the Sun in its quest to support mental health and wellness.

Given Mercury's association with everything cerebral, it's important to incorporate somatic work into your routines to get out of your head and into your body. This is especially important because the full Moon this month is in watery Scorpio. Lunations in Scorpio revolve around the physical body for Gemini. This full Moon illuminates how – or if – you're taking care of your body. This full Moon is the ideal time to go to a doctor or dentist if you've been avoiding doing so. This lunation features the Sun applying to join Uranus in the last degrees of Taurus, spotlighting how, in order to temper the mind, you must first regulate the body. Given this emphasis on mental and physical wellness, this full Moon serves as a resting point in the month for Gemini. The first week was great for socializing, but it's necessary to prioritize downtime too.

On May 20 your solar season begins! Mercury enters Gemini on the 25th and there's a new Moon in your sign on the 26th. On the new Moon there's a 'stellium' or cluster of four planets in Gemini. That's a lot of Gemini energy! Lean into this stellium by scheduling time for what makes you feel most alive. This confluence of Gemini energy will be felt ubiquitously, so expect those around you to ramp up their communication during the last week of the month.

June

Best Days Overall: 3-7
Most Stressful Days Overall: 21-24
Best Days for Love: 11-14
Best Days for Money: 25-28
Best Days for Career: 5-7
Power Word: Measured

Hey, Gemini! The first week of June features several planets switching signs. Venus moves into Taurus on the 6th, followed by Mercury and Jupiter entering Cancer on the 8th and 9th respectively. That's a noticeable change in the cosmic weather. Venus is very happy in Taurus and is focused on security. For Gemini, Venus in Taurus is most concerned that you feel safe. If you haven't identified a 'sanctuary space' to retreat to when you need to recharge, now is the time. Also, monitor your body's innate reaction to being in routine places or with routine people. Mercury's foray into Cancer is short-lived (it ends on the 26th), but Jupiter stays in the sign for close to a year. Jupiter in Cancer is all about financial abundance for Gemini. Jupiter rules growth, expansion, beliefs and conviction. Jupiter in Cancer supports you in the pursuit of new or existing endeavours that inspire others. Jupiter in Cancer can also represent a boon in your partner's finances or prestige.

Speaking of partners, the full Moon in Sagittarius falls in Gemini's 7th house of relationships. This full Moon illuminates your attitude towards relationships. Sagittarius is a very adventurous sign, so lean into spontaneity in this department. If you've got a partner, take them on a spur-of-the-moment trip, even if it's just to a new part of town. If you're single, embrace this adventurous full Moon by putting yourself out there or going on a solo quest to wherever your heart desires.

Cancer's season begins on the 20th, with the new Moon following on the 25th. The new Moon is squaring off with Saturn and Neptune (and was exact on the 22nd and 23rd respectively). This alignment is associated with feeling daunted in the face of tackling tasks, chasing dreams or just managing all the responsibilities you have. Work with this transit by breaking large tasks down into smaller parts. Moreover, this new Moon reminds you that you can't associate your self-worth with productivity. Thankfully, on the 26th the Sun finds harmony with Mars, which will help clear the feeling of doubt and put some fuel back in your tank.

July

Best Days Overall: 7–11
Most Stressful Days Overall: 17–22
Best Days for Love: 2–6
Best Days for Money: 10–13
Best Days for Career: 24–27
Power Word: Honest

Are you ready for some more Gemini energy, Gemini? On July 4 Venus conjoins with Uranus at the last degree of Taurus before hopping into your sign for most of the month. Venus in your sign brings energy around splendour and pleasure, so do try to assign time to treat yourself this first week. Venus–Uranus aspects are social, spontaneous and full of surprises. Uranus enters your sign for the first time since it left it in 1949! This transit affects us on the collective level by ushering in profound innovations around the way we communicate. For you, Uranus will transit your natal Gemini Sun soon if you're an early Gemini or in a few years if you're born later into Gemini season. Uranus transiting your natal

Sun centres around liberation and typically leads to noteworthy shifts in your identity.

On July 10 the annual full Moon in Capricorn occurs. This transit poses the question, 'Do you have a sustainable structure in place to support the financial abundance Jupiter in Cancer could bring?' If the answer is anything but a resounding yes, this lunation will demand you consult with experts on this subject or even educate yourself in the realm of financial literacy. One week later, Mercury turns retrograde in Leo. This transit begins on the 18th, but you will feel it the week before. Mercury is your planetary ruler, so these retrogrades are felt by Gemini. This retrograde especially deals with communication and communication breakdowns. Actively listening is a key skill to work on for this transit.

You know Leo is loud, but this Leo season begins with a roar as the Sun immediately aspects five planets. The new Moon in Leo occurs on the 24th and has all five of these transits built into it. The theme for this new Moon is authenticity. For Gemini, this new Moon specifically promotes speaking your truth. With Mercury being retrograde, there's the added prompt of thinking through what you have to say, but don't shy away from sharing your honest point of view. The Sun opposes Pluto on the 25th, which will further encourage you to shed limiting patterns around communication. This transit also correlates to transformation around education and spirituality for Gemini.

August

Best Days Overall: 21–25
Most Stressful Days Overall: 7–11
Best Days for Love: 12–14
Best Days for Money: 10–14
Best Days for Career: 27–29
Power Word: Diamond

It's a stop-and-start kind of month this August, Gemini. August's astrology begins on the 1st as Venus finds tension with both Saturn and Neptune. Venus squaring off with Saturn typically evokes self-deprecating vibes, so make an extra effort to be a friend to yourself at this time. Moreover, Neptune's involvement stirs up escapist tendencies, so avoid old patterns of dissociative behaviour that may resurface. The good news is this transit yields long-lasting strides in embodying self-love. Remember, it takes pressure to turn carbon into a diamond. On the 6th Mars enters Libra, your fellow air sign. Mars is the planet of assertion and feels a little uneasy being in a sign centred around harmony. For you, Gemini, this transit is about finding integration and balance between your creative pursuits and other aspects of your life. Mars lights a fire under these pursuits and romantic endeavours for the next six weeks.

On the 9th there's a full Moon in Aquarius just as Mars faces off with Saturn and Neptune. This lunation promotes rest over work and will likely force you to trim the fat in your schedule. Productivity does not equal worth, so avoid being hypercritical of yourself if you're feeling like you're moving at a slower pace or can't get everything done. Fortunately, Mercury, your planetary ruler, goes direct two days later. Mercury will still be moving slowly for a few days, but this transit will clear the feeling of being stuck in traffic as Mercury picks up speed over the next couple of weeks.

Virgo's season begins on the 22nd, with the first of two new Moons in the sign occurring the following day. This lunation centres around home and family dynamics for Gemini, and seeks to renew a sense of organization or order within your home or even familial relationships. Renovating, remodelling or reorganizing your space to bring new energy into it are ideal ways to work with the energy of this transit. This new Moon receives scrutiny from Uranus, encouraging you to go to extremes with these themes, so do your best to bring about these changes incrementally or in moderation.

September

Best Days Overall: 18-19, 27-30
Most Stressful Days Overall: 23-26
Best Days for Love: 16-18
Best Days for Money: 5-7
Best Days for Career: 7-12
Power Word: Evolve

It's eclipse season, Gemini! As a reminder, eclipses are evolutionary transits that stimulate growth through destabilization and scrutiny. This eclipse season is particularly potent for your sign, so let's jump right in. On the 7th there will be a full Moon lunar eclipse in Pisces lighting up Gemini's career sector. As discussed in your yearly horoscope, a major theme for this year revolves around the question, 'What do I want my legacy to be and am I on the right track?' This question has been ringing in your ears for a bit and has now attained a louder pitch. Answer the call, Gemini! To really tap into the catalysing energy of this eclipse, it's vital that if you decide to part with existing career goals or roles, you ground yourself in gratitude for all that you have accomplished or learned from this chapter of your life. This eclipse, however, also has a great deal of applicability if you feel as though you're exactly where you need to be in your career or regarding your legacy, although it will demand you shed other aspects of your identity that no longer serve you and may inhibit future growth.

The second eclipse of the month occurs on the 21st in Virgo. While the first eclipse focused on your future and public life, this eclipse has you reconciling the past and your private life. Specifically, this eclipse will likely force you to confront conditioning in your childhood that has locked you into self-effacing patterns of thought or behaviour. While these thoughts or behaviours have become habitual, they absolutely can be rectified with sustained effort. This eclipse is a new Moon solar eclipse, so the end goal is to free you from existing structures in order to usher in a new way of being. Don't feel like you need to tackle this all at once, as this eclipse stimulates these changes over the next six months.

Libra's season begins on the 22nd, and the Sun gets busy aspecting every planet from Saturn to Pluto over the next three days. Libra season and these transits revolve around your relationship to creativity. If you're feeling overly stimulated by all the eclipse energy, lean into creativity as a means of grounding yourself.

October

Best Days Overall: 1-5
Most Stressful Days Overall: 6-12
Best Days for Love: 14-17
Best Days for Money: 25-28
Best Days for Career: 28-31
Power Word: Self-empower

It's October, Gemini! This month's astrology begins with a bright full Moon in Aries on the 6th. This lunation spotlights the groups, communities and organizations you associate with. More specifically, this full Moon actually hearkens back to the new Moon solar eclipse in Aries at the end of March and represents the culmination of the last six months you've spent immersed in these spaces. Since March, how has your dynamic within your various social circles and professional organizations changed? This lunation encourages you to take a close look at whether there's reciprocity in these circles. If the answer is yes, this full Moon will prompt you to deepen your connection within them. However, if you feel as though you give more than you get, this full Moon will spur you to adjust your involvement accordingly.

The second week of the month features Venus aspecting several planets and entering Libra on the 13th. Venus forms connections with Saturn, Uranus, Neptune and Pluto from the 11th to the 15th. As a result, the cosmic weather shifts to focus on your relationship to creativity and romance. More specifically, it demonstrates that you can get in your own way when it comes to creative self-expression and romance. Be open to being shown how you may limit yourself as the cosmic weather seeks to liberate you from this behaviour. Moreover, if you're feeling out of sorts, lean into your favourite forms of creativity as a means to ground yourself. The new Moon in Libra occurs on the 21st, ushering in a new emotional cycle around the role that creativity and romance play in your life. Honour this lunation through allowing yourself the space to explore, play and seek pleasure.

Scorpio's season begins on the 22nd with the Sun immediately aspecting Uranus and Pluto over the following two days. This solar season spotlights your physical wellness routines. In what ways do your daily or weekly routines support or detract from your holistic physical health? On the 28th Mars finds harmony with Jupiter, encouraging you to level up your fitness routines and how you nourish your body.

November

Best Days Overall: 21–24
Most Stressful Days Overall: 8–13
Best Days for Love: 27–30
Best Days for Money: 17–20
Best Days for Career: 22–25
Power Word: Jump-start

Happy November, Gemini! This month's astro-weather begins on the 4th with Mars entering Sagittarius, your polar sign. This transit brings lightning in a bottle to your relationship and dating life. Both extremes apply whether you're single or partnered. If you're single, this transit will find you either feeling incredibly jump-started with dating or extremely frustrated with your current state of affairs. If you're in a relationship, Mars' kinetic energy will either stimulate a lot of passion or a lot of passionate bickering. The key is regression to the mean with this transit. The full Moon in Taurus occurs the next day, shining a light on your mental health and well-ness routines. This lunation inquires if you're able to strike a balance between social time and solo time.

Mercury, your planetary ruler, turns retrograde one last time on the 9th. This retrograde has considerable potential to bring back ghosts from your past, given that it's in Sagittarius, your polar sign. Remember that if this happens, you're being asked to revisit who you were when you were close with this person – or people – in order to reflect on how much you've grown. The Sun forms one of the most harmonious aspects, a grand water trine, with Jupiter and Saturn on the 17th. This transit is mushy and soft, and it supports connecting on a heart level with someone you care about.

The new Moon in Scorpio occurs on the 20th. This lunation encourages you to make a more concerted effort to nourish your body. Check in with it on this date and question what it specifically needs. Unlike our minds, our bodies can't lie to us. On the 22nd Sagittarius season officially begins. This is a visionary time of year for Gemini, during which you dream about what's possible, especially in the realm of partnership and collaboration. If you've got a partner and are planning to level the relationship up in some way, this week is a great time to do so. If you're single, reflect on what qualities you seek to embody in your next long-term relationship.

December

Best Days Overall: 2-5
Most Stressful Days Overall: 9-14
Best Days for Love: 1-4
Best Days for Money: 24-28
Best Days for Career: 21-24
Power Word: Partner

Happy December, Gemini! The big theme for this month is partnership and how it takes two to tango. First up is the full Moon in your sign on the 4th. If a partnership is you plus someone else, this lunation is all about the 'you' in that equation. Your outlook on relationships, temperament in a relationship and common patterns of behaviour will all be up for examination during this full Moon. Individuation versus co-dependent behaviour is also something this lunation illuminates. All of this is ultimately positive because your annual full Moon strongly supports your emotional evolution. In order for a caterpillar to become a butterfly, it has to go through some serious growing pains in its chrysalis phase. Go get your wings, Gemini!

The cosmic weather forces you to step on the brake pedal around the 9th when Mars and Saturn square off. This transit forces you to stop and smell the proverbial roses. Restlessness is a big symptom of this transit, so bunker down and know that frustration is expected – there will be plenty of time later this month for working on future goals. Mercury, your planetary ruler, is direct and forms a number of aspects. Between the 10th and the 13th, Mercury forms aspects with Uranus, Neptune and Pluto, as well as entering Sagittarius on the 11th. These transits bring back the primary theme of relationships and, more so, examine communication. It's a cliché to say that communication is key in a relationship, but it absolutely applies to these transits.

The new Moon in Sagittarius falls on the 19th. This is a visionary lunation, encouraging you to dream up what's possible in existing or future partnerships. If you've got a partner, this new Moon encourages you to have a heartfelt and vulnerable conversation with them about their hopes and dreams, both within the confines of the relationship and in general. If you're single, focusing on the 'you' in the partnership equation and creating a 2026 vision board is a great way to channel the energy of this lunation. Capricorn season begins on the 21st, and 2025 ends with a shift in focus to achieving or maintaining financial abundance.

Cancer

THE CRAB

Birthdays from
June 21
to July 20

Personality Profile

CANCER AT A GLANCE

Element – Water

Ruling Planet – Moon
   Career Planet – Mars
   Love Planet – Saturn
   Money Planet – Sun
   Planet of Fun, Entertainment, Creativity and Pleasure – Pluto
   Planet of Good Fortune – Neptune
   Planet of Health and Work – Jupiter
   Planet of Home and Family Life – Venus
   Planet of Spirituality and Mental Health – Mercury

Totem – the Alchemist

Colours – blue, puce, silver

Colours that promote love, romance and social harmony – black,
   indigo

Colours that promote earning power – gold, orange

Gems – moonstone, pearl

Metal – silver

Scents – jasmine, sandalwood

Quality – cardinal (= activity)

Quality most needed for balance – mood control

Strongest virtues – emotional sensitivity, tenacity, the urge to nurture

Deepest need – a harmonious home and family life

Characteristics to avoid – over-sensitivity, negative moods

Signs of greatest overall compatibility – Scorpio, Pisces

Signs of greatest overall incompatibility – Aries, Libra, Capricorn

Sign most helpful to career – Aries

Sign most helpful for emotional support – Libra

Sign most helpful financially – Leo

Sign best for marriage and/or partnerships – Capricorn

Sign most helpful for creative projects – Scorpio

Best Sign to have fun with – Scorpio

Signs most helpful in spiritual matters – Gemini, Pisces

Best day of the week – Monday

Understanding a Cancer

In the sign of Cancer the heavens are developing the feeling side of things. This is what a true Cancerian is all about – feelings. Where Aries will tend to err on the side of action, Taurus on the side of inaction and Gemini on the side of thought, Cancer will tend to err on the side of feeling.

Cancerians tend to mistrust logic. Perhaps rightfully so. For them it is not enough for an argument or a project to be logical – it must feel right as well. If it does not feel right a Cancerian will reject it or chafe against it. The phrase 'follow your heart' could have been coined by a Cancerian, because it describes exactly the Cancerian attitude to life.

The power to feel is a more direct – more immediate – method of knowing than thinking is. Thinking is indirect. Thinking about a thing never touches the thing itself. Feeling is a faculty that touches directly the thing or issue in question. We actually experience it. Emotional feeling is almost like another sense which humans possess – a psychic sense. Since the realities that we come in contact with during our lifetime are often painful and even destructive, it is not surprising that the Cancerian chooses to erect barriers – a shell – to protect his or her vulnerable, sensitive nature. To a Cancerian this is only common sense.

If Cancerians are in the presence of people they do not know, or find themselves in a hostile environment, up goes the shell and they feel protected. Other people often complain about this, but one must question these people's motives. Why does this shell disturb them? Is it perhaps because they would like to sting, and feel frustrated that they cannot? If your intentions are honourable and you are patient, have no fear. The shell will open up and you will be accepted as part of the Cancerian's circle of family and friends.

Thought processes are generally analytic and dissociating. In order to think clearly we must make distinctions, comparisons and the like. But feeling is unifying and integrative.

To think clearly about something you have to distance yourself from it. To feel something you must get close to it. Once a Cancerian has accepted you as a friend, he or she will hang on to you. You have to be really bad to lose the friendship of a Cancerian. If you are related to Cancerians they will never let you go no matter what you do. They will always try to maintain some kind of connection even in the most extreme circumstances.

Finance

The Cancer-born has a deep sense of what other people feel about things and why they feel as they do. This faculty is a great asset in the workplace and in the business world. Of course, it's also indispensable in raising a family and building a home, but it has its uses in business. Cancerians often attain great wealth in a family business. Even if the business is not a family operation, they will treat it as one. If the Cancerian works for somebody else, then the boss is the parental figure and the co-workers are brothers and sisters. If a Cancerian is the boss, then all the workers are his or her children. Cancerians like the feeling of being providers for others. They enjoy knowing that others derive their sustenance because of what they do. It is another form of nurturing.

With Leo on their solar 2nd money house cusp, Cancerians are often lucky speculators, especially with residential property or hotels and restaurants. Resort hotels and nightclubs are also profitable for the Cancerian. Waterside properties attract them. Though they are basically conventional people, they sometimes like to earn their livelihood in glamorous ways.

The Sun, Cancer's money planet, represents an important financial message: in financial matters Cancerians need to be less moody, more stable and fixed. They cannot allow their moods – which are here today and gone tomorrow – to get in the way of their business lives. They need to develop their self-esteem and feelings of self-worth if they are to realize their greatest financial potential.

Career and Public Image

Aries rules the 10th solar career house cusp of Cancer, which indicates that Cancerians long to start their own business, to be more
active publicly and politically and to be more independent. Family
responsibilities and a fear of hurting other people's feelings – or
getting hurt themselves – often inhibit them from attaining these
goals. However, this is what they want and long to do.

Cancerians like their bosses and leaders to act freely and to be a
bit self-willed. They can deal with that in a superior. They expect
their leaders to be fierce on their behalf. When the Cancerian is in
the position of boss or superior he or she behaves very much like a
'warlord'. Of course, the wars they wage are not egocentric but in
defence of those under their care. If they lack some of this fighting
instinct – independence and pioneering spirit – Cancerians will
have extreme difficulty in attaining their highest career goals. They
will be hampered in their attempts to lead others.

Since they are so parental, Cancerians like to work with children
and make great educators and teachers.

Love and Relationships

Like Taurus, Cancer likes committed relationships. Cancerians
function best when the relationship is clearly defined and everyone
knows his or her role. When they marry it is usually for life. They
are extremely loyal to their beloved. But there is a deep little secret
that most Cancerians will never admit to: commitment or partnership is really a chore and a duty to them. They enter into it because
they know of no other way to create the family that they desire.
Union is just a way – a means to an end – rather than an end in
itself. The family is the ultimate end for them.

If you are in love with a Cancerian you must tread lightly on his
or her feelings. It will take you a good deal of time to realize how
deep and sensitive Cancerians can be. The smallest negativity
upsets them. Your tone of voice, your irritation, a look in your eye
or an expression on your face can cause great distress for the
Cancerian. Your slightest gesture is registered by them and reacted

to. This can be hard to get used to, but stick by your love – Cancerians make great partners once you learn how to deal with them. Your Cancerian lover will react not so much to what you say but to the way you are actually feeling at that moment.

Home and Domestic Life

This is where Cancerians really excel. The home environment and the family are their personal works of art. They strive to make things of beauty that will outlast them. Very often they succeed.

Cancerians feel very close to their family, their relatives and especially their mothers. These bonds last throughout their lives and mature as they grow older. They are very fond of those members of their family who become successful, and they are also quite attached to family heirlooms and mementos. Cancerians also love children and like to provide them with all the things they need and want. With their nurturing, feeling nature, Cancerians make very good parents – especially the Cancerian woman, who is the mother *par excellence* of the zodiac.

As a parent the Cancerian's attitude is 'my children right or wrong'. Unconditional devotion is the order of the day. No matter what a family member does, the Cancerian will eventually forgive him or her, because 'you are, after all, family'. The preservation of the institution – the tradition – of the family is one of the Cancerian's main reasons for living. They have many lessons to teach others about this.

Being so family-orientated, the Cancerian's home is always clean, orderly and comfortable. They like old-fashioned furnishings but they also like to have all the modern comforts. Cancerians love to have family and friends over, to organize parties and to entertain at home – they make great hosts.

Horoscope for 2025

This year is about transmuting your wisdom and experience into gold, Cancer, as you embody your totem, 'the Alchemist'. The year begins with the north node shifting into your 9th house of spirituality, higher education and voyages after spending 18 months in the career sector of your chart. This year is a chapter-turning moment where you'll be directed to draw from your experiences of the last 18 months and make some key decisions that will influence your overarching career trajectory. Getting in touch with your spirituality, identifying the role of education in your life and taking a spirit journey are focus areas to aid you in your journey this year.

This is a unique year because Saturn, Uranus and Neptune (all slow-moving planets) shift signs. These shifts influence the collective and will yield profound societal changes. Saturn moves into Aries after spending 2½ years in Pisces. Saturn in Aries will encourage you to dismantle those career aspirations of yours that no longer align with present-day values and what you seek to be remembered for. Neptune makes the same transition from Pisces to Aries, further emphasizing the need for spiritual fulfilment in your career. Uranus shifts into Gemini this summer, which will catalyse major shifts in the ways we as a society communicate and relate to one another.

In addition to the north node moving into Pisces, there are four planets that will undergo periods of retrograde motion between Aries and Pisces over the course of the year. This is substantial and represents the link between career, legacy, spirituality, higher education and travel. March is one such month that features two of these retrograde periods (Mercury and Venus) plus two eclipses lighting up the career and communication sectors of your chart. The astrology of the spring will be explored in depth in the subsequent sections of this yearly horoscope.

Part of embodying the Alchemist is grounding yourself more deeply in an authentic spiritual value system that not only informs how you navigate life, but also how you approach your relationship with yourself. One of the most harmonious transits of the year for you is when abundant Jupiter enters your sign in June. It does so once every 12 years, so this transit represents the start of a new 12-year cycle centred around how your beliefs and convictions inform your sense of self. More on this transit will be discussed in the self-improvement section of this horoscope.

For a quarterly view of this year, the first quarter focuses on spirituality and higher education, the second features a shift in focus to how your beliefs and values translate in your career trajectory, the third focuses more on career and legacy as well as on your comfortability with communicating your needs, and the last quarter of the year returns the focus to spirituality and higher education, and encourages travel.

Health

(Please note that this is an astrological perspective on health and not a medical one. Any health-related symptoms should be evaluated by a qualified healthcare professional.)

Being ruled by the Moon, eclipse seasons are Cancer's perennial time of focus for health-related matters. March features two eclipses, one in Virgo and one in Aries, plus Mercury, your spiritual and mental health planet, will be retrograde. Maintaining consistency with routines and your spiritual practice during this time is a recommended way to support your well-being. Mercury will be retrograde until April 7, but will not be functioning at full speed until the end of the month. With Jupiter being in Gemini during this time, it's vital you communicate your emotional needs if you feel that you're struggling. September is the other month with a set of eclipses. This month features an eclipse in Pisces and an eclipse in Virgo. Emphasis around gut health is highlighted by the Virgo eclipse occurring during Virgo's season.

Jupiter, your physical health planet, is joyous in your sign, Cancer. Jupiter enters Cancer on June 9 and stays there for the remainder of the year. While abundant, Jupiter does leave you prone to overindulgence, so make a concerted effort to temper hedonistic behaviour while still enjoying yourself. Jupiter in Cancer promotes setting up an exercise space or physical wellness space within your home

– anything from free weights to a designated yoga space – or you might like to build an area in your garden or back yard where you can work out. Jupiter in Cancer promotes nurturing your body, just as a mother would nurture her child. Intuitive eating – also known as listening to what foods your body 'tells you' it needs – is one example of leaning into the energy of this transit.

This year starts off with Mars retrograde, which quickly enters your sign on January 6. Mars stays retrograde in Cancer until February 23 and occupies your sign until April 18. Mars is inflammatory in nature, so take special care to avoid foods or behaviours that cause inflammation. This Mars retrograde functions as an audit of which wellness routines and adjustments need to be implemented to better support your body. Remember, this retrograde ends right before eclipse season begins, so it's essential to align your wellness routines by the end of February.

Mercury, your spiritual and mental health planet, will be retrograde on three occasions. In addition to the spring retrograde, Mercury will be retrograde from July 18 to August 11, and from November 9 to November 29. As recommended with the spring retrograde, maintaining a routine schedule and actively grounding yourself through spiritual practices such as meditation are highly encouraged to mitigate the tension of these retrograde periods. The November retrograde features Mercury transiting through your physical health sector, so be mindful about the role stress plays on your physical body at this time.

Here are the specific areas of the body to focus on this year:

- Stomach, breasts and lymphatic system: these parts of the body are ruled by Cancer in medical astrology and are vital to always stay on top of. Annual examinations of these areas are recommended. Adopting a consistent exercise routine and seeking out a lymphatic massage expert are also recommended to support these parts of the body.
- Head and face: Mars will be retrograde in Cancer's 1st house, which rules the head and face in medical astrology. Internal and external care of this area is important, especially during periods when Mercury is retrograde.

- Lungs and arms: Jupiter, your physical health planet, will be in Gemini for the first five months of the year. Gemini rules these parts of the body, and this is a year to be particularly mindful to avoid deleterious behaviours such as smoking.

Love and Social Life

This is a more neutral area of life this year, as Pluto has finally vacated the relationship sector of your chart and there aren't tense aspects from other planets this year. Your love planet is Saturn, which shifts sign over the summer. Saturn moving from collective-focused Pisces to self-oriented Aries influences how you approach relationships. If you're single, embodying the confidence of Aries will pay dividends in seeking partnership. The Aries archetype follows the mantra 'I with myself', so approaching relationships from the lens of finding someone to complement your already complete life, versus seeking someone to complete you, is strongly promoted with this transit.

Your love and social life undergoes a period of review in March, with Venus turning retrograde from March 1 to April 12. This retrograde is an audit around how your self-esteem and feelings of self-worth translate to how you approach relationships and how you navigate the social circles of which you're a part. A major component of this centres around communication and whether or not you censor yourself for the sake of other people. Allow for this Venus retrograde (and the eclipses occurring at the same time) to spotlight what behaviours you must shed in order to upgrade and evolve in this area of life. Uranus has been occupying the social life area of your chart since 2018 and exits it from July to November. This period from July to November affords an element of stability to your social life.

Career and Finances

As mentioned in the introduction to this horoscope, there are many planetary shifts occurring in the career sector of your chart, most notably by both Saturn and Neptune. This is the first time that the

Saturn transit has occurred since 1999 and the first time in your lifetime for the Neptune transit. Saturn in your career sector forces maturation. This transit is an examination of the existing structures you have in place that support your career trajectory and whether they're really fortified enough to handle the weight of what you seek to accomplish.

Part of this examination is also a litmus test of whether or not there is a sense of spiritual fulfilment in what you seek to do. This need to accommodate your spirituality becomes especially potent once Neptune enters Aries on March 30. This takes place at the tail end of one of the most hectic months of the year for you. Neptune stays in Aries until October 22 and will formally shift into the sign next year. The combination of Saturn and Neptune transiting this area of your chart indicates that true gold can only be created in your career if there's a spiritual alignment. This spiritual alignment will also yield long-lasting sustainability to your career pursuits.

There are peaks and troughs in your finances this year. The Sun is your finance planet, and you'll find that it's continually running through condensed confluences of aspects with the outer planets, who are all hanging out in roughly the same degree. Basically, it's a domino effect for the Sun – when it aspects one planet, multiple others follow over the course of just a few days. Obvious times to adopt a more frugal approach to finances would be the two solar eclipses occurring on March 29 and September 7. Check your monthly horoscope for information about when these condensed periods of activity for the Sun occur. These periods of activity aren't negative financially, but being mindful of whether they are harmonious or tense can inform the level of risk or conservatism you apply to decisions you make.

Two planetary retrogrades occur in the financial sector of your chart this year. First, you enter the year with Mars currently retrograde. Mars in your financial sector is inflammatory and requires a conservative approach to finances. Although Mars dips out of this area of your chart by January 6, the planet returns when in direct motion and stays there from April 19 to June 17. Mars rules drive, ambition and conflict, and brings these themes to your finances during this period. Consulting trusted sources or professionals for advice or guidance is strongly advised during this time of scrutiny. Mercury turns retrograde in this sector of your chart this summer from July 18 to August 11, spurring you to take account of all the pathways by which money enters and exits your account. Make necessary adjustments to income streams after Mercury turns direct in August.

Home and Domestic Life

Your home and domestic life planet is Venus. This is on the whole a more settled area of your life, which is a positive after years of eclipses occurring in this realm. Venus does turn retrograde for the entirety of March and half of April. It should be expected that this period will bring some disruption or confusion to domestic life. Prioritizing quality time with loved ones and housemates is recommended to mitigate the frenetic energy of this month. Cultivating cosiness within the home is also recommended to facilitate a relaxing environment. Cancer is a sign that's emotionally influenced by the energy of the spaces it lives in. Addressing and readjusting the feng shui of your spaces is another recommendation to counterbalance the instability of this month's astrology. Venus will be moving directly and at full speed come May 16 for the rest of the year.

Self-improvement

Your year of embodying the Alchemist hinges upon the necessary self-discovery and exploration of the philosophies that inform your value system. The combination of all the planetary motion to and from Pisces, plus Jupiter entering your sign, means that this is a very spiritual year for you, Cancer. Saturn and Neptune will be co-present in Pisces for the first three months of the year, until Neptune moves into your career sector. These first three months are a hectic time, with Mars retrograde lasting until almost the end of February, and the eclipses plus retrogrades occurring in March. Saturn and Neptune orient you towards grounding yourself through spiritual practice. The first three months are an ideal time in which to discover different types of spirituality so that you can construct a robust spiritual value system.

Jupiter's ingress into Cancer lasts for approximately 12 months and ushers in a new 12-year cycle centred around your redefined spirituality. This transit, paired with the transits in Pisces, promotes taking a trip or voyage as a means to gain perspective around spirituality and your overarching mission in life. If you're unable to travel far away, venturing into nearby nature to get in touch with how your aspirations align with your spirituality works just as well. Moreover, the astrology of 2025 strongly supports you getting more deeply involved in philanthropic or charitable causes. This work will help inform the spiritual value system you seek to create and, in turn, pay dividends towards the maturation you undergo in your career.

Another important area of improvement for you is in how you approach and utilize communication. Both the spring and autumn/fall contain eclipses occurring in your communication sector. Eclipses catalyse evolution through scrutiny and shake-ups. Innovations around methods of communication will only be gaining steam as Uranus enters Gemini this year. Researching and adopting new modalities of communication in all areas of your life will pay long-lasting dividends as these technologies increasingly become part of normal life. Continuing to expand your knowledge around artificial intelligence is also recommended, with your communication sector being spotlighted by both eclipse cycles.

Month-by-month Forecasts

January

Best Days Overall: 8-13
Most Stressful Days Overall: 21-24
Best Days for Love: 27-29
Best Days for Money: 13-17
Best Days for Career: 1-5
Power Word: Ally

Happy 2025, Cancer! This month's cosmic weather begins on the 2nd with Venus entering Pisces. Venus is the planet that rules values, worthiness and intimacy. Venus in Pisces is a dreamy transit that encourages loving wholeheartedly, and finding love for one's self and the collective through spiritual practice. Grounding yourself in routine spiritual practices is going to be important as Mars retrograde enters your sign on the 6th.

Mars' period of retrograde motion through your sign this month is arguably the most noteworthy transit. It encourages profound reflection around how family dynamics affect how you navigate life. This retrograde also has you contemplating your relationship to productivity and whether you tie your worthiness to productivity. It's imperative that you cut yourself some slack and double up on self-compassion this month, especially if you're feeling stalled. This transit brings with it an invitation to incorporate an affirmation practice, journaling or meditation into your wellness routines. Mars retrograde normally instils restlessness and pent-up anger. Utilize your wellness routines as a mechanism to keep yourself present. Lean into creative self-expression if you find that anger is a strong component of how this retrograde affects you.

On the 13th there will be a watery full Moon in your sign. Full Moons represent culminations of emotional cycles and this full Moon revolves around how you treat yourself. Definitely schedule self-care in advance around this date as the vibes very likely will be highly emotional. This transit encourages you to be your biggest cheerleader and to pause to reflect on all the ways your uniqueness betters the world. This is also a great full Moon to nest with family in a place you consider home.

Aquarius' season begins on the 19th, an ideal time to audit your streams of income and follow up on any money you may be owed. The Sun moves directly into its annual meeting with Pluto, which brings with it a rebirth in aspects of your identity. This transit heartens you to shed old characteristics of your identity in order to embody who you currently are. January ends with a new Moon in Aquarius on the 29th, further supporting this evolution. May you be your biggest ally this month, sweet Cancer.

February

Best Days Overall: 23–27
Most Stressful Days Overall: 9–13
Best Days for Love: 1–4
Best Days for Money: 6–8
Best Days for Career: 4–7
Power Word: Fiscal

Happy February, Cancer! This month's cosmic weather begins with a couple of cordial transits and Venus moving into Aries, its fellow cardinal sign. Prior to Venus changing signs, it meets up with Neptune on the 1st. This transit is spiritual in nature and encourages taking action that feeds the soul. This transit is specifically geared towards philosophy and travel for you, so take it upon yourself to seek guidance from those who inspire you or visit a place that helps you connect to the collective. Mercury and Jupiter support each other on the 3rd, which bolsters communication. Venus enters Aries on the 4th, changing its focus to career for you. There are more profound career transits next month, so treat this as an invitation to start ruminating on your current level of satisfaction and long-term aspirations in this department.

February 12 is an important day since there is a full Moon in Leo. This lunation has the added component of forming an almost exact tense aspect with Uranus. Uranus is all about liberation, but it typically catalyses instability as a mechanism for getting us freed from existing structures/systems which no longer serve us. For Cancer, this lunation is financial in nature. There's a huge spotlight on your 2nd house of individual finances. Finances within your locus of control, such as your budget, or hard assets like cash, fall under this umbrella. It's prudent to learn to be more frugal during the week of this lunation. Also, go through your past financial statements to make sure there are no discrepancies. This exercise will also help familiarize you with your spending patterns.

Pisces' season begins on the 18th, bringing more of a spotlight to the overarching yearly theme of spirituality and higher education. Pisces season is the ideal time for Cancer to level up on spiritual practices and routines. This transit is more potent than last month's Venus in Pisces transit, so the invitation stands more firmly. New Moons centre around new emotional cycles, so use the new Moon on the 27th as a day to honour this call. Mars ends its retrograde in your sign on the 23rd, giving you some momentum towards achieving your 2025 goals. Eclipse season is around the corner to get the kinetic energy rolling.

March

Best Days Overall: 22–26
Most Stressful Days Overall: 14–16, 29–30
Best Days for Love: 8–12
Best Days for Money: 20–22
Best Days for Career: 3–8
Power Word: Eminence

March is one of the busiest months of the year astrologically, starting on March 1 with Venus turning retrograde. For you, Cancer, this month has a heavy career focus from end to end. Venus retrograde in Aries first asks if you currently feel valued where you work and/or if you value the work you currently do. Retrogrades force us to reflect in order to course-correct when necessary. It's likely that if the answer to either of these retrograde questions encourages new beginnings, the rest of the cosmic weather for the month will compound or augment your desire for change.

The first eclipse of 2025 occurs in Virgo on March 14. This full Moon lunar eclipse highlights the communication sector of your chart. This is especially important because Mercury will also retrograde one day after the eclipse. Mercury retrograde in Aries audits whether you're verbally advocating for your needs. The eclipse-plus-retrograde pairing absolutely functions as a reckoning if your pattern of behaviour is to not communicate your needs directly. This could be within the confines of a relationship, with friends or at work. Communication isn't just expressive, though. The combination of the eclipse plus retrograde also scrutinizes whether you actively listen as much as you actively speak.

Aries' season begins on March 20 and the second eclipse (also in Aries) follows on the 29th. Both of these transits take your reflections around career desires for the year and transmute them into actionable first steps. Eclipses can catalyse sudden changes, so don't be surprised if your career goals shift as a result of what unfolds with this lunation. These transits also apply to the goals you might have around being famous or public-facing. Actionable first steps towards these dreams are also a part of the cosmic weather for this month. Lastly, Neptune moves into Aries for the first time in our lifetime on March 30. The planet of dreams, illusion and the collective will demands that you feel spiritually fulfilled by your occupation. Concerns around legacy will begin to bubble up and inform the career moves you make this year.

April

Best Days Overall: 3–8
Most Stressful Days Overall: 25–29
Best Days for Love: 19–21
Best Days for Money: 16–18
Best Days for Career: 20–22
Power Word: Connections

Happy April, Cancer! The cosmic weather for the month starts out with a group of soft, supportive transits occurring in the first week. April 5 features a harmonious alignment between Venus in Pisces and Mars in your sign. Around the 5th is a great time to tick things off your to-do list. Mars is soon going to leave your sign, so you definitely want to leverage this once-every-two-years transit. On April 7 Mercury finally ends its retrograde and turns direct. Phew! Mercury direct will cut down on some of the wonkiness you're experiencing around communication, technology and transportation.

On April 12 there's a full Moon in Libra, your fellow cardinal sign. The full Moon in Libra is an emotional lunation centred around collaboration, harmony and relationships. For Cancer, this transit applies specifically to family and home dynamics. This lunation is an important transit for mending relationships within the home or with loved ones if necessary. Regardless, this is a great transit in which to spend quality time with those you love. Venus turns direct as well on the 12th. If you've got a partner, bookmark this lunation as time to do something special with your someone special. If you're single, this lunation is an ideal time to put yourself out there.

On April 19 the Sun enters Taurus. For Cancer, Taurus' season is all about friends, community and how you fit into organizations of which you're a part. The Sun enters Taurus just as Mars aligns with Neptune. This is a dreamy transit inspiring Cancer to leave its nest and go on an adventure with friends. Taurus season occurs in the heart of spring and encourages cultivating all forms of abundance. The month ends with a little bit of turbulent cosmic weather. The new Moon in Taurus occurs just after Mars opposes Pluto. Mars opposite Pluto will unearth inequality in power dynamics within your relationships and groups. It's important to tread lightly when addressing these dynamics while this transit is activated, but it's also necessary to confront and remedy what comes to light in the wake of it.

May

Best Days Overall: 1-6
Most Stressful Days Overall: 9-13
Best Days for Love: 5-8
Best Days for Money: 15-17
Best Days for Career: 20-23
Power Word: Regulate

Happy May, Cancer! May's cosmic weather starts off on the 2nd with Venus meeting up with Neptune in Aries for the first time in your lifetime. This is a soft, supportive career transit for Cancer centred around advocating for your needs in the workplace. Venus and Neptune are not known to be aggressive in nature, so approach this advocacy from a collaborative standpoint. Venus harmoniously aligns with Pluto on the 6th, further lending a hand in the moves you're making to transform career and finances.

On May 12 the full Moon in Scorpio will occur as the Sun aligns to conjoin with Uranus. This is always an emotional period, given the fixed water sign's associations with deep feelings and discovery, and this lunation being influenced by Uranus further contributes to the likelihood of coming to profound realizations around this date. Specifically, these epiphanies centre on your relationship to creativity and/or romance. Given that Mercury is harshly squaring off with Pluto, it's best to lean on your support systems to help digest whatever discoveries or reflections pop up around this date. Therapists, life coaches, astrologers or any sort of advisors are an especially helpful resource at this time. If you're processing with a friend or loved one, make sure there's enough trust established so that you feel safe to be as open and vulnerable as possible.

On May 20 the Sun moves into Gemini. Five days later Mercury follows suit and then there's a new Moon in the sign on the 26th. On this day there will be a four-planet 'stellium' or cluster in Gemini. So much Gemini energy! Gemini falls in Cancer's 12th house of mental health and alone time. If you've been feeling over-stimulated or run down, the astrology of this week fully supports rest and recharging in private. Carve out alone time in your schedule for this week. This energy can also rile up old coping mechanisms to dissociate, so do your best to support your need to recharge in a holistic or healthy way.

June

Best Days Overall: 25-28
Most Stressful Days Overall: 20-23
Best Days for Love: 3-6
Best Days for Money: 11-14
Best Days for Career: 4-7
Power Word: Expand

Hi, Cancer! June's cosmic weather starts off with three planets changing sign, two of which enter your sign. On June 6 Venus enters Taurus, where it promotes celebration and quality time with groups of friends and communities. Venus in Taurus also supports budgeting or wealth-growing strategies as it is strongly associated with security. On the 8th and 9th respectively, Mercury and Jupiter enter Cancer. Mercury is in Cancer every year, but Jupiter only enters your sign once every 12 years. Jupiter was called the 'Greater Benefic' in traditional astrology because the gas giant rules growth and expansion. I hope you have a spacesuit because the 12 months during which Jupiter is in your sign yield an ascension of sorts. Jupiter rules beliefs and convictions, so now more than ever it's important to ground yourself in a value system that serves you in this present moment and corresponds with where you want to go. Draw up an inventory of your long-held values and beliefs, and try to identify what may no longer serve you.

The full Moon in Sagittarius occurs on the 11th, encouraging you to get kinetic. This lunation falls in Cancer's 6th house of physical wellness. Sagittarius is a vivacious fire sign represented by the centaur (half-man, half-horse). This full Moon spurs you to get moving or to go on an adventure to foster a mind-body connection. Sagittarius is associated with teaching as well, so taking an exercise class or some form of physical training is also beneficial to foster this connection.

Happy Birthday! Your solar season begins on the 20th, with the new Moon following on the 25th. Cancer season does start off a little bit bumpily as the Sun squares off with Saturn and Neptune on the 22nd and 23rd. These transits combine, given how close they occur with one another, and they can inspire a feeling of being overwhelmed in the face of trying to achieve your goals. Birthdays always inspire big-picture thinking about the coming year. The best way to navigate this transit is to break up massive goals into smaller goals to accomplish. With Jupiter being in Cancer, this trip around the Sun will be fruitful. You simply need to pace yourself.

July

Best Days Overall: 4-9
Most Stressful Days Overall: 24-28
Best Days for Love: 9-13
Best Days for Money: 22-24
Best Days for Career: 1-4
Power Word: Relational

How are you enjoying Cancer season, Cancer? The cosmic main character for the start of the month is Venus. Venus conjoins with Uranus at the final degree of Taurus before jumping into Gemini on the 4th. Venus in Gemini is a fun social transit, but with Uranus' influence there might be some surprises, so do expect the unexpected. Venus then harmoniously aligns with Saturn and Neptune on the 6th, and with Pluto on the 7th. These transits support finances for Cancer. Also on the 7th, Uranus enters Gemini for the first time since leaving the sign in 1949! Uranus in Gemini collectively changes how we communicate with one another, and how we approach teaching and learning. On the personal level this transit transforms your relationship to finances. This is a very long transit and won't happen overnight, but after Uranus makes its foray through Gemini you'll be in awe over how much has changed.

On July 10 the Moon is full and in Capricorn, your polar sign. This is a relational lunation for you. Capricorn is a structured sign, and this full Moon promotes bringing this energy to your dearest relationships. Set up organizational systems with your partner or your significant others, such as sharing calendars or establishing what your preferred methods of communication are. This will be important because on the 18th Mercury turns retrograde in Leo. Communication breakdowns are common with Mercury retrograde. Make a concerted effort to directly communicate to avoid misinterpretation.

Your season comes to an end with the start of Leo's season on the 22nd. The Sun was busy when it entered Cancer, but it's even busier entering Leo by aspecting five planets in three days. Wow! The new Moon in Leo occurs on the 24th and has all of these aspects baked into it. This lunation ushers in new beginnings around living an authentic life publicly. It's one thing to be comfortable being your genuine self behind closed doors, but a whole other thing to do so in the public eye. Work with this new Moon to allow yourself to shine.

August

Best Days Overall: 10-14
Most Stressful Days Overall: 27-31
Best Days for Love: 12-16
Best Days for Money: 6-9
Best Days for Career: 14-18
Power Word: Empowered

Venus has just entered your sign before this month begins and stirs up some dust on day one, Cancer. On August 1, Venus squares off with Saturn and Neptune, who are still hanging out in Aries, 1 degree apart from one another. Venus is all about pleasure and values, so when it finds tension with Saturn, who rules restriction, old tendencies of self-criticism and being your own worst enemy flare up. Avoid dissociating and stand up to your inner bully, sweet crab. This will unlock some long-lasting self-empowerment. The cosmic weather for a lot of this month revolves around your relationship to money. Venus, Saturn and Neptune will support you in long-term financial growth if you're willing to take an unfiltered look at how you budget and how you spend, and adjust them if they aren't sustainable.

This month's full Moon features Mars trying to one-up Venus by opposing Saturn and Neptune. The full Moon in Aquarius is a financial lunation for Cancer centred around taking stock of your existing streams of income and making sure all your small change is accounted for. Mars' influence through finding tension with Saturn and Neptune typically promotes restlessness or a feeling of being stuck. This is not the time to begin new financial endeavours, but it's a valuable time to circle back to existing money matters you've been avoiding or haven't had the chance to deal with.

On August 11 Mercury turns direct, freeing up some of the feeling of being stuck. Virgo's season begins on the 22nd, with the new Moon following the next day, which strongly revolves around communication for you, Cancer – new Moon, new approach to speaking up. This lunation spurs you to be more direct with your communication, posing the question, 'In what ways or with which people do I silence myself for the sake of others over my own needs?' Virgo is the sign of service, so as well as communication there's a strong prompting to get involved or to give back to your local community.

September

Best Days Overall: 26–30
Most Stressful Days Overall: 7–8, 21–24
Best Days for Love: 12–16
Best Days for Money: 10–14
Best Days for Career: 3–6
Power Word: Perspective

It's eclipse season, Cancer! The first eclipse of September occurs on the 7th and is a full Moon lunar eclipse in Pisces. Eclipses are evolutionary transits that facilitate growth through tension and shake-ups. For Cancer, this eclipse centres on spirituality and education. With regard to spirituality, it is a potent transit stimulating you to define an authentic belief system that reflects your values, not anyone else's. If you've been conditioned to believe or practise spirituality in a specific way, this eclipse will scrutinize whether this truly serves you right now. For education, this eclipse catalyses seeking forms of higher education to support long held career ambitions. This doesn't need to be a four-year programme, but rather any type of course or certification that enables you to explore and acquire the necessary knowledge to take steps towards your overarching goal. This eclipse also has significance around travel, and how it may relate to both spirituality and education for you. Taking some form of trip to gain a different perspective could be a significant move at this time.

The second eclipse of the month occurs on the 22nd and is a new Moon solar eclipse in Virgo. This eclipse carries last month's theme of your relationship to communication and puts it under the proverbial microscope. This is a rare second new Moon in Virgo, and an eclipse at that. The new Moon question from last month, 'In what ways do I silence myself for the sake of others?' is posed even louder if you haven't yet addressed it. If you have made strides towards speaking your truth and vocalizing necessary boundaries, this eclipse will stimulate you in continuing to do so.

Libra's season begins on the 22nd, with the Sun forming aspects to every planet from Saturn to Pluto over the next three days. Libra season focuses on home and family dynamics for you, dear Cancer. If the answer to the new Moon question above involves family members or those you live with, Libra season will demand you address these dynamics. Libra season also serves as an audit of the energy of your home. This solar season could be the perfect time to redecorate or to align your home with the principles of feng shui as a means of revitalizing the heartbeat of where you live.

October

Best Days Overall: 14–18
Most Stressful Days Overall: 23–26
Best Days for Love: 29–31
Best Days for Money: 17–21
Best Days for Career: 2–6
Power Word: Home

Happy October, Cancer! This month starts off with a full Moon in Aries, your fellow cardinal sign, on the 6th. What do you want to be remembered for, sweet crab? This lunation asks this question and spotlights your satisfaction with your current career trajectory, as well as inquiring whether you're feeling seen and heard at work. This lunation represents a culmination of the last six months in this realm. How has your outlook on your career shifted or evolved over the last six months? Sit with this question and, based on your reflections, plan out a couple of actionable next steps to support reaching your overarching 2025 career goals.

Come the 11th, the astro-weather shifts its focus to home and family dynamics. Venus aspects Saturn, Uranus, Neptune and Pluto between the 11th and the 15th, and enters Libra on the 13th. All of this Venusian energy centres around your physical home and relationships you have with family/those you live with. For Cancer, the energy of your home can greatly impact your psyche, so take it upon yourself to view these transits as an invitation to reorganize and revitalize your space. Moreover, if you've been putting off fixing anything within the home that you know needs repairing, now is the time to roll up your sleeves. In addition, the new Moon in Libra on the 21st is an opportune time not only to take care of your physical home, but also to attend to your familial relationships. This new Moon is ripe with potential for establishing more order or harmony with these and other relationships at home. Be mindful that Jupiter is squaring off with Chiron, which can absolutely make you feel a little more raw, so navigate these conversations with a big dose of self-compassion.

The Sun enters Scorpio on the 22nd, bringing its attention to Cancer's creativity and romance sector. This solar season is the ideal time to double up on the unique way in which you creatively self-express. When you find yourself in need of processing or recharging, elect to reflect through your favourite form of creativity. For Cancer, Scorpio season is about finding the time for play and pleasure.

November

Best Days Overall: 15-19
Most Stressful Days Overall: 27-30
Best Days for Love: 20-23
Best Days for Money: 17-21
Best Days for Career: 4-8
Power Word: Support

It's November, Cancer! This month significantly centres around your relationship with your body. On the 4th fiery Mars enters Sagittarius. Mars takes two years to go around the zodiac, so this transit ushers in a new two-year cycle around how you regard and treat your body. If you've been putting off going in for a check-up or even visiting a medical specialist, the cosmic weather strongly encourages you to do so now. Moreover, if you've been meaning to get back into or establish new targets in some form of exercise or sport, this transit will work with you to achieve the goals you've set out for this. The full Moon in Taurus occurs the next day and sheds its light on your social circles. More specifically, are you getting as much support as you're giving among your friends and acquaintances? Taurus has a strong security orientation to it, and it's best to allow this lunation to illuminate which social circles you truly feel secure in.

For one final time this year, Mercury turns retrograde on the 9th. This transit occurs in Sagittarius and compounds the themes described when Mars enters the sign on the 4th. Mercury retrograde is always about 're-' words, such as 'reflect', 're-evaluate' and 'revisit'. This transit seeks for you to reflect on how your routines either support or detract from your overarching physical wellness. When Mercury turns direct on the 29th, you'll be prompted to make necessary adjustments to better cater to your body's needs.

The Sun forms a super-harmonious aspect to Jupiter and Saturn on the 17th. This transit promotes a heartfelt connection with loved ones, as well as enhancing personal development. The new Moon occurs on the 20th, promoting a new cycle around creative self-expression and romance. This lunation honestly just wants you to allocate more time to play and pleasure. Make a concerted effort to strike a better balance between work and play.

Sagittarius' season begins on the 21st and Venus enters the sign on the 30th. November ends with a cluster of Sagittarian energy. In addition to supporting your body, the cosmic weather also pushes you to envision what's possible for you physically. Whether it's running a marathon, doing your first pull-up or effectively meal-prepping for the next month, the Sagittarius transits will work with you to dream big in this regard.

December

Best Days Overall: 1–5
Most Stressful Days Overall: 10–14
Best Days for Love: 21–25
Best Days for Money: 23–27
Best Days for Career: 17–21
Power Word: Balance

Happy December, Cancer! December is all about achieving balance. The cosmic weather begins on the 4th with the full Moon in Gemini. This lunation spotlights whether the ratio of social time to solo time you typically apportion to yourself is conducive to your mental health. Be focused on paying attention to this, especially if there's a big disparity. Moreover, this full Moon is an ideal transit during which to talk about your feelings or mental health needs with someone you trust. This could be a professional or a close confidant. Lastly, this lunation also examines whether you've developed more sustainable stress-coping mechanisms since the new Moon in Gemini six months ago.

On the 9th Mars and Saturn slow things down for you as they square off. This transit can elicit restlessness, although the end goal is getting you to focus on the present. Anxiety is a bio-indicator that while your body's here now, your mind is off in the future. View this transit as an invitation to analyse your full Moon prompt around whether you balance social and solo time. Mercury forms several aspects between the 10th and the 13th, and also switches into Sagittarius on the 11th. These transits function as pressing the start button on taking everything you've learned about your attitudes towards your body during Mercury's retrograde and putting it into action. A balanced body leads to a balanced mind, sweet crab.

Mars enters your polar sign, Capricorn, on the 15th. Mars in Capricorn brings a focus to relationships for the end of the year. If you're partnered, this is an ideal transit to discuss the future and what you seek to achieve together and individually. If you're single, this transit promotes putting yourself out there if you're open to partnership. The new Moon in Sagittarius follows on the 19th. This transit is visionary and encourages you to dream up what's possible in 2026. This especially applies to physical wellness for you, Cancer. Whether it's achieving new personal records in the gym, learning to cook, or nailing down weekly routines, this lunation spurs you to identify your overarching 2026 wellness goals.

Leo

♌

THE LION

Birthdays from
July 21
to August 21

Personality Profile

LEO AT A GLANCE

Element – Fire

Ruling Planet – Sun
  Career Planet – Venus
  Love Planet – Uranus
  Money Planet – Mercury
  Planet of Health and Work – Saturn
  Planet of Home and Family Life – Pluto

Totem – the Knight

Colours – gold, sienna

Colours that promote love, romance and social harmony – black,
  indigo, ultramarine blue

Colours that promote earning power – yellow, yellow-orange

Gems – amber, chrysolite, yellow diamond

Metal – gold

Scents – bergamot, frankincense, musk, neroli

Quality – fixed (= stability)

Quality most needed for balance – humility

Strongest virtues – leadership ability, self-esteem and confidence, generosity, creativity, love of joy

Deepest needs – fun, elation, the need to shine

Characteristics to avoid – arrogance, vanity, bossiness

Signs of greatest overall compatibility – Aries, Sagittarius

Signs of greatest overall incompatibility – Taurus, Scorpio, Aquarius

Sign most helpful to career – Taurus

Sign most helpful for emotional support – Scorpio

Sign most helpful financially – Virgo

Sign best for marriage and/or partnerships – Aquarius

Sign most helpful for creative projects – Sagittarius

Best Sign to have fun with – Sagittarius

Signs most helpful in spiritual matters – Aries, Cancer

Best day of the week – Sunday

Understanding a Leo

When you think of Leo, think of royalty – then you'll get the idea of what the Leo character is all about and why Leos are the way they are. It is true that, for various reasons, some Leo-born do not always express this quality – but even if not they should like to do so.

A monarch rules not by example (as does Aries) nor by consensus (as do Capricorn and Aquarius) but by personal will. Will is law. Personal taste becomes the style that is imitated by all subjects. A monarch is somehow larger than life. This is how a Leo desires to be.

When you dispute the personal will of a Leo it is serious business. He or she takes it as a personal affront, an insult. Leos will let you know that their will carries authority and that to disobey is demeaning and disrespectful.

A Leo is king (or queen) of his or her personal domain. Subordinates, friends and family are the loyal and trusted subjects. Leos rule with benevolent grace and in the best interests of others. They have a powerful presence; indeed, they are powerful people. They seem to attract attention in any social gathering. They stand out because they are stars in their domain. Leos feel that, like the Sun, they are made to shine and rule. Leos feel that they were born to special privilege and royal prerogatives – and most of them attain this status, at least to some degree.

The Sun is the ruler of this sign, and when you think of sunshine it is very difficult to feel unhealthy or depressed. Somehow the light of the Sun is the very antithesis of illness and apathy. Leos love life. They also love to have fun; they love drama, music, the theatre and amusements of all sorts. These are the things that give joy to life. If – even in their best interests – you try to deprive Leos of their pleasures, good food, drink and entertainment, you run the serious risk of depriving them of the will to live. To them life without joy is no life at all.

Leos epitomize humanity's will to power. But power in and of itself – regardless of what some people say – is neither good nor evil. Only when power is abused does it become evil. Without power even good things cannot come to pass. Leos realize this and are uniquely qualified to wield power. Of all the signs, they do it most naturally. Capricorn, the other power sign of the zodiac, is a better manager and administrator than Leo – much better. But Leo outshines Capricorn in personal grace and presence. Leo loves power, whereas Capricorn assumes power out of a sense of duty.

Finance

Leos are great leaders but not necessarily good managers. They are better at handling the overall picture than the nitty-gritty details of business. If they have good managers working for them they can become exceptional executives. They have vision and a lot of creativity.

Leos love wealth for the pleasures it can bring. They love an opulent lifestyle, pomp and glamour. Even when they are not wealthy they live as if they are. This is why many fall into debt, from which it is sometimes difficult to emerge.

Leos, like Pisceans, are generous to a fault. Very often they want to acquire wealth solely so that they can help others economically. Wealth to Leo buys services and managerial ability. It creates jobs for others and improves the general well-being of those around them. Therefore – to a Leo – wealth is good. Wealth is to be enjoyed to the fullest. Money is not to be left to gather dust in a mouldy bank vault but to be enjoyed, spread around, used. So Leos can be quite reckless in their spending.

With the sign of Virgo on Leo's 2nd money house cusp, Leo needs to develop some of Virgo's traits of analysis, discrimination and purity when it comes to money matters. They must learn to be more careful with the details of finance (or to hire people to do this for them). They have to be more cost-conscious in their spending habits. Generally, they need to manage their money better. Leos tend to chafe under financial constraints, yet these constraints can help Leos to reach their highest financial potential.

Leos like it when their friends and family know that they can depend on them for financial support. They do not mind – and even enjoy – lending money, but they are careful that they are not taken advantage of. From their 'regal throne' Leos like to bestow gifts upon their family and friends and then enjoy the good feelings these gifts bring to everybody. Leos love financial speculations and – when the celestial influences are right – are often lucky.

Career and Public Image

Leos like to be perceived as wealthy, for in today's world wealth often equals power. When they attain wealth they love having a large house with lots of land and animals.

At their jobs Leos excel in positions of authority and power. They are good at making decisions – on a grand level – but they prefer to leave the details to others. Leos are well respected by their colleagues and subordinates, mainly because they have a knack for understanding and relating to those around them. Leos usually strive for the top positions even if they have to start at the bottom and work hard to get there. As might be expected of such a charismatic sign, Leos are always trying to improve their work situation. They do so in order to have a better chance of advancing to the top.

On the other hand, Leos do not like to be bossed around or told what to do. Perhaps this is why they aspire so for the top – where they can be the decision-makers and need not take orders from others.

Leos never doubt their success and focus all their attention and efforts on achieving it. Another great Leo characteristic is that – just like good monarchs – they do not attempt to abuse the power or success they achieve. If they do so this is not wilful or intentional. Usually they like to share their wealth and try to make everyone around them join in their success.

Leos are – and like to be perceived as – hard-working, well-established individuals. It is definitely true that they are capable of hard work and often manage great things. But do not forget that, deep down inside, Leos really are fun-lovers.

Love and Relationships

Generally, Leos are not the marrying kind. To them relationships are good while they are pleasurable. When the relationship ceases to be pleasurable a true Leo will want out. They always want to have the freedom to leave. That is why Leos excel at love affairs rather than commitment. Once married, however, Leo is faithful – even if some Leos have a tendency to marry more than once in their lifetime. If you are in love with a Leo, just show him or her a good time – travel, go to casinos and clubs, the theatre and discos. Wine and dine your Leo love – it is expensive but worth it and you will have fun.

Leos generally have an active love life and are demonstrative in their affections. They love to be with other optimistic and fun-loving types like themselves, but wind up settling with someone more serious, intellectual and unconventional. The partner of a Leo tends to be more political and socially conscious than he or she is, and more libertarian. When you marry a Leo, mastering the freedom-loving tendencies of your partner will definitely become a life-long challenge – and be careful that Leo does not master you.

Aquarius sits on Leo's 7th house of love cusp. Thus if Leos want to realize their highest love and social potential they need to develop a more egalitarian, Aquarian perspective on others. This is not easy for Leo, for 'the king' finds his equals only among other 'kings'. But perhaps this is the solution to Leo's social challenge – to be 'a king among kings'. It is all right to be regal, but recognize the nobility in others.

Home and Domestic Life

Although Leos are great entertainers and love having people over, sometimes this is all show. Only very few close friends will get to see the real side of a Leo's day-to-day life. To a Leo the home is a place of comfort, recreation and transformation; a secret, private retreat – a castle. Leos like to spend money, show off a bit, entertain and have fun. They enjoy the latest furnishings, clothes and gadgets – all things fit for kings.

Leos are fiercely loyal to their family and, of course, expect the same from them. They love their children almost to a fault; they have to be careful not to spoil them too much. They also must try to avoid attempting to make individual family members over in their own image. Leos should keep in mind that others also have the need to be their own people. That is why Leos have to be extra careful about being over-bossy or over-domineering in the home.

Horoscope for 2025

Just as a knight charges into battle with conviction, this is your year to courageously face your fears, Leo. In January the north node enters Pisces for the first time since leaving the sign in 2007. The north node functions like a beacon, drawing attention to the over-arching themes of the cosmic weather. For you, Leo, the north node moves into your transformation house, where it will stay for the next 18 months. The north node brings with it eclipses, evolution-ary transits which stimulate growth through tension and shake-ups. Your totem for this year is 'the Knight', as you'll be supported in choosing courage over comfort.

This is a special year astrologically as every slow-moving planet except for Pluto shifts signs at some point during the year. These transits function as a changing of the guard and will profoundly affect society as a whole. One such sign is Uranus, which moves into Gemini for the first time since leaving the sign 76 years ago. Uranus shifting signs will catalyse technological innovation, which starkly affects how we as a society communicate with and relate to one another. Saturn, Uranus and Neptune all dip into their subse-quent sign during this year and then undergo a retrograde period that opens you up to one more pass through the sign they started the year with.

Saturn, the planet that rules discipline, structure and hard work, has been occupying your transformation sector and then moves into your knowledge and spiritual philosophy sector mid-year. Neptune, which rules compassion, makes the same transition from your transformation sector to your spiritual knowledge sector.

These transits emphasize the importance of rooting deeper into a spiritual value system that will afford you the tools to dismantle long-standing anxieties and cultivate self-love. More on this in the subsequent sections of this horoscope.

In addition to spirituality, finances are another hot topic for Leo this year. The north node brings its proverbial magnifying glass and an eclipse to the joint finances sector of your chart. In addition, there are four planetary retrograde periods that will directly impact finances for Leo, and these will be explored in the finance section of this horoscope. Overarchingly, this is a year for frugality and modesty when it comes to all things money. Financial abundance and avoiding debt are at the forefront of your mind this year.

For a quarterly view of the year, the first quarter focuses on conquering fears and joint finances, the second sees a shift in focus to spirituality and higher education as a means to transform yourself, the third further emphasizes these themes and also features some adjustments in social life, while the final quarter once again brings the cosmic weather back to dismantling anxiety and protecting wealth.

Health

(Please note that this is an astrological perspective on health and not a medical one. Any health-related symptoms should be evaluated by a qualified healthcare professional.)

The year of embodying the Knight means being courageous in all sectors of life, health included. Specifically, there's an emphasis on addressing mental health and regulating your nervous system. The year starts off with fiery Mars retrograde in your sign. From January 6 to April 18 the red planet moves into Cancer and occupies the mental health sector of your chart. Mars is inflammatory in nature, so anticipate the year to start off with the feeling of being on edge. Mars irritates in order to direct your attention to what you need to remedy. Mars also rules all things kinetic, so this is your opportunity to mobilize your support systems and begin the process of conquering your fears.

The Moon is your spiritual and mental health planet, so it's important to bookmark the eclipses as times of increased activity – and agitation – around mental health. March's eclipses are especially noteworthy because they occur in tandem with Mercury and Venus retrograde. Re-evaluating patterns of thought and communication will be a key theme during this period, while taming your mind and being able to create some distance from your thoughts are other key themes. The September eclipse season includes an eclipse in your house of transformation, shining a light on anxieties that need to be addressed. A vital task to undertake this year is putting in the hard yards for long-lasting mental and emotional wellness.

On the physical health front, the year starts off with Mars retrograde in Leo. Though Mars moves into Cancer pretty quickly in the year, it's important to note because Mars takes two years to go around the zodiac and has been retrograde in your sign since early December 2024. Managing inflammation is an important intentional step to take at the start of this year. Being disciplined with diet is especially important, given that Saturn is your physical health planet. Saturn rules structure and discipline, and only rewards hard work. Mars returns to your sign from April 19 to June 17, which is an ideal period to increase your exercise load or supplement it with different sports.

Here are the specific areas of the body to focus on this year:

- Heart: this is a perennial area of focus for Leo as it rules this part of the body in medical astrology. Given that the overarching theme of this year is managing anxiety, it's important to support the heart through meditation, exercise and diet.
- Head and face: in addition to this year's focus being regulating your nervous system, the year begins with Mars retrograde in your sign. Moreover, during the summer your health planet enters Aries, which rules the head from a medical astrology perspective. Structure around stress management must be implemented this year.
- Feet: Mars spends the majority of its retrograde in your 12th house, which rules the feet. Mobility and flexibility are an

important focus for this year as tension can be held in the muscles. Routine acupuncture or foot massages are advised.

Love and Social Life

This year begins with your pleasure planet, Jupiter, transiting the friendship sector of your chart. Jupiter rules growth and expansion, so don't be surprised if you find new love blossoming from friendship. Jupiter transits this sector of your chart until June 9. Regardless of your partnership status, Jupiter in your friendship sector bodes well for growing the quantity and quality of your communities. Jupiter will be in the sign of Gemini during this time, supporting you with networking in professional organizations as well. Come June 9, Jupiter will enter the sign of Cancer, promoting softer, sweeter, more touchy-feely summer loving. Moreover, Jupiter in Cancer encourages identifying which of your friends function like family, so that you can ensure you lean into and demonstrate gratitude for these relationships. Embodying the Knight means you'll be spurred to show up for the people in your life who support you day in, day out.

After Jupiter leaves your friendship sector in June, Uranus begins transiting it in July. Uranus is the wildcard planet ruling innovation, instability and individuality, and it will transit your friendship sector from July 7 to November 7. These four months strongly encourage liberating yourself from organizations, communities or friend groups that keep you more stifled than anything else. Social circles that don't validate your individuality are very much on the chopping block during this transit. Uranus in Gemini will also push you to find community through technologically innovative means, such as finding a like-minded community online or through a social media app.

When it comes to long-term partnership, Saturn is your partnership planet. Saturn undergoes a noticeable change in demeanour when it changes sign from Pisces to Aries. Saturn in Aries is more concerned with self-interest, which means that a top priority in relationships is getting your own needs met. If you struggle with advocating for what you want or need, expect this summer to be a watershed moment around this limiting pattern of thinking.

Striving to strike a balance between ensuring your needs are being met in a healthy way as opposed to coming across as selfish will be a test Saturn in Aries administers.

Mercury is your friendship planet and will turn retrograde three times this year. Mercury's first retrograde period occurs in Aries (and Pisces) from March 15 to April 7. This retrograde period overlaps with eclipses, so the probability is high for shake-ups within your friend groups. The second retrograde period occurs in your sign from July 18 to August 11. Miscommunication within your friend groups is especially probable during this retrograde period. The final retrograde period occurs in Sagittarius (and Scorpio) from November 9 to November 29. This final retrograde centres around re-evaluating the ways you participate in recreational activities with others.

Career and Finances

Before Uranus enters your friendship sector, it wraps up its stay in your career sector. Uranus in your career sector has promoted seeking innovative work or incorporating more cutting-edge technology into your career wherever possible. Moreover, joining professional organizations and getting serious about networking is strongly supported by this transit. Venus is your career planet and it undergoes a retrograde period from Aries to Pisces, starting on March 1 and ending on April 12. This retrograde period pairs with the spring eclipse season, creating shake-ups in your career or career trajectory. Inspiration to try your hand at something new is high with this transit as Venus retrograde is all about re-evaluating which values guide your daily decisions. Given that this is your year to embody the Knight, your beliefs and convictions should function as your litmus test for making tough decisions. Venus turns retrograde from your higher education house, which strongly supports pursuing an advanced degree or certification.

As mentioned in the introduction to this horoscope, this is a year for a more conservative or modest approach to money matters. Gambling is ill advised this year. The transformation sector of your chart is also the same place where significations for joint finances lie. The north node is transiting this area of your chart, drawing your attention to the way other people influence profit or loss for you. Both the spring and autumn/fall eclipse cycles have at least one eclipse transiting a financial sector of your chart. Debts, taxes and money from inheritances are all heavily scrutinized this year. In cases where inheritances are acquired, do your due diligence around adhering to all tax-related laws. Mercury, the planet that traditionally rules commerce and trading, will be retrograde in your sign from July 18 to August 12. This retrograde period invites you to conduct a thorough financial review to evaluate the efficacy of existing financial investments. As a result of the confluence of transits occurring around this area of life for you, seeking the advice of a trusted financial advisor is recommended.

Home and Domestic Life

This area of life is not as pronounced for you this year, so things remain more or less in the status quo. That being said, there is some activity to note. First, your home and domestic life planet is Mars. Mars begins the year retrograde in your sign and then in Cancer. Mars rules drive, ambition and conflict, among many other significations. Mars retrograde tends to irritate those relationships that need to align better and would benefit from conflict remediation. This transit occurs from January 1 until February 23. Given March's eclipses, bookmark the first quarter of the year for tension within the home. Mars retrograde can also exacerbate long-standing issues with your physical home that have been left unaddressed.

Similar to how a knight needs to rest after battle, the astrology of the spring also emboldens you to create a nurturing space within your home so you can retreat to it when in need of a recharge. Specifically, Mars' transit in Cancer from January 6 to April 18 would be the time to cultivate this space. The asteroid Vesta, which is associated with warmth and structure, also transits your home and domestic life sector during this time. Addressing the general layout of your home and revitalizing the energy of the space to facilitate an explicitly welcoming tone is strongly recommended. Mars will transit your home and family sector from September 22 to November 4. This is a period of heavy traffic within the home, so make sure you have your supportive spaces fully operational beforehand.

Self-improvement

One thing you may know about knights is that they always go on a quest. There are four planetary retrograde periods beginning in your spiritual philosophy, higher education and travel sector in 2025. The astrology of this year demands that you lean into a combination of some or all of these areas of life as a means of self-improvement. For spirituality, specifically focusing on philosophies and belief systems from cultures outside your own is recommended with these transits. Embrace the curiosity of exploration and venture out on your quest to develop a well-rounded belief system.

This is especially applicable in the spring, when Neptune enters this sector of your chart for the first time in your lifetime. Neptune will stay there until October 22, so there's no need to rush this discovery. Paired with this is the inspiration to travel to places you deem spiritual as a means to build up a robust belief system. Travel to spiritual sites or going on yoga or meditation retreats are all examples of ways to honour the astrology around self-improvement and travel.

Another recommendation for self-improvement is seeking some sort of training or higher education in a creative passion. Your planetary ruler is the Sun, which shines its bright light for all to see. For you, Leo, leveraging creativity will be a modality to courageously navigate fighting your fears or anxieties this year. Bookmark the weeks of the two solar eclipses, occurring on March 29 and September 7, as times to lean heavily into creative self-expression. This recommendation is especially applicable to July Leos, as Pluto has begun to aspect your natal Sun.

Month-by-month Forecasts

January

Best Days Overall: 28-31
Most Stressful Days Overall: 13-16
Best Days for Love: 24-27
Best Days for Money: 8-12
Best Days for Career: 6-9
Power Word: Balance

Happy 2025, Leo! January's cosmic weather begins on the 2nd with Venus moving into idealistic Pisces. This transit encourages leaning into creative self-expression as a means to uplift others and foster intimacy with those you care about. In addition, for Leo there's a fiscal component to this transit, specifically with finances merged with others. If you depend on streams of income stemming from others, dot your i's and cross your t's that everything is flowing as it should. If you've been meaning to get into business with others, this is a positive transit in which to do so.

However, while Venus in Pisces is an ideal time for Leo to discuss all things business, Mars retrograde can create roadblocks if you're going to venture to do this now. We enter 2025 with Mars already retrograde and currently retrograde in your sign. Mars has been in Leo since the beginning of November 2024, so if the past two months have felt especially spicy, you now know why. Mars rules drive, ambition, conflict and carnality, and it has everything to do with forward-moving kinetic energy. When Mars is retrograde, this energy doesn't flow outward as easily. Life typically feels either extra-chaotic or like you're stuck in traffic (one extreme or the other). The key here is to seek balance. Ground yourself in what is in your locus of control and find peace with what isn't.

Mars will re-enter Cancer on January 6 and then, one week later, there's a full Moon in Cancer as well. Both of these transits have everything to do with your spiritual and mental health and wellness. Balance can be found in routines, especially routines that allow for mind-body-spirit alignment. Make a concerted effort to exercise in nature or routinely form a gratitude practice when eating or drinking. Little habitual practices like these will ground you in the present and keep you balanced.

January ends with Aquarius' season beginning on the 19th and the new Moon in Aquarius on the 29th. Both of these transits are relationship-oriented. If you've got a significant other, schedule quality time on a routine basis with them. If you're single, schedule dates solo or with prospective partners routinely. The new Moon ushers in new beginnings, so especially work with the new Moon in the realm of everything to do with relationships.

February

Best Days Overall: 1-6
Most Stressful Days Overall: 9-15
Best Days for Love: 3-7
Best Days for Money: 23-28
Best Days for Career: 5-8
Power Word: Identity

Happy February, Leo! The first few days of the month feature a couple of harmonious alignments: one between Venus and Neptune, the other between Mercury and Jupiter. The Venus-Neptune transit emanates a sweet vibe, which at its core is about spiritual fulfilment. This transit occurs on the 1st, so bookmark this weekend to partake in activities that soothe or feed your soul. This weekend also builds to Mercury and Jupiter's lovely meet-up on the 3rd. Mercury and Jupiter working together is super-helpful for any form of communication. If you're a writer or speaker, this is the ideal transit to get some good work done as it's a useful one in which to express yourself.

The full Moon in your sign occurring on February 12 is especially noticeable given the tense aspect between the Sun and Uranus baked into it. The Sun rules our concept of identity, and Uranus is all about liberation and turbulence. Full Moons are known for being emotional times, and this additional layer to the astrology only adds to that. If you find yourself emotionally agitated on or around this day, it may be wise to spend time exploring the nuance of these feelings. There's a lot of wisdom to be gained in temporary discomfort. In addition to potential dysregulation, this full Moon is a great time to free yourself from labels you or others may put on you. If you've been meaning to reinvent any aspect of your persona, this transit will catalyse these changes.

Pisces' season begins on February 18 with the cosmic weather shifting to focus on finances. This is especially the case for the ways in which you make money with other people or because of others. Do yourself a favour and find ways to reduce debt (if you have any) before the eclipses commence next month. Use the new Moon on the 27th to usher in at least one habit that cultivates a sustainable relationship with money. Pisces transits highlight lack of structure in particular areas of our life. Allow for this solar season to show you in what ways you need to organize your wallet.

March

Best Days Overall: 6-10
Most Stressful Days Overall: 14-18
Best Days for Love: 23-26
Best Days for Money: 2-5
Best Days for Career: 20-24
Power Word: Spiritual

Hi, Leo, there's so much astrology to cover this month so let's jump right in. March's cosmic weather begins on the 1st with Venus turning retrograde. Venus is retrograde in fellow fire sign Aries. Venus' retrogrades always involve some level of re-evaluating our values and relationships. That being said, this specific retrograde for Leo also involves zeroing in on how spirituality informs your values and also how you approach relationships. Mind and body connections are of course important, but this retrograde forces you to ensure there's a spiritual connection in your romantic and platonic relationships.

In addition to the Venus retrograde, March also features both eclipses of 2025's first eclipse season. The first eclipse occurs in

Virgo on March 14 and relates to one of the year's biggest themes for you: finances. As you know from your yearly horoscope, this year is a major turning point in how you make (and spend) your money. This eclipse is one of the hallmark transits of the year, which spurs you into action. Eclipses can be wily and uncontrollable, so this is not the time for extravagant spending. In fact, it's an ideal time for frugality or setting up methods of savings. Research ways in which you can passively grow your money as well. Mercury turns retrograde one day later. Mercury retrograde has us revisiting and reflecting on our patterns of thought and communication. Mercury's retrograde occurring right after the eclipse demands you look at the intersection between your spiritual values and your spending habits. Examples include the call to donate more to philanthropic organizations you care about and whether you could invest more money in financing new aspects of your spiritual routine. On the other hand, the call could be to save your money and find ways to embody your spirituality without having to spend.

Aries' season begins on the 20th, and the second eclipse of the year occurs in Aries on the 29th. In addition to spirituality, these transits also correlate to higher education and far-flung trips. If you're currently at university or college, the confluence of transits in Aries will catalyse important developments in pursuit of your qualification. Be mindful that eclipses tend to shake things up, so don't be alarmed if your expectations around how things will fall into place actually don't materialize according to plan – trust the process. This eclipse, and Neptune moving into Aries on the 30th, also encourages travel as a medium for self-discovery.

April

Best Days Overall: 8–12
Most Stressful Days Overall: 27–30
Best Days for Love: 2–6
Best Days for Money: 17–20
Best Days for Career: 19–22
Power Word: Energize

Happy April, Leo! The first week of this month features a peppering of soft, supportive transits. Specifically, the 5th and the 7th are two days to note. On the 5th Venus harmoniously aligns with Mars in water signs. This is a heart-centred transit – and as you're the sign that literally rules the heart, you know a thing or two about that. Venus–Mars transits are an ideal time in which to cosy up to your special someone or treat yourself to a feelgood activity. On April 7 Mercury ends its retrograde and goes direct. This transit will relieve you of some of the communication breakdowns you've experienced over the last three weeks.

On April 12 there's a full Moon in Libra. Libra is the sign of collaboration, harmony and integration. This transit is centred around communication for Leo. Because this comes on the heels of a Mercury retrograde, it's important to take this opportunity to clarify any lingering conversations that got lost in translation over the last month. This lunation falls in Leo's 3rd house, and is an opportune time for you to explore and support your local community in whatever ways you see fit. The retrograde doesn't function like a light switch, so it will clear gradually over the next three weeks.

On April 18 Mars re-enters Leo for the first time since the beginning of January. Mars rules drive, ambition and assertion. With this transit occurring right after both lesser planetary retrogrades end, there's a lot of momentum to tap into towards achieving year-end goals. Taurus' season begins the next day, which lights up your career sector, and you should definitely make moves to tick things off your to-do list to accomplish your 2025 career goals. The new Moon in Taurus on the 27th is a noteworthy transit because while it's normally centred around security and sensuality, this year's new Moon in Taurus features Mars opposing Pluto. When Mars and Pluto don't see eye to eye, rage is much more easily sparked. You'll be feeling super-energized from Mars entering your sign, so do your best to channel the kinetic energy productively and not detrimentally.

May

Best Days Overall: 20–23
Most Stressful Days Overall: 9–12
Best Days for Love: 1–5
Best Days for Money: 25–28
Best Days for Career: 19–22
Power Word: Community

Happy May, Leo! The first week of this month features social transits for Leo. On May 5 Mercury harmoniously aspects Jupiter in Gemini. This transit encourages social butterfly behaviour. Jupiter is all about expansion, so when it's lovingly greeted by the planet that rules communication and co-mingling, it's time to reach out to those you love to go on an adventure. Your adventure doesn't need to take place on this date, but instead utilize the energy of this cosmic weather to thoughtfully plan an outing or trip with some of your favourite people. Mercury then enters Taurus on the 10th, shifting your focus to career aspirations. As mentioned last month, Taurus is heavily career-oriented for Leo, so continue to leverage the build-up of Taurus energy accordingly.

On May 12 there's a full Moon in Scorpio, your fellow fixed sign. This full Moon sheds its light on home and family dynamics. Scorpio is a heavily analytical water sign, so if there are unasked questions for family or household members, this lunation will bring them to the surface. While the lunation itself isn't tense, Mercury is squaring off with Pluto on this day, which means there will be an on-edge feeling to the week. Mercury–Pluto aspects can elicit obsessive or compulsive thinking. If you have the tendency for hyper-vigilance, plan to get into a supportive routine with your grounding practices before this week starts. The Mercury–Pluto aspect does support any form of discovery, whether it's getting to know someone on a deeper level or doing some form of research.

On May 20 Gemini's season begins, with Mercury joining the Sun in Gemini on the 25th and the new Moon occurring on the 26th. That's a lot of Gemini energy! This new Moon encourages you to go out and explore new groups, organizations or communities. Cultivating community around a passion, hobby or skills during this lunation should yield long-lasting dividends. The new Moon features a supportive alignment with Saturn, which just entered Aries on the 24th. Saturn in Aries ushers in a 2½-year period auditing how spirituality and education influence how you navigate life. Saturn's transit promotes dismantling systems that no longer serve you and catalyses new ways of practising your philosophical beliefs.

June

Best Days Overall: 26–30
Most Stressful Days Overall: 19–23
Best Days for Love: 12–15
Best Days for Money: 1–5
Best Days for Career: 4–8
Power Word: Self-compassion

Hey, Leo! June is an interesting month for you, so let's jump right in. The first 10 days of the month feature three planets changing signs, creating a noticeable vibe change for everyone. Venus enters one of its home signs, Taurus, on the 6th. Venus in Taurus promotes abundance in career pursuits for Leo. Venus in Taurus has a security orientation and best supports accruing abundance through methodical action. If you're looking for a raise or promotion, now is the time to present evidence of how you've demonstrated your abilities, or maybe begin to put together a file for a future discussion. Mercury and Jupiter enter Cancer on the 8th and 9th respectively. Cancer transits centre around mental wellness and being the best parent you can be to yourself. Jupiter will be in

Cancer for close to a year, promoting consistent action around self-compassion and inner-child work.

The full Moon in Sagittarius is romantic and creative for you. This lunation occurs on the 11th and spurs you to go on a creative adventure. If there's a particular form of creative self-expression you love, let that be your guide. If you feel called to do so, bring a special someone along for the ride. The middle of the month also features fiery Mars entering Virgo. Mars in Virgo falls in Leo's 2nd house of finances. Mars in a sign's 2nd house has traditional associations with flagrant spending, so be mindful to budget at this time (especially with your birthday coming up later this summer).

Cancer's season begins on the 20th, meaning that the Sun is only one sign away from Leo! The theme of Cancer season for Leo is, unequivocally, taking care of your mental health. The Sun squares off with Saturn and Neptune on the 22nd and 23rd, just before the new Moon on the 25th. These tense aspects are associated with general feeling of being overwhelmed. Pacing yourself en route to your goals is a must, as is prioritizing the self-compassion mentioned with Jupiter moving into Cancer. You're naturally radiant, so through being kind to yourself you'll radiate an even warmer glow.

July

Best Days Overall: 4–8
Most Stressful Days Overall: 23–27
Best Days for Love: 1–4
Best Days for Money: 21–24
Best Days for Career: 6–10
Power Word: Individuality

Are you ready, Leo? Before we talk about Leo season, we have to discuss the start of the month. July's cosmic weather begins with Venus centre-stage. On the 4th Venus meets up with Uranus at the final degree of Taurus and then subsequently shifts into Gemini. Venus in Gemini is a social transit in general, but especially so for Leo. Venus–Uranus together inject spontaneity and surprises into your social vibe. On July 7 Uranus enters Gemini for the first time since 1949. Wow! Uranus in Gemini affects all of us on the collective level by leading to technological breakthroughs around the ways we communicate and learn. For Leo, this transit ushers in an extended period of changes to the social structures you're enmeshed in.

On July 10 the full Moon in Capricorn shines brightly. This full Moon centres around physical wellness routines for you, Leo. The lunation asks you the question, 'Do I have structures in place to support my physical wellness?' This full Moon demands you take action to implement sustainable routines that support your body. Even small changes that become habits will yield long-lasting dividends. Mercury turns retrograde on the 18th in your sign. This transit can facilitate communication breakdowns and misinterpretation. It's important you communicate directly and actively listen to others.

On July 22 the time has come! Leo is known for roaring, and your season begins loudly. The Sun aspects five different planets within the first three days of Leo season. The new Moon in Leo on the 24th has all of these aspects built into the lunation chart. The new Moon in your sign centres around what makes you uniquely you, stimulating you to view your uniqueness as a major strength and shining your light for all the world to see. There's an element of 'courage over comfort' that comes with this lunation, because vulnerability is not easy. This new Moon catalyses a six-month cycle of being more intentional about being your own cheerleader and being unafraid of showing the world the real you.

August

Best Days Overall: 11–14
Most Stressful Days Overall: 27–31
Best Days for Love: 7–11
Best Days for Money: 22–26
Best Days for Career: 3–7
Power Word: Connection

Happy Leo season, sweet lion! August's cosmic weather starts off with Venus finding tension with Saturn and Neptune. These transits force you to confront limiting patterns of thought and behaviour. This especially includes dissociative or destructive stress-coping mechanisms. The astrology of August centres around ushering in a new year with healthier, more affirming routines. Mars, the planet of ambition, enters harmonious Libra on the 6th. For you, Leo, this transit spurs you to confront negative self-talk and observe how the way you talk to yourself translates to your relationships.

Speaking of relationships, the full Moon this month is heavily centred around partnership for Leo. The full Moon in Aquarius is exact on the 9th. This full Moon spotlights whether you can be your authentic self in partnership and if your partner feels comfortable doing the same. If you're single, this transit would also apply to your most intimate one-to-one connections. The full Moon in Aquarius occurs as Mars faces off with Saturn and Neptune. This transit is frustrating as it limits external productivity as a means to get you to slow down. Mercury is still retrograde for a couple of more days, further complicating communication in partnership. The week of the 11th is an ideal time to move at a slower pace. Mercury turns direct on the 11th, but won't be moving that quickly for another week or so. Venus finds harmony with Jupiter the next day, supporting cosying up to a special someone or having a sweet night in all to yourself.

Leo season ends and Virgo's season begins on the 22nd. The following day there's a new Moon in Virgo centred around finances for you. This new Moon ushers in a new emotional cycle, encouraging the creation of new streams of income or new ways to better manage your finances. Beginning to work with a financial advisor, purchasing budgeting software or identifying a new business venture are all ways to tap into the energy of this lunation. Venus enters your sign on the 25th, prompting you to do something for yourself that functions as an act of self-love.

September

Best Days Overall: 10-14
Most Stressful Days Overall: 23-27
Best Days for Love: 16-19
Best Days for Money: 19-22
Best Days for Career: 1-4
Power Word: Funding

Hi, Leo! This September is also the second eclipse season of the year, so let's jump right in to your monthly horoscope. The first eclipse of September occurs on the 7th and is a full Moon lunar eclipse in Pisces. For everyone, this eclipse season is an audit of interpersonal relationships and the health of these dynamics. For Leo, this first eclipse centres around those relationships with people where your finances are dependent on – or determined by – them. The first important step to take to navigate the scrutinizing energy of this eclipse is asking yourself whether you have a clear picture of how much is entering and exiting your bank account at all times. This eclipse picks up where the last eclipse season left off, focusing on your spending and saving habits. Have you struck more of a balance between the two in the last six months? This eclipse could very well support adopting new streams of income to bolster your overall financial portfolio. Just like with the last eclipse, this one also forces you to confront whether your spending habits align with your spiritual value system.

The second eclipse of the month occurs on the 21st and is a new Moon solar eclipse in Virgo. This eclipse is equally centred on finances for Leo, but is more concerned with the ways you limit your ability to earn. Whether it's a lack of belief in pursuing a money-making endeavour or general ignorance about how to maintain your finances, this eclipse promotes addressing the root blockers between you and fiscal abundance. To get to the bottom of the problem, this Mercury-ruled eclipse would support stream-of-consciousness journaling where you write out everything that comes to mind about how you may get in your own way in this regard. Take what you learn from this exercise and implement one or two small actions that can become habitual and will support growing your wealth.

Libra's season begins on the 22nd with a confluence of transits between the Sun and every slow-moving planet from Saturn to Pluto. This Libra season spurs you to speak your truth more freely. The solar season does start off a little agitated, so make sure you communicate methodically instead of roaring.

October

Best Days Overall: 15–19
Most Stressful Days Overall: 24–28
Best Days for Love: 28–31
Best Days for Money: 3–6
Best Days for Career: 21–23
Power Word: Boundaries

Happy October, Leo! This month's cosmic weather begins with a full Moon in Aries on the 6th. This annual lunation centres around the question of your individual emotional needs being met. Moreover, this full Moon spotlights whether some form of education or adopting a new spiritual practice would help ameliorate these needs. If you've been pondering about going back into education or getting some form of certification, this lunation will push you to do so. Additionally, if you've been feeling like getting into some form of teaching or coaching, this lunation also supports doing so. Full Moons are emotional times, and this lunation highlights whether you have a spiritual practice in place to help soothe yourself when agitated or activated.

The second week of October brings into focus your relationship to communication. While the full Moon helps you identify if your emotional needs are being met, the cosmic weather for the rest of the month centres on if you're comfortable speaking up and asserting yourself. Venus, the planet that rules values and self-worth, aspects every planet from Saturn to Pluto between the 11th and the 15th, and moves into Libra on the 13th. A major component of these transits is identifying the root causes for how you approach communication, especially when it comes to communicating boundaries. The full Moon in Libra occurs on the 21st and furthers this theme. Libra is the sign associated with integration, collaboration and harmony. For Leo, this new Moon serves as the opportunity to usher in more affirmed boundary-setting practices when necessary. Set boundaries as an act of self-love moving forward.

Scorpio's season begins on the 22nd with the Sun immediately aspecting Uranus and Pluto over the next two days. For Leo, Scorpio season centres on home and family dynamics. The theme of this month has been ensuring your emotional needs are being met and advocating for them. This solar season directs your focus to ensuring there's equality in the interpersonal dynamics at home or with your family. Moreover, Scorpio season is the ideal time to refurbish or reorganize the home.

November

Best Days Overall: 20–24
Most Stressful Days Overall: 5–9
Best Days for Love: 26–30
Best Days for Money: 19–22
Best Days for Career: 14–18
Power Word: Petrol

Happy November, Leo! This month's astrology kicks off on the 4th with Mars moving into Sagittarius, your fellow fire sign. Mars rules all things kinetic, and this transit puts some petrol on your creative and romantic fires. If you have the drive and ambition to creatively self-express for a bigger audience, Mars works with you to get the ball rolling. Moreover, this is the ideal energy to go on a romantic date with someone special. Mars will stay in Sagittarius for the rest of the month. The full Moon in Taurus follows the next day, spotlighting security within your career. This full Moon poses the question, 'What do you want your legacy to be?' If you're feeling as though you're currently not setting yourself up on the proper trajectory, this lunation will provide you with an audit around why and how. Be gentle with yourself and know you have time to figure out the next steps (stay tuned for the end of this horoscope).

Mercury turns retrograde one final time this year, on the 9th. This transit invites pause and reflection around your relationship to pleasure. Do you carve out adequate time for play and recreation? Have you struck a proper balance between work and play? This retrograde will spur you to strive for more equilibrium in this regard. On the 17th the Sun forms an incredibly harmonious aspect with Jupiter and Saturn. This transit promotes heartfelt connection and taking action with a higher beneficial purpose.

The new Moon in Scorpio occurs on the 20th. This lunation ushers in a new emotional cycle around home and family dynamics for you, sweet lion. One of the themes of Scorpio's season has been ensuring your emotional needs are being met at home. This new Moon cements whatever work you've done in this regard. Moreover, making necessary changes to your physical home to revitalize the energy of your living space is recommended. Sagittarius' season begins on the 21st. This solar season is visionary and will work with you to help figure out your next steps in the wake of that full Moon in Taurus.

December

Best Days Overall: 22–26
Most Stressful Days Overall: 17–21
Best Days for Love: 1–4
Best Days for Money: 3–6
Best Days for Career: 24–28
Power Word: Community

Happy December, Leo! Creativity and community are the two big keywords for this month. The cosmic weather begins on the 4th with the full Moon in Gemini. This transit is social in nature but also carries a deeper purpose. On the surface, this lunation promotes spending time in your groups and organizations. That's wonderful. The deeper question this full Moon asks you is whether you're experiencing reciprocity in these organizations or putting in more than you're getting out. This full Moon is in Gemini, the sign of the communicator, and it supports really connecting on a deeper level with the communities you immerse yourself in. A great way to honour this transit is through reaching out to express your gratitude to specific friends or community members who support you tirelessly.

Mars and Saturn square off on the 9th, which slows things down to a potentially frustrating pace. The purpose of this transit is to ground you in the present and to force you to only focus your efforts on projects that are already in motion. However, this transit absolutely evokes restlessness and can make you feel like you're stuck in traffic. Channel any frenetic energy into existing endeavours. After Mars is done feuding with Saturn, it moves into Capricorn on the 15th. This transit supports productivity for everyone, although this transit can be inflammatory for you when it comes to physical matters. Now is not the time to mistreat your body or ignore its needs. If you've been putting off going for your annual check-up or seeing a specialist, this transit functions as an invitation to do so.

The new Moon in Sagittarius occurs on the 19th, and centres on ushering in a new cycle around your relationship to creativity and pleasure. More specifically, this new Moon is about taking what you learned during last month's Mercury retrograde and taking actionable next steps around prioritizing a better balance between work and play or work and creativity, usually by ensuring you have more creativity or play in your life. Capricorn's season begins on the 21st. Capricorn is represented by the sea goat, so whether you're metaphorically summiting mountains or swimming to the bottom of the ocean next year, this solar season inspires you to put together your 2026 vision board.

Virgo

♍

THE VIRGIN

Birthdays from
August 22
to September 22

Personality Profile

VIRGO AT A GLANCE

Element – Earth

Ruling Planet – Mercury
  Career Planet – Mercury
  Love Planet – Neptune
  Money Planet – Venus
  Planet of Home and Family Life – Jupiter
  Planet of Health and Work – Uranus
  Planet of Pleasure – Saturn
  Planet of Sexuality – Mars

Totem – the Principal

Colours – earth tones, ochre, green

Colour that promotes love, romance and social harmony – aqua blue

Colour that promotes earning power – jade green

Gems – agate, hyacinth

Metal – quicksilver

Scents – lavender, lilac, lily of the valley, storax

Quality – mutable (= flexibility)

Quality most needed for balance – a broader perspective

Strongest virtues – mental agility, analytical skills, ability to pay attention to detail, healing powers

Deepest needs – to be useful and productive

Characteristic to avoid – destructive criticism

Signs of greatest overall compatibility – Taurus, Capricorn

Signs of greatest overall incompatibility – Gemini, Sagittarius, Pisces

Sign most helpful to career – Gemini

Sign most helpful for emotional support – Sagittarius

Sign most helpful financially – Libra

Sign best for marriage and/or partnerships – Pisces

Sign most helpful for creative projects – Capricorn

Best Sign to have fun with – Capricorn

Signs most helpful in spiritual matters – Taurus, Leo

Best day of the week – Wednesday

Understanding a Virgo

The virgin is a particularly fitting symbol for those born under the sign of Virgo. If you meditate on the image of the virgin you will get a good understanding of the essence of the Virgo type. The virgin is, of course, a symbol of purity and innocence – not naïve, but pure. A virginal object has not been touched. A virgin field is land that is true to itself, the way it has always been. The same is true of virgin forest: it is pristine, unaltered.

Apply the idea of purity to the thought processes, emotional life, physical body and activities and projects of the everyday world, and you can see how Virgos approach life. Virgos desire the pure expression of the ideal in their mind, body and affairs. If they find impurities they will attempt to clear them away.

Impurities are the beginning of disorder, unhappiness and uneasiness. The job of the Virgo is to eject all impurities and keep only that which the body and mind can use and assimilate.

The secrets of good health are here revealed: 90 per cent of the art of staying well is maintaining a pure mind, a pure body and pure emotions. When you introduce more impurities than your mind and body can deal with, you will have what is known as 'dis-ease'. It is no wonder that Virgos make great doctors, nurses, healers and dieticians. They have an innate understanding of good health and they realize that good health is more than just physical. In all aspects of life, if you want a project to be successful it must be kept as pure as possible. It must be protected against the adverse elements that will try to undermine it. This is the secret behind Virgo's awesome technical proficiency.

One could talk about Virgo's analytical powers – which are formidable. One could talk about their perfectionism and their almost superhuman attention to detail. But this would be to miss the point. All of these virtues are manifestations of a Virgo's desire for purity and perfection – a world without Virgos would have ruined itself long ago.

A vice is nothing more than a virtue turned inside out, misapplied or used in the wrong context. Virgos' apparent vices come from their inherent virtue. Their analytical powers, which should be used for healing, helping or perfecting a project in the world, sometimes get misapplied and turned against people. Their critical faculties, which should be used constructively to perfect a strategy or proposal, can sometimes be used destructively to harm or wound. Their urge to perfection can turn into worry and lack of confidence; their natural humility can become self-denial and self-abasement. When Virgos turn negative they are apt to turn their devastating criticism on themselves, sowing the seeds of self-destruction.

Finance

Virgos have all the attitudes that create wealth. They are hard-working, industrious, efficient, organized, thrifty, productive and eager to serve. A developed Virgo is every employer's dream. But until Virgos master some of the social graces of Libra they will not even come close to fulfilling their financial potential. Purity and perfectionism, if not handled correctly or gracefully, can be very trying to others. Friction in human relationships can be devastating not only to your pet projects but – indirectly – to your wallet as well.

Virgos are quite interested in their financial security. Being hard-working, they know the true value of money. They do not like to take risks with their money, preferring to save for their retirement or for a rainy day. Virgos usually make prudent, calculated investments that involve a minimum of risk. These investments and savings usually work out well, helping Virgos to achieve the financial security they seek. The rich or even not-so-rich Virgo also likes to help his or her friends in need.

Career and Public Image

Virgos reach their full potential when they can communicate their knowledge in such a way that others can understand it. In order to get their ideas across better, Virgos need to develop greater verbal skills and fewer judgemental ways of expressing themselves. Virgos look up to teachers and communicators; they like their bosses to be good communicators. Virgos will probably not respect a superior who is not their intellectual equal – no matter how much money or power that superior has. Virgos themselves like to be perceived by others as being educated and intellectual.

The natural humility of Virgos often inhibits them from fulfilling their great ambitions, from acquiring name and fame. Virgos should indulge in a little more self-promotion if they are going to reach their career goals. They need to push themselves with the same ardour that they would use to foster others.

At work Virgos like to stay active. They are willing to learn any type of job as long as it serves their ultimate goal of financial security. Virgos may change occupations several times during their professional lives, until they find the one they really enjoy. Virgos work well with other people, are not afraid to work hard and always fulfil their responsibilities.

Love and Relationships

If you are an analyst or a critic you must, out of necessity, narrow your scope. You have to focus on a part and not the whole; this can create a temporary narrow-mindedness. Virgos do not like this kind of person. They like their partners to be broad-minded, with depth and vision. Virgos seek to get this broad-minded quality from their partners, since they sometimes lack it themselves.

Virgos are perfectionists in love just as they are in other areas of life. They need partners who are tolerant, open-minded and easy-going. If you are in love with a Virgo do not waste time on impractical romantic gestures. Do practical and useful things for him or her – this is what will be appreciated and what will be done for you.

Virgos express their love through pragmatic and useful gestures, so do not be put off because your Virgo partner does not say 'I love you' day in and day out. Virgos are not that type. If they love you, they will demonstrate it in practical ways. They will always be there for you; they will show an interest in your health and finances; they will fix your sink or repair your video recorder. Virgos deem these actions to be superior to sending flowers, chocolates or Valentine cards.

In love affairs Virgos are not particularly passionate or spontaneous. If you are in love with a Virgo, do not take this personally. It does not mean that you are not alluring enough or that your Virgo partner does not love or like you. It is just the way Virgos are. What they lack in passion they make up for in dedication and loyalty.

Home and Domestic Life

It goes without saying that the home of a Virgo will be spotless, sanitized and orderly. Everything will be in its proper place – and don't you dare move anything about! For Virgos to find domestic bliss they need to ease up a bit in the home, to allow their partner and children more freedom and to be more generous and open-minded. Family members are not to be analysed under a microscope, they are individuals with their own virtues to express.

With these small difficulties resolved, Virgos like to stay in and entertain at home. They make good hosts and they like to keep their friends and families happy and entertained at family and social gatherings. Virgos love children, but they are strict with them – at times – since they want to make sure their children are brought up with the correct sense of family and values.

Horoscope for 2025

There are two signs with main character energy this year and you're one of them, Virgo. In January the nodes shift into the Virgo–Pisces axis for the first time in nine years. The nodes are what astrologers use to identify overarching themes for the year because they dictate what signs the eclipses are in. Half of the eclipses this year will be in your sign, a fact of great significance. Eclipses are evolutionary transits that catalyse growth through scrutiny and shake-ups. Spiderman's uncle said it best: 'With great power comes great responsibility.' Your totem is 'the Principal' in 2025 because you're assuming major responsibility and entering a year centred around maturation.

This year features a number of the slower-moving planets – Saturn, Uranus and Neptune – shifting signs. These shifts indicate that you can anticipate major changes occurring worldwide in your macro-environment. On the individual level, many of these planets ingress into highly sensitive and profoundly felt sectors of Virgo's chart. Take the nodes, for example. In January the north node shifts into Virgo's 7th house of partnership. This location of the north node in your chart indicates major increase, so anticipate partnership to be a hot and heavy theme of the year, as will be further discussed in the love and social life section.

Saturn, the planet that rules discipline, restriction and hard work, also occupies your 7th house of partnership for three-quarters of the year. Saturn spends the summer vacationing in your 8th house of joint finances, which shifts its investigative gaze from interpersonal partnership to those relationships of yours where money links you with others. Neptune also oscillates between the same two signs, which only emphasizes how important these themes will be this year.

Aside from relationships, whether romantic or financial, your career and cementing your legacy are also major topics contribut-ing to you embodying the Principal this year. Jupiter, the planet of growth and expansion, is in Virgo's career sector for the first half of the year. Uranus, the planet of innovation, instability and break-throughs, takes over occupying this section of your chart from July to November. There will be more on this in the career and finances section of this horoscope.

For a quarterly view of the year, your focus for the first three months of 2025 centres around relationships and career. Paired with career is a sub-theme of your social standing and responsibil-ity in the organizations of which you're a part. The second quarter of the year features a shift to focus on financial relationships and how your money is tied up with others, the third fully leans into finances and is also a pivotal time for cementing your personal legacy, while the last quarter of 2025 brings the cosmic focus back to relationships and also readily emphasizes friendships.

Health

(Please note that this is an astrological perspective on health and not a medical one. Any health-related symptoms should be evaluated by a qualified healthcare professional.)

The astrology of 2025 overarchingly asks you, 'Do you take responsibility for your physical wellness, Virgo?' This primarily involves identifying the ways in which your relationships and involvement with others take precedence over maintaining your own physical wellness. Given how acutely you're being aspected by several of the most noteworthy transits of the year, upholding consistency with diet and exercise is paramount. Now Virgo, while maintaining this consistency is important, hyper-vigilance around being perfect with diet or exercise is absolutely not sustainable. Mars retrograde at the start of the year primarily transits your house of spiritual and mental health and wellness. In order to establish mental equilibrium, you must focus on achieving homeostasis with your body.

This year starts off with an audit of how your holistic physical fitness correlates to your mental wellness. From a medical standpoint, Mars rules irritation and inflammation, so paying special attention to how your diet affects your mood is vital. The first quarter of the year also features two eclipses, one of which is in your sign. Eclipses are felt in the body, especially if they occur in your sign. Part of why maintaining consistency in wellness routines is vital is because it's important to mitigate the destabilizing aspects of the eclipses this year. Eclipses in your 1st house can also make you want to modify your appearance. Be mindful of what the catalyst is for these changes and ensure that the decision is supportive of your mental wellness.

September is a notable month for health as it's both the second month to feature eclipses and also the time when Saturn moves back into Virgo's relationship sector. During this month it's important for you to evaluate how your relationships impact your physical health. If you find specific relationships to be more taxing than uplifting, definitely determine what boundaries need to be in place to support your physical wellness. September features the second of the two eclipses in your sign. As with March, this is a month in which you should not overexert yourself. Rest and rejuvenation are always important, but scheduling time for them during March and September is paramount.

Here are the specific areas of the body to focus on this year:

- The digestive system: in medical astrology, Virgo rules the intestines and gut, so this is a perennial area of focus for you. This part of the body is especially important, given how crucial diet is to both physical and mental wellness this year.
- The head and face: the two eclipses occurring in the sign of Virgo fall in Virgo's 1st house. From a medical astrology standpoint, the 1st house relates to the head and face. Maintaining consistency in a skincare routine for the face or ensuring an intake of vitamins to support eye health are examples of ways to positively work with the astrology of this year. Also, make sure to thoroughly think through and vet cosmetic alterations to this part of the body this year.
- Reproductive organs: for about half the year, Saturn and Neptune will be transiting Virgo's 8th house, which relates to these parts of the body in medical astrology. Make a concerted effort to consistently integrate foods like berries and cruciferous vegetables, as they contain antioxidants and/or essential vitamins to support these organs.

Love and Social Life

As mentioned in the introduction to this horoscope, relationships and social life are one of the hottest topics for you this year, Virgo. The cosmic weather around love and social life starts almost immediately this year, with the north node moving into Pisces on January 11. The nodes spend 18 months in a sign, so the north node will be occupying the relationships part of your chart all year. This node is inherently linked to the south node, which moves into your sign on the same day. While the north node signifies increase wherever it's transiting, the south node signifies shedding.

Herein lies the first major evolutionary prompt of the year for you. The south node in your sign asks you, 'What aspects of my temperament or identity do I need to shed in order to become more fulfilled in love and my relationships?' You can get to the root of this question in many different ways. I'd recommend leaning into the themes around the north node and asking yourself what qualities you seek to personify within a relationship. Regardless of whether you've already got a partner or not, identifying what you seek to evolve into will allow you to best evaluate what self-effacing patterns of thought and behaviour you must shed.

Jupiter, the planet of growth and expansion, occupies Virgo's 11th house of groups, communities and organizations from June 9 onwards. Jupiter spends a full year in each sign, so this transit only occurs once every 12 years. Jupiter makes this shift and moves into home- and family-oriented Cancer. Jupiter occupying this part of your chart absolutely brings a boost to both the quality and quantity of your friendships. I would recommend spending some time identifying what passions or hobbies bring you the most joy or keep you the most grounded, and then join groups or organizations associated with them come the summer.

Jupiter is also your relationship planet, indicating that there's potency around relationships forming because of your career or through your social circles. This is a major reason why taking an active role in expanding your social circles around your passions is so important. If you're single, definitely leverage Jupiter's shift into Cancer by joining these groups during the summer. Jupiter finds harmony with the Sun and Saturn in mid-November, which is an opportune time to put yourself out there as well.

Lastly, a major relationship theme for you this year is identifying reciprocity within your relationships. Saturn occupies the relationship section of your chart from January until the end of May and then again from September to all the way through December. Saturn is all about structural integrity, and this applies to whether or not your relationships are long-lasting. Thankfully, if there's mutual support and reciprocity in your relationships, transiting Saturn will only bolster them. The only relationships you'll be forced to rethink or outgrow are those that won't support the Principal you're growing into.

Career and Finances

'What do you want to be remembered for, Virgo?' The astrology of 2025 asks you this question. The cosmic weather around career has two chapters, one involving Jupiter and the other involving Uranus. From January to June, Jupiter will be transiting Virgo's 10th house of career and legacy. Jupiter brings expansion and makes things bigger. In one respect, this means the likelihood of assuming more responsibility at work or getting a promotion is high. However, as the Bard wrote, 'Uneasy lies the head that wears a crown.'

Remember that with growth come growing pains. That being said, growth is a fundamentally good thing. Choosing courage over comfort in your career choices can allow you to ascend to heights you didn't know were attainable. The inspiration for your totem, the Principal, comes from the potency around maturation in your career or ascension in your career trajectory. As Jupiter occupies the 10th house, Uranus wraps up its stay in your 9th house of higher education and spirituality. Breakthroughs or shake-ups in your career are likely to be catalysed through seeking newfound certifications or additional education within your field of interest.

Come July, Uranus moves into Virgo's 10th house of career one month after Jupiter leaves it. Uranus brings a more dynamic, albeit frenetic energy to this area of your life. In order to reach the summit of a mountain, you have to leave your basecamp at some point. Uranus brings with it parting with the old in order to usher in the new. Uranus is represented by the Tower card in Tarot, which indicates unexpected changes. The second half of 2025 will likely bring unexpected and potentially exciting career shifts or updates. The 10th house also rules legacy, so these shifts can also be directed towards overarching long-term goals while you remain in the same job.

A big component of this is the prestige and responsibility you hold in professional circles. From June to December Jupiter moves into Virgo's 11th house of groups and organizations. The call to assume additional responsibility in these spaces will be made. Jupiter also rules beliefs and conviction, so use your belief system as a litmus test for whether these newfound roles are right for you.

Your career planet is Mercury, who undergoes three retrograde periods this year, mostly in fire signs. These retrograde periods are times in which to review and reassess your career priorities and how they relate to achieving your overarching career goals. The element of fire relates to passion, so re-evaluating your career goals should be conducted through the lens of what gets you the most fired up. These retrogrades will also encourage looking to the past as a means of showing you how far you've come in your career. Moreover, this exercise will illuminate how you ended up where you are in the present moment and influence the subsequent decisions you make in altering your career trajectory.

Home and Domestic Life

Jupiter is your ruling planet for all things home and domestic, and it starts the year off retrograde. Retrogrades encourage 're-' verbs like 'revisit', 'reflect' and 'rethink'. The first month of 2025 strongly inspires revisiting home-improvement projects you've left lingering for way too long. Typically, there's also the call to confront lingering interpersonal issues within the home during this month as well. Unfortunately, Mars, the ruler of confrontation, will also be retrograde in January, complicating your ability to have constructive conflict at this time. If provoked, do your best to respond instead of reacting. As well as ruling home and domestic life, Jupiter is the planet associated with abundance, so when it turns direct at the start of February it will help break the necessary ice. Jupiter's shift into Cancer in June is joyous. Growing into a new, bigger home or attempting new and exciting improvements or extensions is a high-minded way to work with this transit.

The month with the most potent astrology around home and domestic life is November. November starts off with Mars entering Sagittarius for six weeks. Mars is the planet that rules assertion and confrontation. Although the likelihood of conflict within the home increases, so does the ability to air grievances in order to evolve domestic relationships. The most harmonious transit of the year occurs in November when the Sun, Jupiter and Saturn all align in a grand water trine. This transit inspires profound heart-to-heart connections and can be used to navigate any turmoil you may be experiencing because of the Mars transit.

Self-improvement

Your totem this year is the Principal, so self-improvement centres around assuming responsibility and maturing. The south node occupying your sign for almost the entire year signifies that this year is about stripping away identity markers that no longer serve you, and stepping up or out into the most authentic version of yourself. Part of your eclipse story is shedding the need to put on a facade for other people's comfort at the detriment of living your truth. Both the March and September eclipses in Virgo will create tension around this theme. Remember, it takes tension for muscles to stretch and grow.

Seeking higher education or additional certifications is also a part of this year's self-improvement story for you, Virgo. Uranus wraps up its stay in this area for Virgo, encouraging that prompt in the educational sphere. Pay special attention to a final reminder in this regard in November, when Uranus juts back into Taurus one last time before permanently entering Gemini the following spring. Education is a two-sided coin, so the prompt may be to actually assume a teaching or coaching role.

Month-by-month Forecasts

January

Best Days Overall: 26–31
Most Stressful Days Overall: 2–7
Best Days for Love: 10–14
Best Days for Money: 19–23
Best Days for Career: 15–18
Power Word: Assert

Happy New Year, Virgo! The cosmic weather for 2025 begins with Venus moving into Pisces, your polar sign, on the 2nd. Venus in Pisces is especially relationship-focused as the planet transits your 7th house of partnership. Venus will be in Pisces all month, so schedule routine time to either take yourself on dates or go on dates with a partner. Venus is also slowing down and preparing for its retrograde later this spring, so this transit will also encourage taking a keen eye to reciprocity in partnerships.

We enter 2025 with Mars already retrograde, the fiery planet dipping back into Cancer on January 6. Mars rules conflict, carnality and assertion. When Mars is retrograde, frustration can build up into major powder-keg vibes, so be mindful of how you approach and respond to confrontation. For you, this is especially true for interactions and dynamics within groups and organizations. The full Moon in Cancer on the 13th only compounds this energy. This full Moon and Mars retrograde combination really asks the question, 'Are you getting what you need and what you deserve from the groups and organizations of which you're a part?' Virgo is the sign of service, but being of service should be a two-way street. Monitor these dynamics especially during the week of the full Moon. The full Moon chart features tension between Venus and Jupiter. This aspect reinforces the importance of enforcing boundaries without hesitation.

Aquarius' season begins on the 19th. The Sun in Aquarius functions as a check-in on your physical wellness practices and routines. If you've been feeling sluggish from the end of last year, this is the most opportune time to shed old habits and begin anew. Speaking of which, the Sun forms its annual union with Pluto on the 21st. Pluto rules shedding, unearthing and transformation. Utilize the potent energy of this cosmic weather to turn a new leaf around diet, exercise or holistic wellness. Remember, baby steps are much easier to become habitual, which will lead to long-lasting, positive changes. The new Moon in Aquarius on the 29th is also a great day to focus on implementing new healthy behaviours in your regime.

February

Best Days Overall: 24–28
Most Stressful Days Overall: 9–13
Best Days for Love: 19–23
Best Days for Money: 7–10
Best Days for Career: 1–5
Power Word: Sanctuary

It's February, Virgo! This month begins with a couple of sweet, softer transits, the first of which is Venus meeting up with Neptune on the 1st. This transit is dreamy and revolves around partnership for you, Virgo. If you've got a partner, this is an ideal weekend to go on some adventures with your beau. If you're single, this is a great transit to put yourself out there or take yourself on a cute self-date. Mercury and Jupiter align on the 3rd, which bolsters communication. For you, this transit especially revolves around communication in the workplace.

The most felt transit of the month is unequivocally the full Moon in Leo. As you can imagine, a full Moon in Leo is always loud. This full Moon is especially noticeable because it's squaring off with Uranus. Uranus rules instability, liberation and breakdowns. Full Moons are always emotional, so bookmark this one as a much-needed rest point in the month. This full Moon actually falls in Virgo's 12th house of spiritual and mental wellness, so it's extra important to level up on grounding and protecting your energy. It could be the ideal time to carve out a 'sanctuary space' at your home. A sanctuary space is a space exclusive to you where you can go to retreat and recharge. It can be a room, a bathtub or even an outdoor space. If where you live is unable to accommodate designating a sanctuary space, identify a space nearby that could function as this haven. Hiking trails, public parks and any locations near bodies of water are all great choices. As you know from your yearly horoscope, 2025 is heavily relationship-focused for you, so identifying a space that's exclusive to you will be massively beneficial.

Pisces' season starts on the 18th, with the new Moon following on the 27th. Pisces season means the Sun enters the same sign as the north node. The focus on relationships really begins to ramp up with this transit. The new Moon is a sensitive lunation revolving around how you approach relationships. With Venus about to go retrograde, it's also an audit of which values related to partnership you hold dear or need to re-evaluate.

March

Best Days Overall: 2–8
Most Stressful Days Overall: 12–18
Best Days for Love: 27–30
Best Days for Money: 22–27
Best Days for Career: 24–27
Power Word: Financial

Hi, Virgo! This is one of the most noteworthy months of the year astrologically, featuring two retrogrades, two eclipses and Neptune changing signs for the first time since 2011. On March 1 Venus turns retrograde in Aries. Heads up – there's a confluence of transits happening in the fire sign this month. This Venus retrograde is heavily financial for you, Virgo. Retrogrades force us to embody 're-' words like 'revisit', 're-evaluate' and 'reconsider'. This retrograde spurs you to revisit your budget and take a look at your spending habits. Moreover, there's an added component of analysing money made through other people or money owed to other people. Virgo is known for being meticulous, so it's paramount that you direct your attention to dotting your i's and crossing your t's in the realm of all things money.

Boom! The first eclipse of the year occurs on March 14, and it's occurring in your sign. An eclipse in your sign is holistically felt and signifies that this is a year of massive growth for you. With growth comes change, so do your best to choose courage over comfort when presented with the opportunity to evolve. This eclipse really speaks to the fact that this month Virgo is embodying 'main character energy'. Basically, not only is this an influential month for you, but your ability to influence others is heightened. Wield this power wisely!

The day after the eclipse on March 15, Mercury turns retrograde in Aries. The Sun enters Aries on the 20th and the second eclipse follows suit on the 29th. So much Aries energy! All of these transits compound the financial themes described with the Venus retrograde. There's an added element now of actually advocating for your finances, whether it's the salary you deserve or money you're actually owed. The solar eclipse in Aries is wily, so the frugal mindset that it was recommended you adopt at the start of the month is vital at this time. It's important to note that these transits are not meant to provoke hyper-vigilance, but rather inspire the adoption of sustainable budgeting practices that pay long-term literal and metaphorical dividends. Neptune rounds out the Aries transits on the 30th. This transit has a greater influence next month in April, but be mindful that even at the end of March it can make you see your finances through rose-coloured glasses.

April

Best Days Overall: 7–12
Most Stressful Days Overall: 25–29
Best Days for Love: 13–16
Best Days for Money: 3–7
Best Days for Career: 1–4
Power Word: Service

It's April, Virgo! The cosmic weather for the first week of this month is subtle. On April 5 Venus and Mars support one another, providing soft and sturdy energy. Virgos loves to dot their i's and cross their t's, and that's the vibe for the first week of the month. This is especially true because on April 7 Mercury, your planetary ruler, ends its retrograde and goes direct, which really helps clear the frazzled air for you. If you've been holding off on signing any contracts because of the retrograde, you're now in the clear to do so.

On April 12 Venus follows suit and goes direct, just as the full Moon in Libra occurs. The full Moon in Libra is always relationship-oriented in nature, but for Virgo there's also a financial component to it. Last month's astrology was heavily finance-focused because the cosmic weather was dominated by Aries, Libra's polar sign. This full Moon highlights how your spending practices are affected when you're infatuated by someone. Moreover, this lunation spurs you to consider whether your spending habits grossly change when you're trying to gain favour with someone.

On the 18th Mars enters Leo for the first time since the autumn/ fall of 2024. Themes around mental health and wellness should cycle back. One day later the Sun enters Taurus, a fellow earth sign. Taurus' season is a spiritual time for Virgo. Occurring in the heart of spring, it encourages Virgo to be intentional around channelling its innate sense of service for others in order to cultivate abundance. The 'butterfly effect' is a phenomenon that essentially illustrates that we don't know how great our impact is. Be aware that you're only conscious of a small fraction of the effect you have in all the ways you help others. It's necessary to be grounded on the 27th because the new Moon in Taurus will occur in tandem with Mars and Pluto opposing one another. The vibe around this date is to only be concerned with what you can control; everything else will only drag you out of the present moment.

May

Best Days Overall: 26–31
Most Stressful Days Overall: 9–13
Best Days for Love: 20–24
Best Days for Money: 3–7
Best Days for Career: 1–5
Power Word: Ascend

Hi, Virgo! May begins with Mercury, your planetary ruler, aligning with Jupiter on the 5th. This transit is heavily oriented towards supporting endeavours related to your work and career. Jupiter in Gemini has been hanging out in Virgo's 10th house of career all year, so a harmonious aspect from Mercury provides a jolt in your pursuit of this year's career ambitions. Mercury then enters Taurus on the 10th. Mercury in Taurus encourages you to bolster your mind–spirit connection, be it through travel, prayer or immersing yourself in nature. Mercury in Taurus is more thoughtful with its words as well, so if you're provoked to be critical, think twice about how you respond.

The full Moon in Scorpio occurs on April 12, which is the same day that your planetary ruler squares off with Pluto. The cosmic weather around the 12th is angsty. The full Moon in Scorpio illuminates Virgo's 3rd house of communication and shines its light on your patterns of communication. Do you often censor yourself for the sake of others? Do you speak in a condemnatory fashion to yourself in a way you wouldn't speak to others? This full Moon couples with the Mercury–Pluto aspect to spur you to get to the bottom of this.

The week of May 20 features a major build-up of Gemini energy. May 20 is when the Sun enters Gemini, followed by Mercury on the 25th and the new Moon on the 26th. On the 26th there will be a 'stellium' or cluster of four planets in Gemini. The new Moon in Gemini welcomes new beginnings within your career or your public persona. This doesn't necessarily mean starting from scratch; in fact, it can work well if you reinvent yourself within your current domain or by assuming additional responsibility. If you desire to be in a public-facing capacity or to seek fame, the new Moon strongly supports actionable steps towards these goals.

Saturn enters Aries for the first time in 26 years on the 24th, reintroducing financial themes that arose for you during eclipse season in March.

June

Best Days Overall: 2–6
Most Stressful Days Overall: 9–13
Best Days for Love: 17–20
Best Days for Money: 11–14
Best Days for Career: 26–29
Power Word: Community

Happy June, Virgo! This month's cosmic weather starts off with Mercury, your planetary ruler, finding support with Mars on the 5th. This is a soft productive transit for you, centred around ticking things off your to-do list. On the 8th and 9th respectively Mercury and Jupiter enter Cancer. Mercury will stay in the sign until the 26th, while slower-moving Jupiter will occupy the sign for most of the next 12 months or so. Jupiter in Cancer is a highly social transit for Virgo. Jupiter rules growth and expansion, providing abundance in the realm of community and groups of friends for Virgo. If you're involved in professional organizations or community groups, Jupiter in Cancer supports assuming additional responsibilities that will give you prestige.

The full Moon in Sagittarius, your fellow mutable sign, occurs on the 11th. This full Moon illuminates home and family dynamics. Sagittarius rules truth and wisdom, so this full Moon shines its light on anything that's been left unsaid, either within your home or within specific familial relationships. This full Moon is the ideal time for revitalizing the energy of your living space through feng shui, redecoration or home-improvement work. The full Moon in Sagittarius is also a kinetic lunation, promoting a spontaneous adventure with loved ones or those you live with.

Cancer's season begins on the 20th but starts off with a little bit of turbulence, given that the Sun squares off with Saturn and Neptune on the 22nd and 23rd. Virgo is a heavily systems-oriented sign focused on inputs and outputs. This transit can heighten feelings of being overwhelmed or daunted if you're equating productivity with self-worth. This is noteworthy for Virgo as Mars entered your sign on the 17th for the first time in two years. Mars rules drive, ambition and assertion. When Mars enters our home sign we feel charged up and extra-excited to try and do everything. It's important to not only pace yourself during this week but also break up bigger goals into small goals that add up to the same result. The new Moon in Cancer on the 26th promotes spending time with friends you consider family to support one another through the Sun's squares.

July

Best Days Overall: 3-7
Most Stressful Days Overall: 18-22
Best Days for Love: 10-13
Best Days for Money: 6-9
Best Days for Career: 27-30
Power Word: Flow

Venus is the star of the show for the first week of July, Virgo. On July 4 Venus conjoins with Uranus in the final degree of Taurus and then jumps into Gemini. Venus in Gemini is both a social- and career-oriented transit for you. Uranus' influence adds a bit of spontaneity and the possibility for surprises to both realms. It's time to lean into your mutable nature and go with the flow. Venus finds harmony with Saturn and Neptune on the 6th, and then Pluto on the 7th. There will be constructive energy within the workplace or in whatever endeavours you embark on that are public-facing. On July 7 Uranus enters Gemini for the first time since 1949. Uranus affects us collectively through catalysing profound technological breakthroughs around communication and learning. Uranus transits Virgo's career house now, so the rest of this year gives you a taste of all the growth and changes to come for you in your career.

The full Moon on the 10th is in Capricorn. This lunation being in another structured earth sign is supportive of your intricacies around planning and organizing. Moreover, this lunation illumin-ates Virgo's creativity and romance sector, making it the ideal time to schedule a date with your special someone or take yourself on a self-date. Full Moons in Capricorn can feel a little deflating, so treating yourself to an excursion or spending quality time with your partner is necessary. On July 18 Mercury, your planetary ruler, turns retrograde again. This Mercury retrograde has the potential to cause widespread communication misinterpretation. For Virgo, this Mercury retrograde poses the question, 'Are you making strides to support your mental health on a daily basis?'

Leo's season begins on the 22nd with a roar! The Sun aspects five planets within the first three days of being in Leo. The new Moon on the 24th contains all of these transits baked into it. This new Moon is an ideal time to take action based on your answer to that Mercury retrograde question. Moreover, there's an added prompt to support your mental health through owning your uniqueness or authenticity.

August

Best Days Overall: 21–25
Most Stressful Days Overall: 1–5
Best Days for Love: 10–13
Best Days for Money: 23–27
Best Days for Career: 14–18
Power Word: Routine

It's almost your season, Virgo! The month starts off with the call to give yourself a much-needed pep talk. On the 1st Venus squares off with both Saturn and Neptune. This transit typically materializes with you grappling with your self-esteem or by placing too much emphasis on external validation. These transits encourage you to be your own anchor and combat self-effacing patterns of thought and behaviour. Also, if you're really feeling stressed at this time, do you best to lean into supportive coping mechanisms instead of dissociative ones.

The theme of August and being your own best cheerleader continues with the full Moon in Aquarius. This lunation includes Mars finding tension with Saturn and Neptune. This full Moon calls on you to ground yourself in your body when you're faced with stress or overthinking, spotlighting physical wellness, fitness and dietary routines, and your relationship with your body. In addition to diet and exercise, do you lean into your body as a means of staying in the present? That's the key takeaway from this transit. Venus and Jupiter joyously conjoin a few days later on the 12th. Venus-Jupiter transits are great for all things pleasure, play and romance. Lean into this supportive energy by carving out time around the 12th to do something that will please your inner child.

On the 22nd it's your season! The astrology of Virgo's season starts off one day later with the first of two new Moons. This new Moon is louder than your average Virgo new Moon because of Uranus' influence, and its theme is breaking away from systems and routines that no longer serve you. Virgo typically has a way of doing things day in, day out. After a long period of time you may lose sight of the fact that this regime may have lost its efficacy. Work with this lunation to assess whether it's time to switch things up. The month ends with Venus roaring into Leo and opposing Pluto. This transit can catalyse hyper-vigilance in us, and its purpose is to force you to ground yourself in the present moment rather than unhealthily dwell on the past or future. You've got this, Virgo!

September

Best Days Overall: 16–19
Most Stressful Days Overall: 21–24
Best Days for Love: 7–11
Best Days for Money: 26–30
Best Days for Career: 1–4
Power Word: Shed

It's a noteworthy month for you, Virgo! In addition to the fact that it's Virgo's season for most of the month, it's also officially eclipse season. The first eclipse of September occurs in Pisces, your polar sign, on the 7th. This lunation functions as an audit around partnership and your relationship values. If you've got a partner, this eclipse scrutinizes whether there's reciprocity in your relationship and if you feel comfortable advocating for your needs. Moreover, if you're holding on to long-held beliefs around how to function in this dynamic that no longer serve who you are now, these will reveal themselves for you to address. If you're single, this eclipse will centre around those beliefs of yours that influence your readiness to look for a partner. This could be the ideal time to read up on partnership from relationship experts or to put yourself out there to shed light on these patterns of thought and behaviour.

The second eclipse of the month occurs in your sign at the end of Virgo's season, on September 21. An eclipse occurring in your sign is especially evolutionary, and the energy around this eclipse is reminiscent of an animal shedding its skin. In nature, animals that do this don't understand why they have to rid themselves of the skin they've grown so accustomed to. It's only after the shedding process is complete that they discover the advantages of starting anew. This eclipse applies to you in a similar way, calling on you to part with aspects of your identity that no longer benefit who you are in this present moment. Identify three words you seek to embody over the coming year. Out loud right now, call out what three words come to mind. Then, ponder why this is the case and what small actionable steps you can take to live them more intently.

Libra's season begins on the 22nd with the Sun aspecting several planets over the next three days. This solar season focuses on finances and confronting the ways you may be limiting yourself from making more money. More about this will come to light around the full Moon next month, but open yourself up to being shown answers to this prompt.

October

Best Days Overall: 1–5
Most Stressful Days Overall: 7–11
Best Days for Love: 15–19
Best Days for Money: 13–16
Best Days for Career: 25–29
Power Word: Limit(less)

Happy October, Virgo! I hope you're feeling OK after that eventful eclipse season. October's astrology begins on the 6th with a full Moon in Aries. This full Moon spotlights finances for you, specifically how your money is intertwined with others. Moreover, this lunation asks you whether you're as financially secure as you'd like to be, and, if not, what steps are you willing to take to increase your wealth? This full Moon is all about getting your emotional needs met. Leverage the energy of this lunation by identifying steps you can take over the next month to start building additional financial capital. Examples include educating yourself on fiscal systems you don't know much about, acquiring a financial planner or making some investments.

The focus on finances continues into the second week, when Venus, the modern ruler of personal finances, forms aspects with four other planets between the 11th and the 15th, and shifts into Libra on the 13th. This is transformative energy centred around your relationship to finances and making money! The new Moon in Libra on the 21st is the ideal time to usher in a new venture. Furthermore, this lunation supports identifying new potential streams of income and taking steps to create them. If collaboration is necessary for any existing financial ventures or future endeavours, this energy spurs you to scrutinize any written business agreement or contract to make sure your needs are being met. If you plan on making a large purchase this month that involves a contract, this applies here as well.

The Sun enters Scorpio on the 22nd, bringing another focus of the cosmic weather to communication. Whether it's censoring yourself too often or being too hyper-critical with yourself, this solar season encourages confronting these limiting behaviours around speaking and listening. Jupiter squares off with Chiron on the 23rd, making you feel a little extra-raw, so be gentle with yourself as you explore and speak up for yourself. The month ends with some productive energy as Mars finds harmony with Jupiter. This transit is ideal for whipping out your to-do list and ticking a bunch of items off it.

November

Best Days Overall: 23–27
Most Stressful Days Overall: 3–7
Best Days for Love: 27–30
Best Days for Money: 9–12
Best Days for Career: 14–18
Power Word: Reconsider

Happy November, Virgo! This month's astro-weather begins on the 4th with Mars entering Sagittarius, which brings some kinetic energy to home and family dynamics. If you've been putting off necessary repairs or refurbishment to your home, now is the time to do them. Interpersonal dynamics at home get energized by this transit, essentially amplifying the dynamics currently at play. The full Moon in Taurus occurs on the 5th, centring around spirituality and education for Virgo. This lunation poses the question, 'How do your spiritual beliefs afford you emotional security?' If you feel as though they don't, or that the belief systems that inform your values cause you more stress than security, this full Moon will prompt you to make some adjustments. Tied with this is the encouragement to immerse yourself further in learning or teaching. This could be independent research on a subject where you have knowledge gaps or assuming a role where you're the expert coaching others.

Mercury, your planetary ruler, turns retrograde one last time on the 9th. Mercury joins Mars in Sagittarius and augments the themes described above. In addition, retrogrades spur you to embody 're-' words, such as 'reflect', 'reconsider' and 'revisit'. Remember how I mentioned how important it is to circle back to much-needed home-improvement projects? Well, this retrograde will likely force you to deal with them if you haven't already. Moreover, the possibility of miscommunication is high, especially with loved ones and those you live with, so clarify and actively listen. On the 17th, the Sun, Jupiter and Saturn form one of the most harmonious aspects, a grand water trine. This aspect bolsters heart-to-heart connections and personal development. This is also a transit that takes stock of the hard work you're putting in.

The new Moon in Scorpio occurs on the 21st. With Mercury being retrograde, this lunation especially centres around the theme of your Scorpio season, which is your relationship to communication. New Moons usher in new emotional cycles, so there's no better transit than this lunation during which to update how you approach communication. Sagittarius' season begins the next day, further encouraging you to revitalize or reorganize your living space.

December

Best Days Overall: 24–29
Most Stressful Days Overall: 10–14
Best Days for Love: 16–20
Best Days for Money: 13–17
Best Days for Career: 1–5
Power Word: Locus

This has been an eventful year, Virgo, and it closes out with the question, 'What do you want to be remembered for?' The cosmic weather starts off on the 4th with the full Moon in Gemini. This lunation asks this question of you and encourages you not only to think about it but to communicate it too, whether that means writing it in a journal, creating a vision board or proudly declaring it to those who'll listen. Gemini is the storyteller, so this full Moon helps you write that next chapter. A big theme of the year has been about evolution through shedding what no longer serves you. This lunation is the final notable transit of the year in that regard.

There's a stalling of sorts that occurs around the 9th, when Mars and Saturn will be exactly squaring off with one another. This transit can be frustrating as you're trying to be productive before the end of the year. However, the intention of this transit is for you to slow down and wrap up existing projects before striking out on new ones. There's also the notion of learning to accept what's in your control and what isn't. Anything outside your locus of control is especially irritating to Virgo. Your planetary ruler forms aspects with Uranus, Neptune and Pluto between the 10th and the 13th, as well as entering Sagittarius on the 11th. Mercury in Sagittarius is visionary and offers reinforcement in seeing the big picture. Virgo is really good at zooming in on the fine details, but this transit encourages you to zoom out to the horizon. What are you chasing, Virgo?

Mars enters Capricorn, your fellow earth sign, on the 5th, adding a jolt to how you creatively self-express, approach romance and seek pleasure. Essentially, this transit encourages you to play a little bit more. The new Moon in Sagittarius centres around your home and family dynamics. A key part of writing the next chapter of your story is remembering the beginning. Make an intentional effort to learn more about your family history and observe how this relates to or moulds what you seek to create as a legacy. Capricorn's season begins on the 21st, encouraging you to set your sights on new heights in 2026.

Libra

THE SCALES

Birthdays from
September 22
to October 22

Personality Profile

LIBRA AT A GLANCE

Element – Air

Ruling Planet – Venus
  Career Planet – Moon
  Love Planet – Mars
  Money Planet – Pluto
  Planet of Communications – Jupiter
  Planet of Health and Work – Neptune
  Planet of Home and Family Life – Saturn
  Planet of Spirituality and Mental Health – Mercury

Totem – the Pugilist

Colours – cerulean, jade green

Colours that promote love, romance and social harmony – carmine, red, scarlet

Colours that promote earning power – burgundy, red-violet, violet

Gems – carnelian, chrysolite, coral, emerald, jade, opal, quartz, white marble

Metal – copper

Scents – almond, rose, vanilla, violet

Quality – cardinal (= activity)

Qualities most needed for balance – a sense of self, self-reliance, independence

Strongest virtues – social grace, charm, tact, diplomacy

Deepest needs – love, romance, social harmony

Characteristic to avoid – violating what is right in order to be socially accepted

Signs of greatest overall compatibility – Gemini, Aquarius

Signs of greatest overall incompatibility – Aries, Cancer, Capricorn

Sign most helpful to career – Cancer

Sign most helpful for emotional support – Capricorn

Sign most helpful financially – Scorpio

Sign best for marriage and/or partnerships – Aries

Sign most helpful for creative projects – Aquarius

Best Sign to have fun with – Aquarius

Signs most helpful in spiritual matters – Gemini, Virgo

Best day of the week – Friday

Understanding a Libra

In the sign of Libra the universal mind – the soul – expresses its genius for relationships, that is, its power to harmonize diverse elements in a unified, organic way. Libra is the soul's power to express beauty in all of its forms. And where is beauty if not within relationships? Beauty does not exist in isolation. Beauty arises out of comparison – out of the just relationship between different parts. Without a fair and harmonious relationship there is no beauty, whether in art, manners, ideas or the social or political forum.

There are two faculties humans have that exalt them above the animal kingdom: their rational faculty (expressed in the signs of Gemini and Aquarius) and their aesthetic faculty, exemplified by Libra. Without an aesthetic sense we would be little more than intelligent barbarians. Libra is the civilizing instinct or urge of the soul.

Beauty is the essence of what Librans are all about. They are here to beautify the world. One could discuss Librans' social grace, their sense of balance and fair play, their ability to see and love another person's point of view – but this would be to miss their central asset: their desire for beauty.

No one – no matter how alone he or she seems to be – exists in isolation. The universe is one vast collaboration of beings. Librans, more than most, understand this and understand the spiritual laws that make relationships bearable and enjoyable.

A Libra is always the unconscious (and in some cases conscious) civilizer, harmonizer and artist. This is a Libra's deepest urge and greatest genius. Librans love instinctively to bring people together, and they are uniquely qualified to do so. They have a knack for seeing what unites people – the things that attract and bind rather than separate individuals.

Finance

In financial matters Librans can seem frivolous and illogical to others. This is because Librans appear to be more concerned with earning money for others than for themselves. But there is a logic to this financial attitude. Librans know that everything and everyone is connected and that it is impossible to help another to prosper without also prospering yourself. Since enhancing their partner's income and position tends to strengthen their relationship, Librans choose to do so. What could be more fun than building a relationship? You will rarely find a Libra enriching him- or herself at someone else's expense.

Scorpio is the ruler of Libra's solar 2nd house of money, giving Libra unusual insight into financial matters – and the power to focus on these matters in a way that disguises a seeming indifference. In fact, many other signs come to Librans for financial advice and guidance.

Given their social grace, Librans often spend great sums of money on entertaining and organizing social events. They also like to help others when they are in need. Librans would go out of their way to help a friend in dire straits, even if they have to borrow from others to do so. However, Librans are also very careful to pay back any debts they owe, and like to make sure they never have to be reminded to do so.

Career and Public Image

Publicly, Librans like to appear as nurturers. Their friends and acquaintances are their family and they wield political power in parental ways. They also like bosses who are paternal or maternal.

The sign of Cancer is on Libra's 10th career house cusp; the Moon is Libra's career planet. The Moon is by far the speediest, most changeable planet in the horoscope. It alone among all the planets travels through the entire zodiac – all 12 signs and houses – every month. This is an important key to the way in which Librans approach their careers, and also to what they need to do to maximize their career potential. The Moon is the planet of moods and feelings – Librans need a career in which their emotions can have free expression. This is why so many Librans are involved in the creative arts. Libra's ambitions wax and wane with the Moon. They tend to wield power according to their mood.

The Moon 'rules' the masses – and that is why Libra's highest goal is to achieve a mass kind of acclaim and popularity. Librans who achieve fame cultivate the public as other people cultivate a lover or friend. Librans can be very flexible – and often fickle – in their career and ambitions. On the other hand, they can achieve their ends in a great variety of ways. They are not stuck in one attitude or with one way of doing things.

Love and Relationships

Librans express their true genius in love. In love you could not find a partner more romantic, more seductive or more fair. If there is one thing that is sure to destroy a relationship – sure to block your love from flowing – it is injustice or imbalance between lover and beloved. If one party is giving too much or taking too much, resentment is sure to surface at some time or other. Librans are careful about this. If anything, Librans might err on the side of giving more, but never giving less.

If you are in love with a Libra, make sure you keep the aura of romance alive. Do all the little things – candle-lit dinners, travel to exotic locales, flowers and small gifts. Give things that are beautiful, not necessarily expensive. Send cards. Ring regularly even if you have nothing in particular to say. The niceties are very important to a Libra. Your relationship is a work of art: make it beautiful and your Libran lover will appreciate it. If you are creative about it, he or she will appreciate it even more; for this is how your Libra will behave towards you.

Librans like their partners to be aggressive and even a bit self-willed. They know that these are qualities they sometimes lack and so they like their partners to have them. In relationships, however, Librans can be very aggressive – but always in a subtle and charming way! Librans are determined in their efforts to charm the object of their desire – and this determination can be very pleasant if you are on the receiving end.

Home and Domestic Life

Since Librans are such social creatures, they do not particularly like mundane domestic duties. They like a well-organized home – clean and neat with everything needful present – but housework is a chore and a burden, one of the unpleasant tasks in life that must be done, the quicker the better. If a Libra has enough money – and sometimes even if not – he or she will prefer to pay someone else to take care of the daily household chores. However, Librans like gardening; they love to have flowers and plants in the home.

A Libra's home is modern, and furnished in excellent taste. You will find many paintings and sculptures there. Since Librans like to be with friends and family, they enjoy entertaining at home and they make great hosts.

Capricorn is on the cusp of Libra's 4th solar house of home and family. Saturn, the planet of law, order, limits and discipline, rules Libra's domestic affairs. If Librans want their home life to be supportive and happy they need to develop some of the virtues of Saturn – order, organization and discipline. Librans, being so creative and so intensely in need of harmony, can tend to be too lax in the home and too permissive with their children. Too much of this is not always good; children need freedom but they also need limits.

Horoscope for 2025

There's tons of cosmic weather to discuss with you, Libra, given the plethora of planets occupying air signs and Aries, your polar sign, throughout the year. Health and relationships are especially up for review, given that both Saturn and Neptune oscillate between Pisces and Aries. The back and forth between these two signs functions like a magnifying glass, shifting its focus between physical wellness and partnership all year. Venus, your planetary ruler, will turn retrograde in Aries, and vacillate similarly between Aries and

Pisces for all of March and half of April, only further strengthening the glass's lens. The good news is that Saturn and Neptune overlap for a lot of their stays in each sign, so there should be a noticeable feeling of understanding which particular aspect of your life is being highlighted during these transits.

Saturn and Neptune aren't the only slow-moving planets spending time in more than one sign this year. Uranus will oscillate between Taurus and Gemini, your fellow air sign. Uranus is all about break-throughs, innovation and liberation, and it will be a major player in informing your spirituality this year when it spends its tenure in Gemini (July 7 to November 7). Uranus transiting this sector of your chart also invites more spontaneous trips and adventures. Outside of this time frame, Uranus will continue its transit through the sector of your chart devoted to combating fears and anxieties. This is a noteworthy year for choosing courage over comfort.

For the first time in your lifetime Pluto will stay in Aquarius for the entire year, moving from centring around your home/domestic life to centring around themes of creativity, romance and children. Pluto rules transformation, so anticipate this year to revamp how you creatively self-express and how you approach romance. More detail to be shared in the relationship section, but definitely note the importance creativity and romance will play in your life this year.

Your totem this year is the Pugilist, someone like Rocky Balboa, the protagonist of the eponymous series of films about boxing. Given that the main headlines of the year are physical health and relationships, it is an apt totem to ground your understanding of the astrology of 2025. Embodying the Pugilist's resilience and grit in the face of cosmic scrutiny, this year will surely yield prized dividends by the year's end.

For a quarterly view of the year, your focus for the first three months of the year is holistically centred around physical health and routines. Examples include diet, exercise and time management. In the second quarter of the year, the shift to an emphasis around relationships and social life takes effect. Reviewing relationships takes centre-stage in the third quarter of the year, while the last quarter includes growth and expansion in your career, plus an audit around how habitual your adjustments to physical health routines have become.

Health

(Please note that this is an astrological perspective on health and not a medical one. Any health-related symptoms should be evaluated by a qualified healthcare professional.)

Embrace your inner pugilist this year, Libra. The cosmos appears to be asking you the question, 'How does the structure of my physical wellness routines or lack thereof affect my closest relationships?' Saturn, the planet that rules consequences and structure, starts the year off and stays in your house of physical health until May 24. Neptune will also co-reside in this house with Saturn until March 30. Neptune rules dreams, compassion and rose-coloured glasses, among many other significations. Here lies that question noted above, because both the planet of discipline and the planet that rules metaphorical tunnel vision are probing your physical health. Sometimes the hustle and bustle of daily life is so frenetic that we don't stop to take stock of such basic things as wellness routines. It would behove you to contemplate this question during the first three months of the year and make the appropriate healthy changes accordingly.

March is also an important month for mental health as there's a total lunar eclipse occurring on the 14th in your 12th house of mental wellness. Eclipses are frenetic evolutionary transits that linger long past the day on which they occur. This eclipse further emphasizes the importance of updating your physical wellness routines, given that a primary way to calm the mind is through regulating the body. With Jupiter, your health planet, being in Gemini and Cancer, it's extra important to brush up on breath work and other practices that utilize breathing as a grounding agent. This is the first of many eclipses occurring in the Virgo–Pisces axis, all of which will revolve around physical or mental wellness and the way in which they're linked.

The eclipses are now occurring in Virgo and Pisces because on January 11 the north node re-enters Pisces for the first time since it left it in December 2007. This also means the south node enters Virgo on January 11 for the first time since December 2007 as well. Wherever the north node transits your chart, we can anticipate an increase. Wherever the south node transits, we're prompted to shed limiting patterns of thought and behaviour. Just like Rocky trained for his first big fight by evolving his exercise, diet and holistic wellness routines, this profound nodal shift invites you to do the same. The north node will stay in Pisces all year, so implement your new wellness routines in bite-sized chunks to ensure they'll stick.

Here are specific areas of the body to focus on this year:

- Libra always rules the kidneys, so given the focus on health this year it's important to double-up on supporting these vital organs. Be more intentional about incorporating kidney-supportive foods like red bell peppers, berries and fish into your diet.
- Lung health is very important as well, with Jupiter, your health planet, spending the year between Gemini (ruled by Mercury) and Cancer (the sign which rules the lungs). Avoid practices or behaviours that could harm the lungs. This is an opportune year in which to include vitamins or supplements supporting lung health in your diet.
- Foot health continues to be an important area to focus on. The north node in Pisces brings eclipses into your health house in the sign that rules the feet. Foot strengthening and massaging could be an important addition to your physical wellness routines at this time. Also, increasing foot dexterity and mobility this year will pay long-lasting dividends.

Love and Social Life

Next to health, the other headline theme for this year is relationships. For the first time in your lifetime, Neptune will assume a tenure in Libra's house of relationships (from March 30 to October 22). Neptune rules compassion, spirituality and rose-coloured glasses. Expect relationships to have a dreamier feel. In addition, expect spiritual chemistry to matter a lot more. While physical turn-ons won't dissipate, they'll matter less when you realize that a spiritually compatible partner can fuel your soul. Neptune also rules illusion, so it's important to note that the dates during which it's in Aries are a time when rose-coloured glasses are more likely to abound. Lean on your closest confidants during this period to temperature-check and support your tactics of grounding yourself in reality. Thankfully, Saturn functions as a mitigator, clearing some of that rosy fog when it joins Neptune in your house of relationships on May 24.

Saturn's stint through your house of relationships occurs from May 24 to September 1. Saturn is like the tax agency of the cosmos, so expect an audit around the sustainability and quality of your relationships during this time. Saturn rules consequences, highlighting the fact that they're a heavyweight around the theme of accountability in relationships. You'll become increasingly aware of reciprocity in your relationships during the summer as Saturn stays in Aries. This may be a sobering transit, but it comes with a helpful invitation. You've got the opportunity to stop pouring more into cups that pour very little into yours. Furthermore, you've also got the opportunity to lean into and bask in the joy of relationships that are rooted in reciprocity.

Mars, your relationship planet, starts the year doing the moonwalk (in other words it's retrograde). Given that Mars will be retrograde in Cancer for the majority of this transit, it's highly likely there will be an interplay between family dynamics and the dynamics at home on the one hand and your other closest relationships on the other. Libra is strongly associated with collaboration and harmony, but that doesn't mean you can't assert yourself. It's crucial that you address relationship quarrels or conflicts as directly and responsibly as possible during this retrograde. Mars retrograde is a time that typically limits direct communication, and this is only compounded when the fiery planet is in Cancer. Furthermore, it's probable that you'll encounter passive-aggressiveness during this time. Do not engage in behaviour that negates your ability to drive or repair any necessary aspect of your relationship during this time. Mars leaves its retrograde on February 23, but lingers in a slow post-retrograde haze until May 2. Come that date, Mars will be flying at its normal speed and enters five signs through the remainder of the year.

Venus, your general planetary ruler, also has a period of being retrograde this year. Venus will be retrograde in your house of relationships from March 1 until March 27. This retrograde functions as a review of whether your needs are being met in existing relationships. Libra is the sign associated with integration. This retrograde will serve as an inventory of whether you're able to individuate appropriately in relationships. Your values are put to the test during these retrogrades. Allow for this retrograde to show you if you need to realign your values to support your ability to maintain autonomy while fully being present in relationships. If you're single, this retrograde and inventory will highlight what qualities you may desire to embody in order to support future partnerships.

With Venus' retrograde beginning on March 1, Neptune entering Aries on March 30 and the solar eclipse in Aries occurring on the 29th, bookmark the spring for a radical time of growth, shifts and evolution in your relationships. Saturn entering your house of relationships at the end of May lends structure – albeit with a touch of restriction – to this theme of life. If you ground yourself in your values and choose courage over comfort, you'll look back on this year in awe of how much you grew in this department.

Career and Finances

Important long-term career decisions are likely to be made this year. The year starts with Mars in your 10th house of career from January 6 to April 1. Mars rules drive, ambition and assertion. The fiery planet will be retrograde from the start of the year until February 23. This transit tends to spur us to making dynamic career decisions through facilitating a 'stuck in traffic' feeling. When Mars is retrograde, all of that outward drive and ambition feels blocked or unsettled. Use this retrograde to explore the restless feelings that likely will come up around career and legacy. Wait until after February 23, if possible, to make any major career moves.

It's especially important to mind this retrograde because Mars is also your financial planet. Money may not feel like it's flowing at the very start of the year, but things should ease up after Mars goes direct on February 23. If you plan on making any major financial decisions or moves, waiting until the retrograde is over is preferred so that you can budget additional time during the retrograde to review the decision. Although Mars goes direct on February 23, it takes a couple more months to regain functioning at full speed. Mark May 2 as the first day on which Mars is fully liberated from its retrograde period, meaning that your financial planet is fully uninhibited. It's ideal, if possible, to wait until this date before making major financial decisions.

At the same time that Mars is in your career house, Uranus will be wrapping up its multi-year tenure in your house of shared finances and joint ventures. Uranus is all about innovation and liberation, and it will revolve around these themes from January 1 to July 7, encouraging the continued development of additional streams of income. January features Uranus mimicking Mars, as Uranus will also be retrograde until January 30. January functions as an essential month in which to revisit your various forms of finances, including debts that are owed to you or that you yourself owe. Do your best to resolve your debts before eclipse season begins in March, due to the eclipses' associations with your mental health and holistic wellness.

Pluto will finally stay in Aquarius after wandering back and forth between it and Capricorn for a few years. The planet of transformation moves into your house of creativity for 20 years. When thinking about additional streams of income or ways to make money, now is the time to lean into creative self-expression. If you're born in the first three to four days of Libra, Pluto will be explicitly aspecting your natal Sun this year. You should note, however, that all Libras receive this aspect by sign as Pluto will be in your fellow air sign.

Home and Domestic Life

For your home and domestic life it's important to look at Saturn's activity this year. Saturn has been in Pisces for the last two years, encouraging you to make your home more amenable to health-related routines. Saturn stays in Pisces for the first half of the year, finally shifting into Aries on May 24. Saturn in Aries centres around making sure our needs are met, so view this important transit as an invitation to address long-overdue home-improvement projects that will provide you with a better quality of life. This is especially auspicious from May 24 to July 12 while Saturn is still moving direct. However, if there are home-improvement projects that have been in the works for several years, Saturn's retrograde period is actually an ideal time to refocus your attention on finishing them. Saturn will be retrograde from July 13 to November 27.

Mars dips into your 4th house at the end of year, from December 15 to the 31st. Whenever Mars is in the 4th house, there's a lot of kinetic energy in our domestic lives. Prepare for this to be a busy time, with family and people coming and going in your home. In anticipation for this transit, spend time decluttering and organizing your belongings in the weeks leading up to mid-December. Mars is associated with confrontation, so be sure to respond and not react if provoked during this period.

Self-improvement

Libra is ruled by Venus and is associated with integration, collaboration and harmony. Venus will spend more time in Aries than almost any other sign this year, encouraging you to take strides towards advocating for your needs and assuming greater autonomy. Venus will be in Aries from February 5 to March 27, then again from May 1 to June 7. These time spans also encourage a levelling-up around how you assert yourself. With your planetary ruler in fiery Aries for such an extended period of time, seek out practices or disciplines that assist with self-assertion, such as studying a martial art or routinely participating in a bootcamp, so that you truly embody 'the Pugilist'.

Mars, the planet that rules drive, ambition and assertion, enters your sign on August 6 and stays in Libra until September 22. Mars in your sign is an ideal time to step into whatever form of spotlight appeals to you. Vlogging, performing, visual art and competitions are all examples of media to lean into during this period. Venus follows suit, entering Libra on October 14 and ending its tenure in Libra on November 7. These three weeks are an auspicious occasion for self-improvement since the planet of self-worth and values will meet up with your Sun sign. Honour this transit through writing out all the ways you've grown since the year started and pause to congratulate yourself on your evolution.

Month-by-month Forecasts

January

Best Days Overall: 27–31
Most Stressful Days Overall: 16–20
Best Days for Love: 21–24
Best Days for Money: 23–26
Best Days for Career: 8–12
Power Word: Legacy

Happy 2025, Libra! Family dynamics, home and real estate are all at the top of your mind this month. It's a good month to focus on rethinking career aspirations and planning long-term career pivots, but not the month to act on them. Come the 2nd of the month, it's important you identify and carve out a sanctuary in your home to which you can retreat to be alone in order to ground yourself or cool down when necessary. Lean into grounding practices like meditation, mindfulness and somatic work in this space. If you're unable to establish this kind of sanctuary in the home, identify a space nearby in nature or your local community that can function in the same way.

Venus, your planetary ruler, will be in Pisces virtually the entire month. This transit normally instils daydreaming or aspirational thinking, so allow yourself to dream this month as this will be a good period to revisit during the multiple planetary retrogrades occurring this year. The first week of the year is an ideal time to take pen to paper and journal about your daydreams or aspirations. The second week of the year features a full Moon in Cancer. This lunation asks you to contemplate the question, 'What do I want to be remembered for?' No biggie. Make sure you carve out some time to think about this question on or within a few days of the 13th.

Aquarius' season begins on the 19th, encouraging you to get creative and romantic. There's a ton of cosmic weather that week, so it's an ideal time to test out those grounding practices if you feel overwhelmed. The 21st features the Sun's annual meet-up with Pluto. If possible, schedule in self-care the day before and/or on the 21st itself. This could be something as simple as budgeting in time at the end of your day to properly unwind, or something more elaborate such as a massage. The last week of the month includes a new Moon in Capricorn. Capricorn is a sea goat that looks to the top of a mountain or the bottom of the ocean, knowing that it may take a while to get there, but step by step it'll make it. Apply that same logic to how you approach long-term career goals moving forward.

February

Best Days Overall: 6–10
Most Stressful Days Overall: 12–16
Best Days for Love: 1–5
Best Days for Money: 24–27
Best Days for Career: 25–28
Power Word: Peacemaker

Happy February, Libra! This month's cosmic weather begins with a couple of harmonious transits and your planetary ruler changing signs. The first weekend of the month features a beautiful meet-up between Venus and Neptune. Venus is your planetary ruler, and just before it moves into Aries it conjoins with the planet of dreams, idealism and the collective. For everyone this transit is about doing activities that are spiritually fulfilling. For you, Libra, this transit links the body with the spirit. Get out in nature, eat delicious natural food or spend time with animals. Mercury and Jupiter form a lovely aspect on the 3rd, then Venus moves into Aries on the 4th. There's a lot of energy supporting communication in your partnerships at this time.

A noteworthy component of February's astrology is the potent full Moon in Leo occurring on the 12th. Bookmark this full Moon in your calendar because you, and everyone around you, will feel it. This full Moon is strong because the lunation is in a tight and tense configuration with Uranus. Uranus rules break-ups, breakdowns, breakthroughs and liberation. This full Moon likely will rock the boat among groups of your friends, so definitely proceed with caution and do your best not to stoke the flames. Fortunately, this lunation can also illuminate which of your friends are solid and whose closeness to you is grounded in reciprocity. If you have to participate in any sort of extended trip or long event with a group or organization, lean into Libra's orientation towards harmony and peacemaking.

The Sun joins the north node in Pisces with the start of Pisces' season on the 18th. One of the major themes of your year is physical health routines. The Sun is like a bright spotlight on this theme. If you haven't begun implementing new and sustainable wellness practices, use the new Moon in Pisces on the 27th to do so. During this time Mars will also finally go direct on the 23rd. Mars direct clears the path for you to make moves around your career, so work with the new Moon in Pisces to begin actionable next steps towards your career goals for 2025.

March

Best Days Overall: 22–27
Most Stressful Days Overall: 1–5
Best Days for Love: 20–24
Best Days for Money: 6–10
Best Days for Career: 27–31
Power Word: Relationship

Hi, Libra! March is a major month astrologically, with a confluence of transits in Aries, your polar sign, plus two eclipses. The cosmic weather starts off on March 1 when Venus in Aries turns retrograde. Venus retrograde always involves some level of reflection on our relationships, but this is especially true for Libra. This transit spurs you to assess whether the dynamic of your closest relationships and partnership are still uplifting or supporting you according to your needs. If you've not got a partner, this retrograde inspires you to evaluate how you approach relationships, while also providing the setting to update what you value most in relationships.

On March 14 the first eclipse of 2025 occurs in Virgo. Eclipses are evolutionary transits that promote growth through making us uncomfortable or forcing necessary change. This eclipse heavily centres on your mental wellness and how your day-to-day routines either promote or detract from it, comprising a watershed transit around behaviours you've avoided addressing that hurt more than they help. Dissociative behaviour is a great example of what the eclipse will force you to confront. It's important to note that this isn't scrutinizing productive coping mechanisms, just those that don't support your holistic growth or limit you in one way or another. Mercury turns retrograde in Aries the day after the eclipse. This retrograde compounds with Venus retrograde and adds an additional layer of focus to your patterns of communication in relationships. Do you feel as though you can wholeheartedly and directly speak your truth in your existing relationship? If you're single, do you feel as though direct communication is something that comes easily to you in relationships? This eclipse, combined with Mercury retrograde, dissuades avoidant behaviour, especially around communication with partners.

Aries' season begins on March 20, with the second eclipse following suit in the sign on the 29th. With the eclipse occurring in the sign of partnership for Libra on the 29th, there's a lot more potency around your needs being met for the continued health of your individual relationships. Aries is the cardinal fire sign ruled by Mars, so it's important to approach potential necessary confrontations from a grounded position. Neptune moves into Aries for the first time in your lifetime on the 30th. This transit makes you aware of the importance of spiritual compatibility, in addition to physical chemistry.

April

Best Days Overall: 8–13
Most Stressful Days Overall: 25–29
Best Days for Love: 16–20
Best Days for Money: 20–23
Best Days for Career: 1–5
Power Word: Grow

It's April, Libra! The first week of this month features several soft and supportive transits. Venus, your planetary ruler, aligns with Mars on April 5. This is a productive transit for Libra, so if you have items on your to-do list that would support you in your career or your pursuit of career goals, this is the week to put your nose to the grindstone. On April 7 Mercury ends its retrograde and turns direct. Mercury moving direct supports Libra's pursuit of keeping a routine.

On April 12 not only is there a full Moon in your sign, but your planetary ruler also turns direct. Yay! This full Moon is especially potent for you because it's in your sign. Full Moons are emotional culminations, and this one functions as a checkpoint since it's the first new Moon in Libra since last October. A lot has transpired since October 2, 2024, and this lunation implores you to pause and take stock of all the ways in which you've grown. Specifically, this lunation centres around personal growth and your relationship with yourself. With Venus moving direct, this is the ideal day to be intentional around supporting yourself in the ways you know you need to.

On April 19 the Sun enters Taurus. Taurus is a fixed earth sign that is especially financial in nature for Libra. Taurus cares about security above all else. Taurus' season is the time when Libras should audit their finances and make sure every stream of income is vetted. Monitor all the ways money enters and exits your accounts. The new Moon in Taurus on the 27th would normally be a time to get involved in new financial ventures, but this one is different. On the same day Mars opposes Pluto, bringing a modicum of frustration to the surface for everyone. Ideally, wait about a week before diving headfirst into new financial endeavours. Your planetary ruler re-enters Aries on the 30th. Venus in Aries is a transit that reminds you that you'll struggle to love others if you don't love yourself first. Be mindful around both negative self-talk and prioritizing the needs of others over your own.

May

Best Days Overall: 5–10
Most Stressful Days Overall: 14–19
Best Days for Love: 22–26
Best Days for Money: 3–7
Best Days for Career: 1–5
Power Word: Us

Happy May, Libra! The cosmic weather for this month begins on the 2nd with Venus, your planetary ruler, conjoining with Neptune in Aries for the first time in your lifetime. Aries is your polar sign and this transit is heavily relationship-oriented for you. The energy this transit facilitates is a combination of rose-coloured glasses and 'Don't worry, be happy'. If you're going on a first or second date, have a great time but be mindful that your judgement is likely clouded a little bit. This is 'lovey dovey' energy, so spend the occasion with your special someone or a loved one.

The full Moon in Scorpio occurs on May 12 just as Mercury and Pluto square off. Appreciate that the few days before and after this transit will likely be highly emotional. This lunation has the potency to elicit some obsessive, compulsive or hyper-vigilant tendencies in others and yourself. For Libra, full Moons in the sign of Scorpio are fiscal in nature. This full Moon serves as the first financial check-in since the new Moon in Scorpio last November. Addressing spending patterns or looking at any noteworthy investments you've made since the new Moon would be advised at this time.

On May 24 Saturn moves into Aries for the first time in 26 years. Saturn rules discipline, restriction and structure, and Saturn in Aries brings a maturity to how you approach existing and future relationships. If you've got a partner, Saturn functions like a building inspector making sure the structure of your relationship passes the appropriate regulations. If you're single, Saturn will force you to deepen your understanding of what you want out of a relationship.

The last week of the month features a build-up of Gemini energy. In addition to the Sun entering Gemini on the 20th, Mercury enters Gemini on the 25th and the new Moon follows one day later. This confluence of energy supports pursuits in education and/or spirituality for you. Additionally, the new Moon supports travel as a mechanism for reflection, and is especially fruitful if you're seeking to further any form of studies, acquire a certification, plan a voyage or are looking to book a session with a spiritual practitioner.

June

Best Days Overall: 4–8
Most Stressful Days Overall: 21–25
Best Days for Love: 25–28
Best Days for Money: 1–4
Best Days for Career: 26–30
Power Word: Aspire

Let's talk about your career, Libra! June starts off with the first of two planets moving into Cancer. Mercury enters Cancer on the 8th and Jupiter follows on the 9th. Jupiter was called the 'Greater Benefic' in traditional astrology because the gas giant rules growth and expansion. Jupiter is a slower-moving planet and will spend about 12 months in a sign. Transits in Cancer centre around career for Libra, so it's very exciting for this transit to be beginning again. Think back to where you were 12 years ago and what career aspirations you had then. Which goals have changed since that time and which have stayed constant? Jupiter entering Cancer ushers in a new 12-year cycle centred around your career journey.

The full Moon in kinetic Sagittarius occurs on the 11th. Sagittarius is associated with the preacher archetype, and this lunation gives off those vibes. The potential for you to get on your soapbox is high with this full Moon. It's important for you to speak your truth, but just make sure you're preaching to a receptive audience. This full Moon is always adventurous and spontaneous in essence. With this lunation falling in Libra's 3rd house of local community, it's the ideal lunation for you to immerse yourself in your neighbourhood. Check out the local farmers' market, an interesting event in town, or lean into Sagittarius' association with education and take a class offered locally.

There's more Cancer energy this month, Libra, with the Sun moving into Cancer on the 20th. It's important to note that the Sun then quickly squares off with Saturn and Neptune on the 22nd and 23rd. These transits usually bring a sense of being overwhelmed or feeling daunted around career objectives. That being said, the goal is to get you to reduce your pace and tackle things in bite-sized chunks, with the moral of the story being 'slow and steady wins the race'. The new Moon in Cancer on the 25th will work with you to help with the first steps towards your new or revamped career goals.

July

Best Days Overall: 4–8
Most Stressful Days Overall: 19–23
Best Days for Love: 7–10
Best Days for Money: 28–31
Best Days for Career: 10–13
Power Word: Company

Hi, Libra! Venus, your planetary ruler, is the star of the show for the first week of July. On July 4 Venus meets up with Uranus in the last degree of Taurus before switching into Gemini. Venus in Gemini is a social transit for everyone, and for Libra it centres around travel and spirituality, with Uranus' influence adding spontaneity to the mix. This transit supports travel as a means of gaining perspective or grounding yourself. Given the social angle Gemini brings, this travelling could be equally or more beneficial if undertaken with others. Venus in Gemini harmoniously aspects Saturn and Neptune on the 6th and Pluto on the 7th. These transits further support transformation around spirituality or finding space for a transformative travel experience. On July 7 Uranus enters Gemini for the first time since leaving the sign 76 years ago! Uranus in Gemini affects society through catalysing incredible innovations that support how we learn and communicate.

The full Moon this month spotlights home, family and real estate for Libra. This lunation in Capricorn occurs on the 10th, so if you're in the process of moving, definitely make a note in your calendar of the days just before and after this full Moon so you can double up on patience and poise. This will be especially beneficial because Mercury is very slow and will retrograde soon. The full Moon spotlights relationships with family or those you live with as well. If there's been communication that's so far been avoided but that is necessary to get out in the open, do it now before Mercury retrogrades. On the 18th Mercury is officially retrograde in Leo, and communication breakdowns and technology mishaps can abound. The goal of Mercury retrograde is for you to slow down and reflect on your patterns of communication and thinking. Address themes like being your own biggest critic at this time.

Leo's season begins with a loud roar on the 22nd. Within the first three days of this solar season, the Sun will aspect five planets. The new Moon in Leo on the 24th contains them all. This lunation asks the question of you, 'Can you be authentically yourself within your groups of friends or organizations? If not, what is holding you back?' Embracing your individuality and finding your tribe who unequivocally loves you for you will be the name of the game with this lunation.

August

Best Days Overall: 10-14
Most Stressful Days Overall: 25-29
Best Days for Love: 6-9
Best Days for Money: 7-10
Best Days for Career: 29-31
Power Word: Unique

Happy August, Libra! This month's cosmic weather begins with Venus, your planetary ruler, finding tension with both Saturn and Neptune. This transit can provoke a sense of despondency, with feelings of self-doubt and needing to seek external validation being typical side-effects. The purpose of this transit is to force you to become your own best ally. Additionally, this transit has a financial and relationship component to it for Libra. Remember, when it comes to partnership, you're already whole and a partner is only supposed to add to the cup that you filled yourself. For career, this transit spurs you to *not* compare yourself or your performance with your colleagues'. Mars enters your sign for the first time in two years on the 6th. This transit typically revs your engine, so channel this energy constructively!

On the 9th the full Moon in Aquarius spotlights creativity and romance for Libra. This lunation pairs with the theme of the new Moon in Leo two weeks ago by focusing on authenticity. However, instead of living your truth with your friends, this full Moon shifts the focus to whether you can embrace your unique creativity and individuality when it comes to romance. There's only one you, Libra, and your ability to create and be expressive is unique. This full Moon features Mars playing a tug of war in your sign with Saturn and Neptune. This transit can make you feel like you're stuck in traffic. The purpose of this lunation is to not rush progress or tangible outputs. Whether it's with how you creatively self-express or progress within your career, this transit will only reward you for putting in the time and not taking the easy route.

Virgo's season begins on the 22nd and the new Moon follows on the 23rd. This new Moon centres around mental health for Libra.

Virgo is a sign heavily associated with routine and structures. This new Moon promotes examining and creating new systems that support your mental wellness. This new Moon also encourages finding more balance between social time and solo time. The month ends with Venus and Pluto tensely aspecting each other. This transit will highlight which aspects of your mental health you need to focus on and precisely where you should create those new systems to support you.

September

Best Days Overall: 15–19
Most Stressful Days Overall: 21–25
Best Days for Love: 26–30
Best Days for Money: 1–4
Best Days for Career: 8–12
Power Word: Liberate

It's almost your season, Libra! September is one of the most noteworthy months of the year astrologically, so let's jump right in. As a reminder, eclipses are evolutionary transits that stimulate growth through scrutiny and shake-ups. This month features the final two eclipses of the year. The first eclipse of September occurs on the 7th in Pisces. One of your major themes in 2025 is physical health and wellness. This eclipse functions as an audit of the steps you've taken to support your body this year. Paired with this is a cosmic examination of how your daily routines benefit your physical well-being or prevent you from nurturing your body in the ways you desire. Eclipses are transits that can be felt profoundly in the body, so make a concerted effort not to overexert yourself this month and be intentional about scheduling in just as much rest as work or play.

The second eclipse of the month occurs in Virgo on the 21st. While the first eclipse focused on your relationship with your body, this eclipse focuses on your relationship with your mind. Mental health and wellness are what this new Moon solar eclipse centres on. Did you know, leading anxiety experts state that the primary way to calm the mind is through regulating the body? These eclipses work in tandem to propel you to find greater mind–body alignment. Furthermore, this eclipse is all about confronting limiting patterns of your thoughts and behaviour. For Libra, this is specifically around the ways you convince yourself that your goals or dreams are unattainable. In order to liberate yourself from the shackles of your own mind, you must confront the root causes of this conditioned mindset. This eclipse is likely to feel a bit like a crucible, but it takes extreme pressure to turn carbon into a diamond.

Your solar season begins on the 22nd. Happy Birthday! Libra season this year starts off bumpily because of Mars squaring off with Pluto on the 24th. This transit is associated with unearthing buried rage, so do your best to respond instead of reacting if provoked. Treat this transit as an invitation to prioritize a self-care outing in the first week of Libra season.

October

Best Days Overall: 13–17
Most Stressful Days Overall: 6–10
Best Days for Love: 28–31
Best Days for Money: 25–28
Best Days for Career: 3–6
Power Word: Partner

Happy Birthday, Libra! This month's cosmic weather begins on the 6th with a full Moon in Aries, your polar sign. The Aries full Moon is all about making sure your emotional needs are being met. For Libra, this especially applies to your needs in a relationship, but if you don't have a partner, this full Moon will spotlight whether or not there's anything lacking for you emotionally and if you're open to a new relationship. This lunation is actually a great transit to put yourself out there if you're seeking partnership. If you're in a relationship, it will prompt you to correct your course with your partner.

Venus, your planetary ruler, gets very busy by aspecting Saturn, Uranus, Neptune and Pluto between the 11th and the 15th. In addition, Venus enters your sign on the 13th. These transits shift the focus from partnering with others to how you partner with yourself. How can you be better about supporting yourself, and in what ways are you the biggest blocker to your emotional needs being met? Allow these transits to suggest answers for you. The new Moon in Libra occurs on the 21st and is an ideal time to usher in a new emotional cycle around being your best ally. Whether that's seeking out professional support, adopting small, healthy practices at the start or end of each day, or just cutting yourself more slack, this new Moon spurs you to uplift yourself routinely and innately. It's also the ideal transit in which to adopt a change to your appearance, even if it's something as minor as a new haircut.

Scorpio's season begins on the 23rd, which adds finances to the focus of the cosmic weather for you. The Sun in Scorpio squares off with Pluto two days later, meaning that there's a component of transformation around money matters in the air. If you're considering a new financial venture or thinking about making a large purchase, you should audit the figures with a trusted third party. The month's cosmic weather ends with Mars finding support with Jupiter, a vigorous transit that supports you tackling the major items on your to-do list.

November

Best Days Overall: 26–30
Most Stressful Days Overall: 6–10
Best Days for Love: 24–28
Best Days for Money: 2–6
Best Days for Career: 15–19
Power Word: Heartfelt

Happy November, Libra! Are you feeling your post-birthday glow? The cosmic weather for November kicks off on the 4th with Mars entering fiery Sagittarius. This transit can have you losing your filter a bit when you communicate, so be mindful around how you say what you want to say. The full Moon in Taurus occurs one day later, spotlighting finances for you, and the financial concerns that have been present since April are reaching a climax around this date. One astrological theme that was present at that time was how other people influence your relationship to money. This full Moon encourages you to assume greater responsibility for your financial well-being, and how you approach spending and saving.

Mercury turns retrograde one last time in Sagittarius, making communication ripe for misinterpretation. For Libra, this transit lights up your communication sector, so it's especially noteworthy for you. Remember, communication is just as much about actively listening as it is about speaking. On the 17th the Sun, Jupiter and Saturn all team up to form one of the most harmonious aspects – a grand water trine. This is a great day to open up or connect on a deep level to someone.

The new Moon in Scorpio occurs on the 20th and is also a financial lunation. This lunation strongly supports trying to start new financial ventures or streams of income if you're planning to do so. Although Mercury is still retrograde, this lunation would suggest making larger purchases if you were planning to do so or need to do so. Please make sure to carefully read all the small print with a third party.

Sagittarius' season begins on the 21st, with the Sun aspecting Uranus and Neptune on the same day. This solar season inspires you to start dreaming up your 2026 goals. Mercury finds harmony with Saturn the following day, which is an opportune time to journal or put together a vision board for next year. This transit also supports being scrupulous about the details of any purchases if you are leaning into the new Moon energy around spending. November ends with Venus entering Sagittarius, stimulating you to go on a spontaneous adventure as a self-date or with a special someone.

December

Best Days Overall: 1–5
Most Stressful Days Overall: 9–12
Best Days for Love: 23–27
Best Days for Money: 15–19
Best Days for Career: 26–30
Power Word: Brake

It's December, Libra! With 2026 just around the corner, the cosmic weather for this month has you looking to the horizon. The full Moon in Gemini starts the astro-weather off this month on the 4th, illuminating the roles education and spirituality currently play in your life and how these two can evolve in the coming year. This full Moon serves as a check-in since the last new Moon in Gemini in June, which promoted seeking education in either a completely new subject or advancing your learning in your current discipline. If you followed that prompt, this full Moon will be an emotional milestone in your journey, as well as mirroring that call to action if you hesitated at the time. In addition, this lunation strongly encourages leaning into your spirituality as a means of grounding yourself. Whether that's getting out in nature, connecting to a higher power or being of service to others, the full Moon reminds you to connect to the macro-environment and not get swept up in your own world.

Mars and Saturn slow things down for everyone around the 9th when they square off with one another. This transit can provoke frustration given the feeling of being stuck and/or restlessness that this transit can instil in you. As I mentioned, this month is about looking to the horizon and this week intentionally pumps the brakes so that you can tie up any loose ends in your to-do list.

After this transit dissipates, Mars enters Capricorn on the 15th and the new Moon in Sagittarius occurs on the 19th. These transits revolve around the interplay of family dynamics and how you approach communication. Do you censor yourself for the sake of specific loved ones? Does your temperament around communication morph in the home? Both of these are up for review for you to redefine with this new lunar cycle. Mars in Capricorn is also a significantly productive transit. With Capricorn's season beginning on the 21st, now is the time to not only set intentions around what you seek to accomplish in 2026, but also to proudly proclaim it to loved ones and your support systems.

Scorpio

♏

THE SCORPION

Birthdays from
October 23
to November 22

Personality Profile

SCORPIO AT A GLANCE

Element – Water

Ruling Planet – Pluto
  Co-ruling Planet – Mars
  Career Planet – Sun
  Love Planet – Venus
  Money Planet – Jupiter
  Planet of Health and Work – Mars
  Planet of Home and Family Life – Uranus

Totem – the Bon Vivant

Colour – cyan

Colour that promotes love, romance and social harmony – green

Colour that promotes earning power – blue

Gems – bloodstone, malachite, topaz

Metals – iron, radium, steel

Scents – cherry blossom, coconut, sandalwood, watermelon

Quality – fixed (= stability)

Quality most needed for balance – a wider view of things

Strongest virtues – loyalty, concentration, determination, courage, depth

Deepest needs – to penetrate and transform

Characteristics to avoid – jealousy, vindictiveness, fanaticism

Signs of greatest overall compatibility – Cancer, Pisces

Signs of greatest overall incompatibility – Taurus, Leo, Aquarius

Sign most helpful to career – Leo

Sign most helpful for emotional support – Aquarius

Sign most helpful financially – Sagittarius

Sign best for marriage and/or partnerships – Taurus

Sign most helpful for creative projects – Pisces

Best Sign to have fun with – Pisces

Signs most helpful in spiritual matters – Cancer, Libra

Best day of the week – Tuesday

Understanding a Scorpio

One symbol of the sign of Scorpio is the phoenix. If you meditate upon the legend of the phoenix you will begin to understand the Scorpio character – his or her powers and abilities, interests and deepest urges.

The phoenix of mythology was a bird that could recreate and reproduce itself. It did so in a most intriguing way: it would seek a fire – usually in a religious temple – fly into it, consume itself in the flames and then emerge a new bird. If this is not the ultimate, most profound transformation, then what is?

Transformation is what Scorpios are all about – in their minds, bodies, affairs and relationships (Scorpios are also society's trans- formers). To change something in a natural, not an artificial way, involves a transformation from within. This type of change is rad- ical change as opposed to a mere cosmetic make-over. Some people think that change means altering just their appearance, but this is not the kind of thing that interests a Scorpio. Scorpios seek deep, fundamental change. Since real change always proceeds from within, a Scorpio is very interested in – and usually accustomed to – the inner, intimate and philosophical side of life.

Scorpios are people of depth and intellect. If you want to interest them you must present them with more than just a superficial image. You and your interests, projects or business deals must have real substance to them in order to stimulate a Scorpio. If they haven't, he or she will find you out – and that will be the end of the story.

If we observe life – the processes of growth and decay – we see the transformational powers of Scorpio at work all the time. The caterpillar changes itself into a butterfly; the infant grows into a child and then an adult. To Scorpios this definite and perpetual transformation is not something to be feared. They see it as a normal part of life. This acceptance of transformation gives Scorpios the key to understanding the true meaning of life.

Scorpios' understanding of life (including life's weaknesses) makes them powerful warriors – in all senses of the word. Add to this their depth, patience and endurance and you have a powerful personality. Scorpios have good, long memories and can at times be quite vindictive – they can wait years to get their revenge. As a friend, though, there is no one more loyal and true than a Scorpio. Few are willing to make the sacrifices that a Scorpio will make for a true friend.

The results of a transformation are quite obvious, although the process of transformation is invisible and secret. This is why Scorpios are considered secretive in nature. A seed will not grow properly if you keep digging it up and exposing it to the light of day. It must stay buried – invisible – until it starts to grow. In the same manner, Scorpios fear revealing too much about themselves or their hopes to other people. However, they will be more than happy to let you see the finished product – but only when it is completely unwrapped. On the other hand, Scorpios like knowing everyone else's secrets as much as they dislike anyone knowing theirs.

Finance

Love, birth, life as well as death are Nature's most potent transformations; Scorpios are interested in all of these. In our society, money is a transforming power, too, and a Scorpio is interested in money for that reason. To a Scorpio money is power, money causes change, money controls. It is the power of money that fascinates them. But Scorpios can be too materialistic if they are not careful. They can be overly awed by the power of money, to a point where they think that money rules the world.

Even the term 'plutocrat' comes from Pluto, the ruler of the sign of Scorpio. Scorpios will – in one way or another – achieve the financial status they strive for. When they do so they are careful in the way they handle their wealth. Part of this financial carefulness is really a kind of honesty, for Scorpios are usually involved with other people's money – as accountants, lawyers, stockbrokers or corporate managers – and when you handle other people's money you have to be more cautious than when you handle your own.

In order to fulfil their financial goals, Scorpios have important lessons to learn. They need to develop qualities that do not come naturally to them, such as breadth of vision, optimism, faith, trust and, above all, generosity. They need to see the wealth in Nature and in life, as well as in its more obvious forms of money and power. When they develop generosity their financial potential reaches great heights, for Jupiter, the Lord of Opulence and Good Fortune, is Scorpio's money planet.

Career and Public Image

Scorpio's greatest aspiration in life is to be considered by society as a source of light and life. They want to be leaders, to be stars. But they follow a very different road than do Leos, the other stars of the zodiac. A Scorpio arrives at the goal secretly, without ostentation; a Leo pursues it openly. Scorpios seek the glamour and fun of the rich and famous in a restrained, discreet way.

Scorpios are by nature introverted and tend to avoid the limelight. But if they want to attain their highest career goals they need to open up a bit and to express themselves more. They need to stop hiding their light under a bushel and let it shine. Above all, they need to let go of any vindictiveness and small-mindedness. All their gifts and insights were given to them for one important reason – to serve life and to increase the joy of living for others.

Love and Relationships

Scorpio is another zodiac sign that likes committed, clearly defined, structured relationships. They are cautious about marriage, but when they do commit to a relationship they tend to be faithful – and heaven help the mate caught or even suspected of infidelity! The jealousy of the Scorpio is legendary. They can be so intense in their jealousy that even the thought or intention of infidelity will be detected and is likely to cause as much of a storm as if the deed had actually been done.

Scorpios tend to settle down with those who are wealthier than they are. They usually have enough intensity for two, so in their partners they seek someone pleasant, hard-working, amiable, stable and easy-going. They want someone they can lean on, someone loyal behind them as they fight the battles of life. To a Scorpio a partner, be it a lover or a friend, is a real partner – not an adversary. Most of all a Scorpio is looking for an ally, not a competitor.

If you are in love with a Scorpio you will need a lot of patience. It takes a long time to get to know Scorpios, because they do not reveal themselves readily. But if you persist and your motives are honourable, you will gradually be allowed into a Scorpio's inner chambers of the mind and heart.

Home and Domestic Life

Uranus is ruler of Scorpio's 4th solar house of home and family. Uranus is the planet of science, technology, changes and democracy. This tells us a lot about a Scorpio's conduct in the home and what he or she needs in order to have a happy, harmonious home life.

Scorpios can sometimes bring their passion, intensity and wilfulness into the home and family, which is not always the place for these qualities. These traits are good for the warrior and the transformer, but not so good for the nurturer and family member. Because of this (and also because of their need for change and transformation) the Scorpio may be prone to sudden changes of residence. If not carefully constrained, the sometimes inflexible Scorpio can produce turmoil and sudden upheavals within the family.

Scorpios need to develop some of the virtues of Aquarius in order to cope better with domestic matters. There is a need to build a team spirit at home, to treat family activities as truly group activities – family members should all have a say in what does and does not get done. For at times a Scorpio can be most dictatorial. When a Scorpio gets dictatorial it is much worse than if a Leo or Capricorn (the two other power signs in the zodiac) does. For the dictatorship of a Scorpio is applied with more zeal, passion, intensity and concentration than is true of either a Leo or Capricorn. Obviously this can be unbearable to family members – especially if they are sensitive types.

In order for a Scorpio to get the full benefit of the emotional support that a family can give, he or she needs to let go of conservatism and be a bit more experimental, to explore new techniques in childrearing, be more democratic with family members and to try to manage things by consensus rather than by autocratic edict.

Horoscope for 2025

This is your year to enjoy the finer things, Scorpio. The year begins with a strong overarching shift in energy as the north node leaves Aries after 18 months and enters Pisces. In doing so, it brings its focus and magnifying glass to the pleasure, creativity and romance sector of your chart. As a result, your totem for the year is 'the Bon Vivant', which translates from French as someone who lives well. This year absolutely has some challenges, but there's a focus on prioritizing pleasure and creativity. This must be highlighted and used to anchor 2025's more frenetic moments.

Given that several slow-moving planets shift signs, 2025 is an important year for the collective. One such planet is Saturn, which has spent 2½ years in Pisces and will spend the summer in Aries, before exiting Pisces next year. Saturn's restrictive presence has been transiting the pleasure sector of your chart for the last 2½ years, making the vibe 'all work, no play'. Essentially, Saturn's summer vacation is also your summer vacation, Scorpio. More on this will be discussed in the later sections of the horoscope.

Neptune follows a similar path as Saturn in that it takes a respite from occupying Pisces for part of the year and moves into Aries. Neptune takes 160 years to go around the zodiac and has consistently been in Pisces since 2012! Neptune's foray into Pisces was creative but not grounded, so its ingress into Aries provides a level of reassurance or permission to prioritize fun. Uranus is the other slow-moving planet shifting signs, but instead of moving away from your pleasure sector, it exits your house of partnership, stabilizing this area of life.

It's important to note that while the overarching theme of the year is to embody the Bon Vivant, the year starts off with some turbulence given that Mars, your planetary ruler, has been retrograde and will stay that way until late February. This retrograde will be discussed in the career and finances section of this horoscope as it's a primary focus for you. Abundant Jupiter's ingress into your house of higher education will also be discussed in this section.

All of these planetary shifts result in many of the planets coexisting in ways that mean they interact in groups with other, faster-moving planets. As a consequence, this year is rife with energetic peaks and troughs. For a quarterly view of the year, the first quarter focuses on your career and social life, while the second features a shift in scrutiny towards wellness and routines, with the focus turned away from pleasure and creativity. The third quarter further cements this and brings additional focus to money matters, and the final quarter centres more around your social life and finances.

Health

(Please note that this is an astrological perspective on health and not a medical one. Any health-related symptoms should be evaluated by a qualified healthcare professional.)

According to the official dictionary definition for your totem, the Bon Vivant is 'a sociable person who has cultivated and refined tastes, especially with respect to food and drink'. For you, Scorpio, this year will be about refining and disciplining your diet and wellness routines, given the multiple planetary shifts into the physical health sector of your chart. This year there are four planetary retrograde periods that occur between Aries and Pisces. This means there's a significant amount of time in which several planets will transit your physical health sector while retrograde. Retrograde periods embody 're-' verbs such as 'reflect', 're-evaluate' and 'reconfigure', and they will spur you to reflect on your current routines around physical wellness and make revisions that better support your physical wellness. Ceres, the dwarf planet associated with food and how we take care of ourselves, also transits Pisces and Aries for almost the entire year, further reinforcing these themes.

Saturn is the planet that rules discipline, restriction and hard lessons, among many other significations. Saturn enters your physical health sector on May 24 and stays until September 1. Saturn is all about reaping what we sow, and its energy can be leveraged through diligent work and taking responsibility for ourselves. In addition, Saturn rules mastery and expert opinion, so it's a good idea to consult professionals in the wellness space to best set yourself up for success. Neptune also moves into Aries, but does so two months earlier at the end of March. March is a significant month for your health sector, not only because both Mercury and Venus will be retrograde in this sector of your chart this month, but also since it features the first set of eclipses for 2025. Supporting mental health and wellness through emotional regulation practices is strongly recommended too, as Venus is your spiritual and mental health planet.

Your physical health planet is Mars, which begins the year retrograde. Mars will be retrograde in your career and social-standing sectors, so there's an added emphasis on focusing on how career influences your ability or inability to support your physical wellness. Mars will be retrograde this year from January 1 to February 23. Be open to being shown in what ways you can mature and better support yourself in this area of life. In order to fully enjoy this year as the Bon Vivant, you must give your body the TLC it deserves.

Here are the specific areas of the body to focus on this year:

- Reproductive organs: these are a perennial area of focus for you, as Scorpio rules this part of the body in medical astrology. Checking in with your doctor on how to supplement your diet to support these organs is strongly recommended, given the number of health transits that are present this year.
- Lymphatic system: Mars is your physical health planet and spends the majority of its retrograde in 2025 in Cancer, which rules this bodily system. In addition to staying on top of hydration, managing stress is especially important to support the lymphatic tubes and nodes. March and September, the two eclipse periods, are especially vital times for emotional regulation.

- Heart and circulatory system: Mars begins the year retrograde in Leo, which rules the heart. Maintaining a heart-healthy diet, especially in the months Mars is in Leo (January, April, May and June) is recommended.

Love and Social Life

One of the most significant transits influencing love this year is Uranus finally leaving Taurus after staying in the sign since 2019. Uranus rules innovation and instability, so occupying the relationship sector of your chart for this length of time brought a great many changes. Uranus takes a leave of absence from your 7th house of partnership during the same year as Saturn takes his summer vacation out of Scorpio's 5th house of pleasure and romance. There's a buoyancy to the energy around relationships as these planets move themselves away from these sectors of your chart.

That said, your love planet is Venus, which does undergo a period of retrograde motion from March 1 to April 12. March is a month of holistic reflection, given the multiple planetary retrogrades and eclipses, with relationships being an area you'll be encouraged to re-evaluate. Relationships based on mutual support will only be bolstered by this period of reflection. Relationships that feature unequal power dynamics are likely to incur significant tension in order to catalyse necessary adjustments to the dynamic. This also applies to friend groups and indeed your social life in general, as Mercury, your socializing planet, is also retrograde during this month. Mercury's spring retrograde period occurs from March 15 to April 7.

Jupiter is influential in love and social life, as it rules your house of creativity and romance. If you're single, recreation and creative self-expression are useful ways of meeting prospective partners this year. If you've got a partner, being intentional about scheduling more time for shared creativity or play time is strongly encouraged. Jupiter's foray into Cancer in June means that spiritual beliefs will become a litmus test for existing and prospective partnerships. Essentially, it will become crucial for both of you in a relationship to align spirituality or operate within a similar belief system. If you're looking for partnership this year, places that unite community through spirituality are linked to partnership through this transit.

The eclipses this year strongly emphasize love and social life. The first eclipse in March lights up the sector of your chart related to community and groups of friends. This eclipse occurs in tandem with Venus retrograde and functions as a values alignment transit with those you associate with. Which friends share your values and are people with whom you can be authentically yourself? This eclipse will illuminate to whom you should be allocating your energy. The eclipses in the autumn/fall function as a repetition of this theme as well.

Career and Finances

There are two planetary retrograde periods occurring in your career sector this year, the first of which is Mars retrograde. Although brief – Mars technically leaves this area of your chart on January 6 – Mars will have spent a full month in this sector prior to departing. Mars retrograde will have you questioning your overarching career goals for the year, as Mars rules drive, ambition and forward momentum. The best way to work with this retrograde period is to evaluate whether you feel the proverbial wind in your sails at work or if you find your job to be emotionally draining. Mars moves from your career sector to your higher-education sector during this period. As a result, the astrology at the start of the year will very likely also have you questioning whether you should seek additional or brand new educational opportunities.

Mercury's second retrograde period occurs in your career sector. Mercury will be retrograde in Leo from July 18 to August 11. Mercury retrogrades are times to reflect on how you approach patterns of thinking or communication. This retrograde period occurs as the collective astrology shifts away from scrutinizing relationships and pleasure towards looking at your routines and finances. As a result, this retrograde period revolves around the correlation between your work and your physical health. Does your current career support your physical body? If not, are there adjustments within your role at work that you can make to better accommodate a healthy lifestyle?

The astrology around finances for you this year is complex. On one hand, Jupiter, your finance planet, makes one of its most joyous shifts in sign to Cancer. This transition occurs in June, and Jupiter will stay in the sign for the remainder of the year. Jupiter in Gemini has been a time to focus on increasing your wealth through trading and commerce. Jupiter's ingress into Cancer brings the focus more on ensuring your finances support home, family and emotional support. Investing in real estate is an ideal way to honour this transit. On the other hand, Uranus, the wild card of the cosmos, shifts into the sector of your chart relating to how your finances are intertwined with others. Uranus makes this move in July. Typically, the recommendation around this transit would be to adopt a more frugal approach to finances. Moreover, Uranus is the innovator, so this could be an ideal time to cultivate new and innovative streams of income.

Home and Domestic Life

Your home and domestic life planet is Saturn, which changes sign this year. Saturn has been in Pisces since 2023, taking the focus away from the self when it comes to the needs of your home and family. Saturn's ingress into Aries this summer prioritizes your needs as a means of supporting those within the home and/or family. An ideal time to move this year, or do some form of home improvement, would be when Saturn forms a harmonious grand water trine with the Sun and Jupiter in November. More information on this transit can be found in your November horoscope. Pluto occupies this sector of your chart for the entire year, bringing with it the urge to transform and change. Addressing and improving the feng shui of your living space this year are highly recommended.

March is a month in which there may be some disruption within the home or to domestic life as a result of the confluence of transits. March features two planetary retrogrades plus two eclipses.

Establishing a sanctuary space within your home to retreat to in order to recharge is highly recommended. This space should be a place you can go to for alone time and where others need permission to join you. If such a space within the home is not available, identifying somewhere in your local community like a nature trail would be perfectly suitable. This recommendation is further supported given that the asteroid Vesta, associated with safety within the home, occupies your sign from January 3 to September 13.

Self-improvement

The year begins with a focus on this area of life as Mars, your planetary co-ruler, is retrograde. Embracing your authenticity is one theme this retrograde spurs you to confront. Your ability to embody the Bon Vivant and the goals you seek to achieve this year will be influenced by whether or not you embrace your individuality. Connected to this is the question of whether you're able to incorporate more pleasure or play into your life. The September 7 eclipse is noteworthy with regard to spotlighting your relationship to pleasure and play. This eclipse encourages leaning more heavily into creative self-expression as a means to ground and centre yourself.

Spirituality is an area of self-improvement that absolutely grows this year thanks to Jupiter. Jupiter's ingress into Cancer reinforces the role your spiritual value system plays in how you navigate life. This summer is an ideal time in which to explore new philosophies and schools of thought to update and improve your relationship with spirituality. Spending time in nature and connecting to Mother Earth are strongly reinforced for you by Jupiter in Cancer. Jupiter in Cancer also supports travel as a means for Scorpio to gain perspective. This trip need not be a far-flung voyage, but it should take you away from your daily grind.

Month-by-month Forecasts

January

Best Days Overall: 25-29
Most Stressful Days Overall: 2-6
Best Days for Love: 11-14
Best Days for Money: 13-16
Best Days for Career: 17-20
Power Word: Roots

Happy January, Scorpio! This year begins with Mars, your planetary co-ruler, still being retrograde. This means that it may take a little time to get your engine revved up this month. This month's cosmic weather begins on the 2nd with Venus moving into delicate, dreamy Pisces. This is a beautiful transit centring around creativity and romance for you. If you're feeling sluggish at the start of the year, utilize this transit by using creative self-expression as a means of getting started. Venus will be in Pisces for the entire month, so this energy is at your disposal for all of January.

Mars is travelling backwards through the zodiac and on January 6 will re-enter Cancer, your fellow water sign. Mars retrograde in Cancer typically features potent energy around how home and family ties inhibit or enable your ambitions. This transit spurs you to take a good look at the ways in which family and upbringing have moulded the values and goals that still may be central to who you currently are. Do you need to shed any outdated values or goals? Remember, a tree grows from the roots, so use this opportunity for reflection and rectification in order to grow on a sturdy foundation.

January's full Moon is in Cancer on the 13th. Full Moons are all about the culmination of emotional cycles, and this full Moon only accentuates the vibe of Mars' retrograde in Cancer. Additionally, this full Moon encourages leaning into spirituality as a means of grounding yourself, asking whether grounding practices such as meditation or mindfulness are a part of your daily/weekly wellness routines. Because full Moons tend to be emotional occasions, now is the time to regulate your body, which in turn will calm your mind.

Aquarius' season begins on the 19th. The Sun in Aquarius builds on the astrological themes of home and family for this month. If you've been meaning to do any form of home-improvement project or feng shui work, now is the time! You'll be wowed by how the energy and flow of your space can affect your psyche. The new Moon in Aquarius on the 29th is a great day to usher in a new layout of your home or to spend quality time with family. Overall, January's astrology urges you to reflect on your past in order to create your desired future.

February

Best Days Overall: 24–28
Most Stressful Days Overall: 11–15
Best Days for Love: 1–4
Best Days for Money: 3–7
Best Days for Career: 12–15
Power Word: Forward

Hey, Scorpio! The cosmic weather this month kicks off with a couple of sweet transits. Venus and Neptune meet up on Saturday the 1st to inspire you to take action that will uplift your spirit or do something that will become fuel for your dreams. The first weekend of the month also has Mercury and Jupiter building towards a harmonious alignment on the 3rd. Mercury and Jupiter working together is the ideal time to write or communicate. This is an excellent weekend for journaling, public speaking or initiating important conversations.

The full Moon in Leo on the 12th is extra-hot given the tense aspect it forms with Uranus. The full Moon in Leo is always a career-oriented lunation for you. This full Moon likely inspires a feeling of restlessness or aspiration for something new, fresh or more exciting in this realm. Uranus rules liberation at all costs and sometimes creates feelings of instability to catalyse change. If you've been meaning to change careers, this lunation will augment those feelings. If not, this is still a lunation that poses the question, 'What do I want to be remembered for?', subsequently prompting you to evaluate whether the path you're currently on aligns with your answer.

Pisces' season begins on the 18th, with the new Moon in Pisces following on the 27th. This is noteworthy because the Sun is meeting up with the north node, which just moved into Pisces last month. As mentioned in your yearly horoscope, a major theme of this year is your relationship to creative self-expression and romance. The Sun functions as one big spotlight in this regard. Allow yourself the time and space to explore the nuances of how you approach creativity and romance. The new Moon is an ideal time to commence some practice or behaviour that centres on either theme.

Lastly, I'm excited to report that Mars, your planetary co-ruler, finally ends its retrograde period on the 23rd. Mars rules drive, ambition and assertion, and while it will barely be moving this month, at least it will be moving forward. This is major unsticking energy!

March

Best Days Overall: 7-12
Most Stressful Days Overall: 14-18
Best Days for Love: 21-25
Best Days for Money: 3-8
Best Days for Career: 6-10
Power Word: Regulate

March is one of the most dynamic months of 2025, Scorpio, so let's dive right in. March 1 features Venus, the planet of values, worthiness and intimacy, turning retrograde. Venus will be retrograde for the entire month. This Venus retrograde centres around how you value your body and whether your choices align with this mindset. In addition, the end of the retrograde will prompt you to re-evaluate your relationship to romance and creativity.

Not only is there a noteworthy planetary retrograde, but March is also the start of eclipse season. Eclipses are evolutionary transits that spur profound changes through forcing necessary growth or shedding. The first eclipse occurs on March 14 and is a full Moon lunar eclipse in Virgo. This eclipse shines its light on Scorpio's 11th house of groups, communities and organizations. Navigate whatever turbulence might arrive as gracefully as possible, and identify whether the groups, communities or organizations you engage in support you in this present moment. If you hold leadership positions in any group or organization, there's additional scrutiny around the efficacy of you and your fellow leaders. An eclipse in Virgo also poses the question, 'Have I been of sufficient service to the communities I care about?' This eclipse could also catalyse promotions or changes in career path.

On March 15 Mercury mimics Venus' motion by turning retrograde. This Mercury retrograde builds on the attention the Venus retrograde pays to your physical wellness routines, so it's a critical time in which to meal prep and explicitly carve out time in your schedule for exercise. Aries' season begins on the 20th, with the second eclipse, a solar eclipse in Aries, occurring on the 29th. In addition to physical wellness, this eclipse will also make you aware if you've got a tendency to overwork. Just as it's important to carve out time for exercise, it's equally important to be intentional around rest. Periods of inactivity are just as vital to help you achieve long-term career goals or sustain challenging routines as periods of activity. Progress will be made through balancing work and rest.

April

Best Days Overall: 4–8
Most Stressful Days Overall: 26–29
Best Days for Love: 13–16
Best Days for Money: 6–10
Best Days for Career: 18–22
Power Word: Balance

Spring has sprung, Scorpio! The first week of April features multiple soft and harmonious transits. On April 5 Venus aligns with Mars in water signs. This is super-supportive energy for you, given that you round out the water trio, Scorpio. The vibes are productive with this transit, so put your gloves on and you'll accomplish a whole lot. On April 7 Mercury finally ends its retrograde and goes direct, rectifying the communication wonkiness that you've likely been experiencing over the last few weeks. This transit isn't like a light switch, though, so allow for Mercury to pick up speed over the next several days.

On April 12 there's a full Moon in Libra. Full Moons are always emotional, but this one is a little extra for Scorpio as it falls in your 12th house. The 12th house is all about spirituality, mental wellness and isolation. Isolation is tricky because sometimes the best thing for our mental health is being by ourselves, although it's deleterious to our mental health if we avoid human contact for too long. Libra is all about balance, so be intentional about balancing time alone and time with others. Venus turns direct on this day as well, which ramps up romance and creativity for you!

On April 19 the Sun enters Taurus, your polar sign. Taurus season is a heavily relationship-oriented time of year for you. If you've got a partner, the Sun shines its light on the dynamics of this relationship. Work with the luminary by prioritizing quality time with your special someone. If you're single, Taurus' season is the ideal time to put yourself out there. If you've always been approaching dating or meeting people in the same way, now is the time to get innovative. The new Moon in Taurus on the 27th is a lunation you can work with to accomplish this. Mars, your planetary co-ruler, opposes Pluto as the new Moon occurs, so do what you can to prevent hyper-vigilance around this. Also, Mars–Pluto transits can make things feel edgier, so put in some extra effort to keep things light.

May

Best Days Overall: 1–6
Most Stressful Days Overall: 11–15
Best Days for Love: 6–11
Best Days for Money: 4–7
Best Days for Career: 24–27
Power Word: Physical

Happy May, Scorpio! May's astrology begins with a couple of Venus transits. On May 2 Venus meets up with Neptune in Aries for the first time in your lifetime. Venus–Neptune transits elicit 'Don't worry, be happy' vibes; these are nice, but they can also promote escapist behaviour. Be mindful around prioritizing rest that's recharging in nature and not simply dissociative. Venus harmoniously aligns with Pluto on the 6th, encouraging physical transformation for Scorpio. This transit supports efforts you make to improve your diet or physical fitness. Scorpio has been navigating a great deal of Aries energy this year, which centres around the body. Support your physical form at this time through healthy nourishment, especially with Saturn entering Aries later this month.

There's a full Moon in your sign on the 12th. The full Moon in Scorpio is a waymarker for you, given that you're halfway through this trip around the Sun. Take stock of all the ways in which you've grown and all the things you've already accomplished in the first six months of this solar cycle. The full Moon in your sign is an especially reflective period, so anticipate some big emotions to really rise to the surface around this date. Mercury will be squaring off with Pluto at this time, which supports any form of investigation (particularly self-discovery). However, Mercury–Pluto transits can elicit obsessive, compulsive or hyper-vigilant behaviour for those who are prone to it. Do your best to ground yourself in the present moment and focus on what is in your locus of control.

Saturn enters Aries for the first time in 26 years on the 24th. Saturn is the great auditor of the cosmos and, as mentioned above, transits in Aries centre around the physical body for Scorpio.

Saturn in Aries will scrutinize how much you nurture your physical body and prioritize maintaining it. The Sun enters Gemini on the 20th, with the new Moon following on the 26th. This new Moon is financial in nature for Scorpio and specifically strongly supports business ventures that involve collaboration with others. It also provides an ideal time to resolve any debts you may owe in order to free yourself up for new fiscal endeavours.

June

Best Days Overall: 4-9
Most Stressful Days Overall: 19-23
Best Days for Love: 16-18
Best Days for Money: 11-15
Best Days for Career: 24-28
Power Word: Journey

Hi, Scorpio! June's astrology begins with not one, not two, but three planets changing signs in the first 10 days. Venus enters Taurus, your polar sign, on the 6th, bringing its influence to relationships. If you've got a partner, this is the ideal time to lean into the Taurus-ruled theme of sensuality and indulge in one or more of the five senses with your special someone. Yummy dinner time! If you're single, go out of your way to pamper yourself in this regard: massages, delicious food or beautiful sights are all very much in line with this transit. Mercury and Jupiter enter Cancer on the 8th and 9th. Jupiter hasn't been in Cancer for 12 years, and it ushers in a new cycle around education and spirituality for you, Scorpio. Where has your educational journey over the last 12 years led you? How has your spiritual value system evolved during that period? You're endeavouring to start afresh with new beginnings based on these journeys.

The full Moon for this month is in Sagittarius and occurs on the 11th. For Scorpio, a full Moon in the mutable fire sign is financial in nature. This full Moon represents a culmination of your relationship with money over the last six months. As mentioned last month with the start of Gemini season, you've been in a period

centred around auditing spending patterns and budgeting practices. This full Moon is a check-in on how that's going.

Cancer's season begins on the 20th, with the new Moon in
Cancer following on the 25th. Cancer season starts off a little rock-
ily, as the Sun quickly squares off with Saturn and Neptune right
after entering Cancer. The 22nd is the exact aspect with Saturn,
followed by the 23rd for the Sun-Neptune alignment. The combination of these transits is felt as being overwhelmed in pursuing or
achieving big goals. Managing mounting daily responsibilities can
also feel heavier at this time. Now is the time to get methodical,
Scorpio! Based on necessity and importance, categorize all the
things you have to do and want to achieve. Break down each item
into smaller, more bite-sized tasks. Lastly, this energy reminds us
that estimating our worth by our productivity is a limiting pattern
of thought. Be gentle with yourself, Scorpio!

July

Best Days Overall: 5-9
Most Stressful Days Overall: 23-26
Best Days for Love: 12-16
Best Days for Money: 1-4
Best Days for Career: 4-8
Power Word: Cents/Sense

Hi, Scorpio! July's cosmic weather begins with a confluence of
transits involving Venus. On the 4th Venus conjoins Uranus at the
very end of its stay in Taurus and subsequently enters Gemini.
Venus in Gemini is a social transit for everyone and has an added
financial component for Scorpio. Specifically, Venus moves into
Scorpio's joint finances sector so income dependent upon or made
as a result of others takes centre-stage. Uranus' influence adds an
element of spontaneity and surprise to both the social and the
financial side of this transit. If you're managing money in a lot of
different places, doing a quick audit as to whether everything's
working according to plan is recommended (especially with
Mercury's retrograde coming soon). On July 7 Uranus enters

Gemini for the first time since it left the sign in 1949! Uranus in Gemini will affect us collectively through revolutionizing the ways we as a society approach learning and communicating. For Scorpio it will also bring new and innovative ways you generate income over the seven years it spends in Gemini.

The full Moon in Capricorn is bright and juicy on the 10th. This full Moon spotlights your relationship to communication, picking up where you left off with the new Moon in Capricorn at the end of last year. What patterns of communication have come to light in the last six months? This is an important question to reflect on as Mercury turns retrograde on the 18th. Mercury will be retrograde in Leo, which affects Scorpio's career sector. There's great potential at this time for miscommunication and misinterpretation in the workplace and/or among colleagues. Do your due diligence to clarify things when necessary.

Leo's season begins on the 22nd and the Sun immediately gets extra-busy. The Sun aspects five different planets in the first three days of being in Leo. The new Moon on the 24th includes all of these aspects, and centres around authenticity in your career and within the workplace. Can you be authentically yourself at work? Does your current career align with your genuine career aspirations? This new Moon ushers in a six-month cycle of taking steps towards finding greater alignment between your individuality and your career.

August

Best Days Overall: 22–26
Most Stressful Days Overall: 6–10
Best Days for Love: 12–16
Best Days for Money: 11–14
Best Days for Career: 3–6
Power Word: Constructive

Happy August, Scorpio! This month starts off with a call for you to cut yourself some slack as Venus squares off with Saturn and Neptune on the 1st. This transit can trigger you becoming a bit of a bully to yourself, so be mindful of your internal dialogue. Mercury is still retrograde, prompting a re-evaluation of communication, including communication with yourself. Mars, your planetary ruler, enters peaceful, balance-oriented Libra on the 6th. For Scorpio, this transit focuses on finding balance when it comes to mental wellness. Coupled with this is a prompt to evaluate if there's a sustainable balance between social time and alone time. Do you give yourself enough time to recharge? Do you isolate yourself a little too much? The cosmic weather encourages you to find more balance in this department.

The full Moon in Aquarius occurs on the 9th, spotlighting home and family dynamics for Scorpio. Your planetary ruler finds itself at odds with Saturn and Neptune as this lunation lights up the night's sky, illuminating whether aspects of your family dynamics or the dynamics within the home are stifling your evolution. Work with the full Moon to identify this, and then, when Mercury ends its retrograde on the 11th, go ahead and have constructive conversations related to this topic with loved ones. Boundaries aren't easy to enforce, but they're both necessary and a form of self-love. An ideal day to have these conversations would be on the 12th, given that's when Venus and Jupiter harmoniously conjoin, promoting spending quality time with those you love. Moreover, for Scorpio, this transit also encourages leaning into spiritual practices to ground yourself in the present moment.

Virgo's season begins on the 22nd, and on the 23rd there's a new Moon in the sign. This transit is very social for Scorpio. As mentioned earlier, a theme for this month is striking a balance between socializing and quiet time. This lunation will spur you to make necessary adjustments if you haven't already, given Uranus' influence. Its influence on this new Moon also encourages Scorpio to be more spontaneous with their friends. Grab a few people who you're close to and go on an adventure around this date.

September

Best Days Overall: 16-20
Most Stressful Days Overall: 23-28
Best Days for Love: 5-9
Best Days for Money: 1-3
Best Days for Career: 27-30
Power Word: Tightrope

Happy September, Scorpio! This month is the second eclipse season of the year, so buckle up. To remind you, eclipses are evolutionary transits that promote growth through tension and shake-ups. The first eclipse of September occurs on the 7th and is a full Moon lunar eclipse in Pisces. As you know from your yearly horoscope, a major theme for you in 2025 is your relationship to creativity and romance. Eclipses catalyse transformation, so expect this month to precipitate a six-month growth phase in these departments. More specifically, this eclipse spurs you to incorporate creative self-expression more intentionally into your life on a routine basis. If you're already doing so, the eclipse promotes incorporating this form of creativity in your relationship by approaching it in new and exciting ways. This eclipse applies to romance in your life, whether you're single or have a partner. Regardless of your relationship status, it strongly encourages adopting new and innovative takes on how you approach romance, which could mean being more spontaneous or creative.

The second eclipse of the year is a new Moon solar eclipse in Virgo on the 21st. This eclipse is actually the second new Moon in Virgo of the year and amplifies the theme of last month's lunation, further examining whether you've struck a productive balance between social time and quiet time. If you haven't, you're likely going to feel run down as eclipses are felt in the body. Do your best to better accommodate play and rest. This eclipse also audits whether there's reciprocity in the social circles or organizations in which you're immersed. Does your cup get filled by these groups as much as you fill everyone else's cup? If it does, this eclipse will support further immersing yourself in these communities. If not, it will spur you to reconsider how much energy you're expending if it's not being matched.

Libra's season begins on the 21st, and three days later Mars, your planetary ruler, squares off with Pluto. This transit is associated with a fair amount of anger for you, Scorpio. Mars is in your sign, revving your engine. Channel all the kinetic energy into building your empire instead of clashing with others.

October

Best Days Overall: 27-31
Most Stressful Days Overall: 11-15
Best Days for Love: 3-7
Best Days for Money: 16-19
Best Days for Career: 1-4
Power Word: Embody

It's almost your season, Scorpio! This month's cosmic weather starts off on the 6th with a full Moon in Aries. This full Moon hearkens back to the new Moon lunar eclipse in Aries at the end of March, illuminating your relationship to your physical body and your tendency to overwork. With regard to the former, this lunation prompts all of us to make sure our emotional needs are being met. For you, this specifically has to do with whether your body's needs are being met. Are you nourishing your body and moving it as it needs? Tune into your body and ask it how it would like to be treated this month. With regard to working, this lunation will spotlight whether you're a chronic overworker. If you're feeling frazzled or pulled in too many directions around this date, it's your cosmic invitation to trim the fat out of your schedule for a few weeks and focus solely on what absolutely cannot be put off.

Venus stirs up a ton of astrological activity by aspecting Saturn, Uranus, Neptune and Pluto between the 11th and the 15th, and entering Libra on the 13th. Venus rules self-worth and values. While the full Moon revolves around your physical body, these transits centre around your mental health and wellness. It's vital at this time to affirm your boundaries in order to preserve your peace. The new Moon in Libra is an ideal transit during which to usher in a more intentional practice of making and sticking to boundaries. This new Moon also supports identifying ways to strike a better balance between work, rest and play.

Your solar season begins on the 23rd and the Sun in Scorpio finds tension with Pluto two days later, this transit prompting self-transformation. Given that your birthday is right around the corner, choose three words that you seek to embody this coming year. Pause and reflect on why you seek to embody these words. If you do a meditation practice, integrate these words into your routine. If not, be intentional about finding ways of actualizing these words.

November

Best Days Overall: 3-7
Most Stressful Days Overall: 11-15
Best Days for Love: 17-19
Best Days for Money: 28-30
Best Days for Career: 20-24
Power Word: Venture

Happy Birthday, Scorpio! This month's astro-weather begins on the 4th with Mars, your planetary ruler, entering Sagittarius. One of the themes for this month is financial well-being, with this transit being the first to revolve around your relationship to money. Mars is kinetic and inflammatory, so be mindful around excessive spending. The full Moon in Taurus occurs one day later, spotlighting partnership and collaboration for you. Taurus is a security-minded earth sign, so this lunation prompts you to contemplate feelings of security or self-assurance around partnership. If you've got a partner, the full Moon can absolutely breed significant intimacy if that sense of safety is there. If it isn't, this full Moon will likely spur you to have some tougher conversations to advocate for your needs. If you're single, this full Moon centres around your emotional availability for a relationship.

Mercury turns retrograde one more time in 2025, on the 9th. This transit occurs in Sagittarius and is also financial in nature for Scorpio. Mercury retrograde is a time to revisit, re-evaluate and reflect. For you, Scorpio, this retrograde will first promote taking stock of all your assets, and really understanding where and why money enters and exits your bank account. Additionally, if there were any financial ventures that you contemplated in the past, this will be the time to rethink whether or not they're still possible. On November 17 the Sun forms a super-harmonious grand water trine with Jupiter and Saturn. This transit is incredibly supportive of creating tangible outcomes for all the hard work you've been putting in. Whether it's in your business, schooling or another area of life, now is not the time to slow down.

The new Moon in your sign occurs on November 20, the last day of Scorpio season. This lunation encourages proudly proclaiming your 2026 goals and taking steps towards getting the ball rolling early. Furthermore, this new Moon supports new beginnings around aesthetics and identity. Changes to your look or how you seek to be regarded are encouraged with this lunation. Sagittarius' season begins on the 21st, bringing more attention to your relationship with your wallet. Remember that it's sustainable to spend as long as you're also saving.

December

Best Days Overall: 1–5
Most Stressful Days Overall: 9–14
Best Days for Love: 15–20
Best Days for Money: 19–23
Best Days for Career: 21–24
Power Word: Visionary

Happy December, Scorpio! Are you ready for 2026? Well, before we get there, there are a few more transits that we've got to cover. First, the full Moon in Gemini lights up the December sky on the 4th. Gemini is all about embodying duality, and this full Moon has you confronting the many different facets that make you unique.

More specifically, this lunation encourages doing some much-needed shadow work. Shadow work is essentially exploring the parts of ourselves that we hide, ignore or resist. Gemini is also associated with learning, so if you venture into this, do so with a professional. The only way to get to buried treasure is to dig it up. Believe it or not, learning to love the parts of ourselves we resist is the best way to get unstuck.

This is especially important because Mars, your planetary ruler, squares off with Saturn, which slows momentum down significantly around the 9th. The vibe is restless with this transit and is best met by pivoting to focus on things within your control. For you, this is the opportune time for introspection. It's also important because the second half of December, starting with Mars entering Capricorn on the 15th, picks up steam and encourages visionary thinking about the following year. For Scorpio, this is a heavily communication-oriented transit. Mars rules assertion, so mental and verbal acuity are heightened over the next six weeks. Leverage this transit through planning out your next steps for your own unique form of metaphorical world domination.

The new Moon in Sagittarius is the last major financial transit for Scorpio in 2025. In addition to the themes highlighted in Sagittarius season around starting new ventures, this transit also supports seeking out education as a means of growing wealth in the long term. Go get that certification or hone that specialty! Capricorn's season begins on the 21st and Venus follows the Sun there on the 24th. This build-up of Capricorn energy reinforces the importance of structure and routine in achieving your goals. While Sagittarius season was all about dreaming about them, Capricorn season is all about taking the tangible steps to materialize precisely what you want.

Sagittarius

THE ARCHER

Birthdays from
November 23
to December 20

Personality Profile

SAGITTARIUS AT A GLANCE

Element – Fire

Ruling Planet – Jupiter
  Career Planet – Mercury
  Love Planet – Mercury
  Money Planet – Saturn
  Planet of Health and Work – Venus
  Planet of Home and Family Life – Neptune
  Planet of Spirituality and Mental Health – Pluto

Totem – the Mighty Oak

Colours – blue, dark blue

Colours that promote love, romance and social harmony – yellow, yellow-orange

Colours that promote earning power – black, indigo

Gems – garnet, citrine, turquoise

Metal – tin

Scents – carnation, jasmine, myrrh

Quality – mutable (= flexibility)

Qualities most needed for balance – attention to detail, administrative and organizational skills

Strongest virtues – generosity, honesty, broad-mindedness, tremendous vision

Deepest need – to expand mentally

Characteristics to avoid – over-optimism, exaggeration, being too generous with other people's money

Signs of greatest overall compatibility – Aries, Leo

Signs of greatest overall incompatibility – Gemini, Virgo, Pisces

Sign most helpful to career – Virgo

Sign most helpful for emotional support – Pisces

Sign most helpful financially – Capricorn

Sign best for marriage and/or partnerships – Gemini

Sign most helpful for creative projects – Aries

Best Sign to have fun with – Aries

Signs most helpful in spiritual matters – Leo, Scorpio

Best day of the week – Thursday

Understanding a Sagittarius

If you look at the symbol of the archer you will gain a good, intuitive understanding of a person born under this astrological sign. The development of archery was humanity's first refinement of the power to hunt and wage war. The ability to shoot an arrow far beyond the ordinary range of a spear extended humanity's horizons, wealth, personal will and power.

Today, instead of using bows and arrows we project our power with fuels and mighty engines, but the essential reason for using these new powers remains the same. These powers represent our ability to extend our personal sphere of influence – and this is what Sagittarius is all about. Sagittarians are always seeking to expand their horizons, to cover more territory and increase their range and scope. This applies to all aspects of their lives: economic, social and intellectual.

Sagittarians are noted for the development of the mind – the higher intellect – which understands philosophical and spiritual concepts. This mind represents the higher part of the psychic nature and is motivated not by self-centred considerations but by the light and grace of a Higher Power. Thus, Sagittarians love higher education of all kinds. They might be bored with formal schooling but they love to study on their own and in their own way. A love of foreign travel and interest in places far away from home are also noteworthy characteristics of the Sagittarian type.

If you give some thought to all these Sagittarian attributes you will see that they spring from the inner Sagittarian desire to develop. To travel more is to know more, to know more is to be more, to cultivate the higher mind is to grow and to reach more. All these traits tend to broaden the intellectual – and indirectly, the economic and material – horizons of the Sagittarian.

The generosity of the Sagittarian is legendary. There are many reasons for this. One is that Sagittarians seem to have an inborn consciousness of wealth. They feel that they are rich, that they are lucky, that they can attain any financial goal – and so they feel that they can afford to be generous. Sagittarians do not carry the burdens of want and limitation which stop most other people from giving generously. Another reason for their generosity is their religious and philosophical idealism, derived from the higher mind. This higher mind is by nature generous because it is unaffected by material circumstances. Still another reason is that the act of giving tends to enhance their emotional nature. Every act of giving seems to be enriching, and this is reward enough for the Sagittarian.

Finance

Sagittarians generally entice wealth. They either attract it or create it. They have the ideas, energy and talent to make their vision of paradise on Earth a reality. However, mere wealth is not enough. Sagittarians want luxury – earning a comfortable living seems small and insignificant to them.

In order for Sagittarians to attain their true earning potential they must develop better managerial and organizational skills. They must learn to set limits, to arrive at their goals through a series of attainable sub-goals or objectives. It is very rare that a person goes from rags to riches overnight. But a long, drawn-out process is difficult for Sagittarians. Like Leos, they want to achieve wealth and success quickly and impressively. They must be aware, however, that this over-optimism can lead to unrealistic financial ventures and disappointing losses. Of course, no zodiac sign can bounce back as quickly as Sagittarius, but only needless heartache will be caused by this attitude. Sagittarians need to maintain their vision – never letting it go – but they must also work towards it in practical and efficient ways.

Career and Public Image

Sagittarians are big thinkers. They want it all: money, fame, glamour, prestige, public acclaim and a place in history. They often go after all these goals. Some attain them, some do not – much depends on each individual's personal horoscope. But if Sagittarians want to attain public and professional status they must understand that these things are not conferred to enhance one's ego but as rewards for the amount of service that one does for the whole of humanity. If and when they figure out ways to serve more, Sagittarians can rise to the top.

The ego of the Sagittarian is gigantic – and perhaps rightly so. They have much to be proud of. If they want public acclaim, however, they will have to learn to tone down the ego a bit, to become more humble and self-effacing, without falling into the trap of self-denial and self-abasement. They must also learn to master the details of life, which can sometimes elude them.

At their jobs Sagittarians are hard workers who like to please their bosses and co-workers. They are dependable, trustworthy and enjoy a challenge. Sagittarians are friendly to work with and helpful to their colleagues. They usually contribute intelligent ideas or new methods that improve the work environment for everyone. Sagittarians always look for challenging positions and careers that develop their intellect, even if they have to work very hard in order to succeed. They also work well under the supervision of others, although by nature they would rather be the supervisors and increase their sphere of influence. Sagittarians excel at professions that allow them to be in contact with many different people and to travel to new and exciting locations.

Love and Relationships

Sagittarians love freedom for themselves and will readily grant it to their partners. They like their relationships to be fluid and ever-changing. Sagittarians tend to be fickle in love and to change their minds about their partners quite frequently.

Sagittarians feel threatened by a clearly defined, well-structured relationship, as they feel this limits their freedom. The Sagittarian tends to marry more than once in life.

Sagittarians in love are passionate, generous, open, benevolent and very active. They demonstrate their affections very openly. However, just like an Aries they tend to be egocentric in the way they relate to their partners. Sagittarians should develop the ability to see others' points of view, not just their own. They need to develop some objectivity and cool intellectual clarity in their relationships so that they can develop better two-way communication with their partners. Sagittarians tend to be overly idealistic about their partners and about love in general. A cool and rational attitude will help them to perceive reality more clearly and enable them to avoid disappointment.

Home and Domestic Life

Sagittarians tend to grant a lot of freedom to their family. They like big homes and many children and are one of the most fertile signs of the zodiac. However, when it comes to their children Sagittarians generally err on the side of allowing them too much freedom. Sometimes their children get the idea that there are no limits. However, allowing freedom in the home is basically a positive thing – so long as some measure of balance is maintained – for it enables all family members to develop as they should.

Horoscope for 2025

How deep do your roots run, Sagittarius? This year you'll be prompted to explore this concept as the north node enters your home and domestic life sector in January. The north node hasn't been in this part of your chart for over 18 years, and it brings with it the eclipses. The north node functions like a beacon, illuminating which areas of life are highlighted in a given year. For you, centaur, the cosmic weather focuses on family dynamics, real estate and your physical home.

This year is a unique year astrologically as several slower-moving planets shift signs. This means you can anticipate influential societal shifts, in addition to the changes happening to you in your micro-environment. The north node shifts into Pisces, meaning that the south node shifts into Virgo. This is notable for Sagittarius because it shares an important quality, its modality, with these signs, and as a result is profoundly affected by this shift. In addition to home and domestic life, the shift brings a heavy astrological focus on themes of career and/or legacy for Sagittarius.

Two of the slower-moving planets shifting signs this year are Saturn and Neptune, both of which are moving from Pisces to Aries. Saturn rules discipline, restriction and hard work; it has spent the last 2½ years in your home and domestic life sector, and will shift into your recreation and pleasure sector over the summer. Neptune is moving into this sector as well, for the first time in your lifetime. Your comfort around allowing yourself to play instead of work is undergoing a metamorphosis this year.

This is also a year where every possible planet that could retrograde will be retrograde at some point. Four of these retrograde periods occur from Aries to Pisces. Although potentially frustrating, retrogrades are not negative transits; they are periods of forced reflection along the themes of the planet in retrograde motion. The astrology of 2025 functions as a chapter-turning moment with the planetary shifts in signs, and these retrogrades prompt audits of several themes of life. This year you will embody 'the Mighty Oak' as your totem emphasizes home and domestic life, as well as encouraging you to bolster your sense of self amid the energetic shifts.

For a quarterly view of the year, the first quarter features a strong emphasis on home and domestic life, plus some financial themes. The second quarter features an additional focus on your relationship to pleasure and some themes around career/legacy, while the third features additional scrutiny around recreation and creativity, plus more financial themes. The final quarter of the year returns to the overarching focus on home and domestic life.

Health

(Please note that this is an astrological perspective on health and not a medical one. Any health-related symptoms should be evaluated by a qualified healthcare professional.)

March and September are two noteworthy months for this domain of life, given they feature the two eclipse cycles of 2025. Eclipses are evolutionary transits that encourage growth through scrutiny and shake-ups. In addition to the fact that eclipses are felt in the body, March's eclipses occur in tandem with Venus, your health planet, being retrograde. Having your health planet retrograde functions like an audit of your routines and behaviours, centred around physical wellness. This includes, but is not limited to, diet, exercise and sleep. Be prepared for the eclipses to illuminate dysfunctional patterns of behaviour that are deleterious to your health. When revealed, the astrology of March implores you to not only confront these behaviours, but also take decisive action. There will be a recitation of these themes with the second eclipse cycle in September.

Your spiritual and mental wellness planet is Mars, which begins the year retrograde. Mars is inflammatory in nature and this transit functions to spur you to address the ways you self-sabotage. Mars rules drive and ambition, and, when retrograde, reveals the ways we stifle ourselves. For you, Sagittarius, patterns of thought that are self-effacing are especially brought up by this transit. This retrograde supports working on your mental health with a professional if you don't already. Embodying the Mighty Oak means erecting supportive processes that bolster your sense of self.

Here are the specific areas of the body to focus on this year:

- Hips and thighs: these are a perennial area of focus for Sagittarius, as your sign rules them in medical astrology. Focusing on mobility and flexibility, in addition to strengthening, is vital for holistic physical wellness.
- Bladder and reproductive organs: Mars will primarily be retrograde in Sagittarius' 8th house, which rules these parts of the body in medical astrology. They are a particular area of focus for the first four months of the year.
- Digestive system: two of the four eclipses this year occur in Virgo, ruler of this system. Be particularly mindful around diet during the March and September eclipse seasons.
- Feet: the north node moves into Pisces, which rules your feet. Routine foot reflexology or massages are recommended.

Love and Social Life

This year begins with Jupiter, your planetary ruler, transiting your 7th house of partnership. This affords Sagittarius abundant energy around this area of life. Jupiter rules growth, expansion and the philosophies we follow to navigate life. Jupiter transiting your relationship sector for the first five months of the year places an emphasis on growing within existing partnerships or creating new ones. Given Jupiter's association with beliefs and conviction, those who are single will find a heavier weighting around spiritual or philosophical compatibility in seeking new partners. Those with existing partnerships will find abundance in partaking together in activities aligned with mutually shared spirituality.

Jupiter exits your relationship sector in June, but the sector isn't left empty for long, as Uranus enters it in July. Uranus is the planet of innovation, instability and individuality. It takes 84 years to go around the zodiac, so this is likely the first time in your lifetime you'll be encountering this transit. If you're single, Uranus in your partnership house demands you seek partnership in new and innovative ways. Leveraging technology as a means to find prospective partners is encouraged. Uranus rebels against tradition, so it's vital you rethink your approach to dating if you're looking for a partner. If you are already partnered, Uranus in this area of your chart encourages injecting more spontaneity into the mundane routines of the everyday life of your partnership. If you function best in highly structured systems, explicitly schedule open-ended spontaneous time with your partner on a consistent basis. Uranus in your partnership house does facilitate an air of 'expect the unexpected'. This transit is likely to exacerbate any anxiety you might have around trying to control partners or aspects of the relationship outside your control. The purpose of this irritation is to confront the root causes of the behaviour.

The play and pleasure sector of your chart is significantly activated this year by the four planetary retrogrades occurring in Aries in 2025. In March, both Mercury and Venus turn retrograde. These periods function as a review of your relationship to pleasure and how you approach it. Mercury is your partnership planet and Venus functions as your social life planet, so these retrogrades will be felt. All retrogrades encourage embodying 're-' words like 'rethink', 're-evaluate' and 'reconsider'. These retrogrades will specifically encourage re-evaluating how you approach recreation and with whom. Inspiration to adopt new forms of creativity or recreational outlets are encouraged by this transit. Mercury's and Venus' retrograde periods occur in March and early April.

While Mercury and Venus move quickly, Saturn and Neptune, the other two planets who will retrograde in Aries, move very slowly and will be occupying this region of your chart for longer. Saturn will be in your play and pleasure sector from May 24 to September 1 this year. Given Saturn's association with work and restriction, recreation time will need to be more intentionally sought out during this transit. Saturn encourages you to create structures around how you approach creative self-expression and recreation. Neptune will be occupying this region of your chart from March 30 to October 22. Neptune rules spirituality, and this transit intertwines your personal spirituality with how you approach creative self-expression and recreation. Neptune seeks to elevate why you create or how you seek pleasure with a higher purpose. How can you leverage your own unique creativity or forms of recreation to support others?

Career and Finances

As mentioned in previous sections, March's astrology features a confluence of transits, including two eclipses and two retrograde periods. March is a noteworthy month for career and legacy for you, Sagittarius. The first eclipse of 2025 is a total lunar eclipse in Virgo occurring in Sagittarius' career sector. This eclipse occurs a day before Mercury, your career planet, turns retrograde. Changes to career trajectory abound with this astrology. In fact, the entire month of March is rife with change in this regard. September also features an eclipse in Virgo and sets itself up as another month where change is afoot in this realm. When the north node moves into your home and domestic life sector in January, the south node moves into your career sector. This means the overarching career theme for you this year is shedding what no longer serves you. This could be dreams that no longer apply, a role which you've outgrown or a business collaboration that has run its course. View 2025 as a trimming-of-the-fat year when it comes to your career.

Financially, the year starts off a little volatile, with Mars retrograde in your 8th house of joint ventures. This retrograde scrutinizes the way you give and receive money from others. Mars will be retrograde from the start of the year until February 23, but it stays in this sector of your chart until April 18. This is the time to avoid acquiring debts, if possible, and outstanding debts are likely to become a noticeable thorn in your side at this time as well. The period of Mars moving directly in this sector of your chart (February 23 to April 18) encourages long-term investments that grow and accrue in value over a number of years. These themes, along with any joint ventures you are involved with, will likely be emphasized in March and September as well by the eclipses.

Saturn is your finance planet. With Saturn moving into your creativity and recreation sector, new streams of income can be accrued from creative self-expression. Saturn will be in this sector of your chart from May 24 to September 1. This is the last year that Saturn will be in the real estate sector of your chart (January 1 to May 23; September 2 to December 31). Financial ventures in real estate should be especially scrutinized when Saturn is involved. More on this in the home and domestic life section that follows.

Home and Domestic Life

Your home and domestic life planet is Jupiter, which enters the sign of its exaltation, Cancer, in June. Jupiter is the great expander and, when in Cancer, is focused on growing abundance within the home. There is noteworthy energy centred around real estate this year, especially during the summer, when Jupiter moves into Cancer and Saturn leaves the home and domestic life sector of your chart. Planning home renovations or revitalizing the feng shui of your home is also opportune during this period. Jupiter will be in Cancer from June 9 until the end of the year, so real estate opportunities can also abound after Saturn returns to the 4th house of your chart. However, Saturn's presence in your home and domestic life sector (September 2 to the end of the year) brings more scrutiny around the fine details. Ensure a thorough inspection of any property you are interested in buying is done by an independent inspector and have a professional review any financial contracts. Embodying the Mighty Oak means rooting yourself into the ground and creating a home. The ultimate purpose of Jupiter in Cancer is for your living space to feel safe, secure and like home.

In addition to Saturn's return to this sector of your chart, September is also an important month for home and domestic life because there will be a new Moon solar eclipse occurring on the 21st. Anticipate some disruption within the home or within interpersonal relationships in the home. It's not advised to begin home-improvement projects on this day, and ones in progress should be monitored carefully. Being the caretaker and steward within your family unit is highlighted by this eclipse, so make sure to advocate for your needs as well when this arises.

Self-improvement

Embodying the Mighty Oak this year entails providing yourself with the tools and support system needed the reach the heights of all your 2025 goals. Jupiter, your planetary ruler, entering nurturing Cancer mid-year highlights the importance of innerchild work or becoming the best parent to yourself. This transit encourages challenging struggles you may have with vulnerability by identifying and addressing their root causes. Jupiter rules the philosophies and belief systems we abide by to navigate life. Transiting Jupiter spurs you to explore various schools of thought that promote a healthy relationship with vulnerability. Travelling to any ancestral family homeland is another Jupiter-in-Cancer activity that could spur meaningful healing for you this year, Sagittarius.

Communication is an ever-evolving area of life for you, now that Pluto has entered and will stay in this sector of your chart for over 20 years. With Saturn being your communication planet and Pluto transiting this region of your chart, 2025 will be a year of confronting limiting patterns of behaviour around communication. Bookmark Mercury's retrograde periods to be especially reflective in this regard. Mercury will be retrograde in Aries (and Pisces) from March 15 to April 7, in Leo from July 18 to August 11 and in Sagittarius (and Scorpio) from November 9 to 29.

Month-by-month Forecasts

January

Best Days Overall: 28–31
Most Stressful Days Overall: 1–5
Best Days for Love: 17–20
Best Days for Money: 19–22
Best Days for Career: 8–12
Power Word: Intertwine

Happy New Year, centaur! January's cosmic weather starts off on the 2nd with Venus moving into dreamy Pisces. This transit will be in effect for the entire month, encouraging you to spend quality time at home and with your loved ones. Be intentional about scheduling time to do so before you start galloping towards the horizon, dear Sagittarius.

We begin 2025 with Mars already retrograde. On January 6 the fiery planet re-enters Cancer. This transit is financial in nature for you, revolving around your income streams and all the places you spend your money. Mars rules inflammation, and when this planet's focus is financial we can absolutely overspend or lose sight of aspects of our finances. It would definitely be in your best interest to partake in financial forecasting for the fiscal quarter or year if you don't actively follow a budget.

On January 13 there's a full Moon in Cancer, which builds on this theme of financial auditing. Full Moons shine their light on aspects of our lives, and this one illuminates the way in which your finances are intertwined with others. This can be as a result of joint ventures, familial ties, or debts owed to you or that you owe. Having finances intertwined with others isn't a negative, but this transit wants you to dot your i's and cross your t's that all of these dynamics are functioning as supportively as possible.

Aquarius' season begins on January 19, encouraging you to immerse yourself in the communities and groups of people who uplift you. The Sun has its annual meet-up with Pluto, the planet that rules shedding, unearthing and transformation. This means the inverse is also true. If you feel as though there are communities or groups of people that take more than they give or do not uplift you, now may be the time to review how often you gather with them. The new Moon on the 29th is a lovely lunation focused on positive, joyous community involvement, so gather with your favourite herd during this new Moon, centaur.

February

Best Days Overall: 4–9
Most Stressful Days Overall: 10–15
Best Days for Love: 2–6
Best Days for Money: 24–28
Best Days for Career: 14–18
Power Word: Thoughtful

Happy February, Sagittarius! Mercury and Jupiter start things off this month by harmoniously aligning on the 3rd. This transit bolsters communication, which is great, but just be mindful of not falling victim to 'foot-in-mouth syndrome'. Basically, be intentional about having a filter when opening your mouth. Venus enters Aries the next day, which heats things up romantically and creatively for you, centaur. Venus will be in Aries all month now, so there's no need to rush in these departments. Say yes to any opportunities to lean into your favourite forms of creativity.

The full Moon in Leo on the 12th is intense, given that the lunation is tensely aspecting Uranus. Uranus rules instability, innovation and individuality, as well as sudden changes. This is important to note because this full Moon is very much a powder keg. There's no need to be hyper-vigilant, but it's important to be mindful that the energy around this date is wired to be explosive. If you do find that you're getting roared at like a lion, ground yourself if possible in active listening and a thoughtful response. For Sagittarius, this lunation falls in the 9th house of higher education, spiritual philosophy and travel. If you're travelling on or around this date, be especially careful around stoking conflict. In addition, this lunation supports educating yourself through spirituality or philosophical belief systems.

Pisces' season begins on the 18th. As mentioned in your yearly horoscope, home and family dynamics are two major themes for you this year. The Sun moving into the same sign as the north node only highlights these themes. If you've been thinking about moving or taking action related to real estate, Pisces season is a critical time of year to get your ducks in a row. Furthermore, if you've been considering making money in real estate, Mars goes direct in Cancer on the 23rd, which clears a path for this. The new Moon in Pisces occurs on the 27th, an ideal time to begin anything new related to home or real estate. The energy around this new Moon is nesting energy, so you'll want to snuggle up with loved ones.

March

Best Days Overall: 20-26
Most Stressful Days Overall: 1-3, 13-16
Best Days for Love: 7-12
Best Days for Money: 4-7
Best Days for Career: 7-12
Power Word: Pleasure

This is a big month, Sagittarius! March's cosmic weather begins on the 1st with Venus turning retrograde in Aries. For Sagittarius, this transit zeroes in on how you approach romance. If you've got a partner, this is your opportunity to assess the contours of your relationship and vocalize where you desire your needs to be met better. If you're single, you'll reflect on how you approach romance and identify if these methods are sustainable or fruitful. This Venus retrograde is also extremely creative for Sagittarius, providing a great opportunity to revisit forms of creative self-expression you've long overlooked or haven't partaken in for some time.

Bam! The first eclipse of 2025 occurs on March 14. Eclipses are evolutionary transits that typically promote growth through shake-ups and scrutiny. Career promotions, kerfuffles at work and even major career changes are all possible with this transit. If you're happy in your current place of employment, definitely dot your i's and cross your t's this month (especially around the eclipse). It's important to do so because one day after the eclipse occurs, Mercury joins Venus by turning retrograde in Aries. This transit, in conjunction with the Venus retrograde, could bring 'ghosts' from your past back into the picture. This occurs in order to reflect back to you how much you've grown, evolved or changed since they were a more prominent part of your life.

Aries' season begins on the 20th, there's a solar eclipse on the 29th and Neptune moves into Aries for the first time in your life-time on the 30th. Aries season is the time of year when creativity and/or romance are the bottom line. This Aries season is super-special because of the retrogrades, the eclipse in Aries and Neptune's historic move into the sign. The eclipse is a watershed moment when it comes to how creativity is integrated into your everyday life. This eclipse also very likely will influence super-romantic experiences for you. Neptune in Aries ushers in a new era of how your creative self-expression is influenced by your spiritual-ity (and vice versa).

April

Best Days Overall: 3-8
Most Stressful Days Overall: 25-30
Best Days for Love: 17-20
Best Days for Money: 4-6, 21-23
Best Days for Career: 16-19
Power Word: Community

Happy April, centaur! This month starts off with a confluence of soft and supportive transits during the first week. Venus aligns with Mars, which in turn aligns with Saturn on the 5th. This is a super-productive coupling of transits, so lean into the energy and take care of business. Mercury ends its retrograde and goes direct on the 7th. While this transit won't cure Sagittarius' foot-in-mouth tendencies, it does clear the general wonkiness you've been experiencing around transportation, communication and technology.

On April 12 there's a bright full Moon in Libra. The full Moon in Libra is always a relational lunation, but this one is especially so for Sagittarius. The focus for this full Moon is friends and community. This lunation illuminates which groups of friends or communities are there for you through thick or thin. Honour this transit by planning an adventure with those people who first come to mind, or reach out to a grouping of them to express your gratitude. Venus ends its retrograde and goes direct on this day as well. Venus direct will officially lighten the vibe, helping you navigate whatever fallout occurred in the wake of last month's eclipses and retrogrades.

On April 19 it's officially Taurus' season. Taurus season for you is your annual spotlight on physical wellness and routines. Now that spring has sprung, it's time to thaw out of winter and get physical. Saturn meets up with the north node on the 21st, creating a regimented, structured air that's perfect for grounding yourself in healthy routines. If you feel as though you already have your physical wellness regime down pat, then use this transit to support loved ones with their routines. The new Moon in Taurus occurs on the 27th. This lunation and all its energy absolutely function as the start of a new emotional cycle around diet, exercise or holistic wellness work. The month ends with Venus entering Aries, your fellow fire sign. Venus in Aries is a romantic and creative transit for you. Plan some dates with your special someone or yourself in May, and carve out time to enable yourself to have play time with friends.

May

Best Days Overall: 1-5
Most Stressful Days Overall: 13-18
Best Days for Love: 4-9
Best Days for Money: 20-24
Best Days for Career: 6-11
Power Word: Play

It's May, Sagittarius! The cosmic weather for this month begins on the 2nd when Venus meets up with Neptune in Aries for the first time in your lifetime. This Venus–Neptune transit is incredibly creative and romantic for Sagittarius. Such a dreamy alignment can promote rose-coloured glasses, so don't give away all your secrets at once if you're meeting new people. On the 5th Mercury supports Jupiter, your planetary ruler. This transit heightens the relational quality of the Venus–Neptune transit. The Mercury–Jupiter transit would support you if you were seeking to profess your love or admiration for someone special. Additionally, this transit would be equally supportive if you were seeking to creatively self-express using a linguistic form of communication (singing, writing, poetry, etc).

On May 12 it's the full Moon in Scorpio. Scorpio Moons are always emotional, but this full Moon is especially so for Sagittarius as it falls in its 12th house of spirituality, mental health and isolation. This full Moon reminds you, centaur, that sometimes you have to take a rest from all the galloping and chill out in the stables. May 12 also features Mercury and Pluto squaring off with one another. Mercury–Pluto transits are investigative in nature. Utilize the downtime this full Moon promotes by making space for some necessary self-discovery.

On May 24 Saturn enters Aries for the first time since leaving the sign in 1999. Saturn rules discipline and structure, and in Aries it facilitates a 2½-year period of maturation around creativity, recreation and romance. This period will likely require you to be increasingly intentional about carving out time for creative self-expression and play. Saturn promotes maturity and doles out responsibility, so you'll need to evolve your ability to time-manage. Furthermore, it's important you prioritize your needs if you have a busy schedule or are in a relationship. Speaking of relationships, the Sun enters Gemini on the 20th and the new Moon occurs in the sign on the 26th. This lunation welcomes new beginnings or new adventures in relationships. Lean into the calling to budget time for pleasure, however you see fit.

June

Best Days Overall: 5–9
Most Stressful Days Overall: 20–24
Best Days for Love: 11–15
Best Days for Money: 26–30
Best Days for Career: 25–29
Power Word: Adventure

Hi, Sagittarius! On June 6 Venus enters its home sign of Taurus. Venus in Taurus benefits Sagittarius' kinetic tendencies. It's time to run, bike, skate or gallop! Venus in Taurus supports efforts you've been making or are seeking to make towards improving your physical fitness or nutrition. Mercury and Jupiter both enter Cancer, on the 8th and 9th respectively. Jupiter is your planetary ruler and is very happy in the sign of Cancer. Jupiter rules growth, expansion, beliefs and conviction, and in the sign of Cancer there's an orientation towards improving the dynamics of home and family. This applies literally to the home, whether that's moving to a bigger place or revitalizing your existing space through redecoration, feng shui or home improvement. Jupiter in Cancer encourages expanding upon the ways you nurture others and spend time with those that nurture you. Moreover, there's ample energy to enable you to tap into well-vetted fiscal endeavours with others. There are also significations around debt with the transit, however, so be very careful about taking out loans and be responsible with any existing debts you might owe.

On the 11th it's your annual full Moon. The full Moon in Sagittarius is a lunation that promotes adventure. This is a spiritual lunation as well, and sometimes the best way to gain perspective is through travel, so take even a small trip or go on a short exploration around this date if possible. Full Moons are associated with a change in mood, and this one will amp you up exponentially. Channel this fire wisely. This is important to note because on the 17th Mars enters Virgo. Mars rules forward momentum, with this transit supporting your career hustle.

On June 20 Cancer's season begins. Things then get a little rocky, as the Sun squares off with Saturn on the 22nd and Neptune on the 23rd. These two transits are associated with feeling exasperated around all that you're expecting to get done. Essentially, this transit is heightened if you associate your worth with productivity. Do your best to avoid this point of view, and also be measured in the face of accomplishing large tasks. Slow and steady wins the race, centaur.

July

Best Days Overall: 25–29
Most Stressful Days Overall: 15–19
Best Days for Love: 7–12
Best Days for Money: 4–8
Best Days for Career: 27–31
Power Word: High-minded

Happy July, centaur! This month's cosmic weather starts off by focusing on relationships as Venus enters Gemini, your polar sign, on the 4th. Venus also forms harmonious aspects with Saturn, Uranus, Neptune and Pluto during this week. If you're single, channel the chatty energy of Venus in Gemini by putting yourself out there. If you've got a partner, this is an ideal week to come up with a list of fun/vulnerable/curious questions for your partner so you can get to know each other on a deeper level. Uranus enters Gemini for the first time since leaving the sign 76 years ago! Uranus is the planet of innovation, instability and individuality, and when it's in Gemini it will usher in profound technological innovations that alter the way people relate to, communicate with and learn from each other.

The full Moon in Capricorn shines its bright light on your finance sector on the 10th. This full Moon demands you cultivate more structure around budgeting and finance, and it's an ideal time in which to invest your money or work with a financial professional on identifying ways to grow it. If you plan to do this, take the opportunity to do so prior to the 18th, when Mercury turns retrograde in Leo. This Mercury retrograde period centres around spirituality and higher education for you. You may be rethinking going back to college or getting a certification at this time. This Mercury retrograde prompts you to reconnect with your spirituality as a mechanism to ground yourself when stressed.

Leo's season begins on the 22nd with a louder roar than usual, as the Sun aspects several planets within the first three days of this transit. The new Moon in Leo on the 24th has all of these transits baked into it. This new Moon ushers in a new emotional cycle around how you practise spirituality and seek out educational opportunities. If you're feeling stuck, this lunation prompts you to travel as a means of gaining a fresh perspective on the situation. July ends with Venus entering Cancer, encouraging you to nest at home or do something productive that helps soothe anxiety.

August

Best Days Overall: 14–18
Most Stressful Days Overall: 1–5
Best Days for Love: 16–20
Best Days for Money: 25–29
Best Days for Career: 22–25
Power Word: Present

Happy August, centaur! It's time to confront any hyper-critical tendencies you have towards yourself. On the 1st Venus finds tension with Saturn and Neptune. This transit typically brings to the surface that bullying voice in our heads. The purpose of this transit is not to shy away from the bully but to confront it. Stand up to your inner saboteur with compassion and love. This is a big theme of the month for you, with this transit being the first opportunity to make headway. Mercury is still retrograde for part of August, so revisiting patterns of communication is on the docket.

Speaking of patterns of communication, the full Moon for this month – occurring on the 9th in Aquarius – is heavily focused on communication for you. In addition to the ways in which you often communicate with yourself, this lunation also highlights limiting patterns of communication with others. Examples of this include censoring yourself around certain people, not actively listening as much as you actively speak or saying yes when you actually want to say no. This full Moon includes a tussle between Mars, Saturn and Neptune built into it, making you feel like you're stuck in traffic. As a result, restlessness can manifest around this date. The key is to ground yourself in the present moment and tie up any loose ends of what's currently on your plate before galloping off to complete future tasks. This absolutely pertains to the primary theme of addressing your styles of communication. Thankfully, Mercury ends its retrograde on the 11th, removing some wonkiness around communication over the next few weeks.

Jupiter, your planetary ruler, has a lovely meeting with Venus on the 12th. This transit encourages spending quality time with those you love. The new Moon in Virgo occurs on the 23rd, a day after Virgo's season formally begins. This lunation is all about legacy for Sagittarius. Uranus has a heavy influence with this new Moon, so expect the unexpected when it comes to your career or your public-facing persona. New Moons usher in new emotional cycles, so if you have goals for 2025 that you haven't yet met, lean into this Virgo energy by breaking one of those large goals into three smaller goals. Then go for it!

September

Best Days Overall: 10-14
Most Stressful Days Overall: 3-7
Best Days for Love: 26-30
Best Days for Money: 9-12
Best Days for Career: 18-21
Power Word: Sustainable

Happy September, centaur! This month is the second and final month of eclipses this year. As a reminder, eclipses are evolutionary transits that facilitate growth through shake-ups and scrutiny. The first eclipse of this month is a full Moon lunar eclipse in Pisces. Major themes of 2025 for you are your family dynamics, home and real estate. This eclipse is one of the year's noteworthy transits, making these areas of your life of central importance. This eclipse absolutely can catalyse necessary changes in family dynamics, although not in a negative way; it will simply help any interpersonal dynamic that needs to evolve for the sustainability of the relationship. Furthermore, this eclipse also applies to your physical home. If you know there are overdue repairs or inspections needed to your home, don't wait until this eclipse forces your hand. One beneficial way to positively leverage the energy of this lunation is through reorganizing your space or doing some feng shui to revitalize the space. Lastly, this eclipse has implications around real estate, so if you're planning to move, make sure you inspect every nook and cranny of the new space (as well as the contract!).

The second eclipse of the month is a new Moon solar eclipse in Virgo on the 21st. While the first eclipse revolved around your private life, the second concerns your career and public life. This eclipse will force you to confront those limiting patterns of thought or behaviour that prevent you from achieving your overarching career goals. What do you want to be remembered for, dear centaur? This eclipse desires to liberate you from the self-made blockers you've put in your way that prevent you from cementing your legacy.

Libra's season begins on the 22nd, with the Sun aspecting several planets over the next three days. This solar season spotlights the groups and communities you're immersed in; more specifically, which social circles might be holding you back (or limiting you) and which stoke your fire to achieve all that's possible. Speaking of stoking fires, Mars squares off with Pluto on the 24th, making anger a much more knee-jerk reaction. This is a week in which to be highly intentional about having a filter on how you communicate.

October

Best Days Overall: 13-16, 30-31
Most Stressful Days Overall: 7-8, 22-26
Best Days for Love: 28-31
Best Days for Money: 1-5
Best Days for Career: 4-8
Power Word: Immerse

Happy October, centaur! How are you feeling after a kinetic September? This month's cosmic weather begins on the 6th with a full Moon in Aries. For everyone, this lunation centres around making sure your emotional needs are being met. For you, Sagittarius, there's an added focus on creative self-expression, romance and recreation. This full Moon calls into question whether you're budgeting enough time to lean into your creativity, explore romance or simply allow yourself the bandwidth for play. After last month's eclipse season, the cosmic weather in October promotes lightening your load and making a concerted effort to have a good time. This full Moon also serves as a culmination of the last six months with regard to whether you've been able to effectively integrate creativity and leisure into your routine schedule in a balanced way. If not, this lunation spurs you to do so.

The cosmic weather shifts its focus to your social circles come the second week of the month. Between October 11 and the 15th Venus will form aspects with Saturn, Uranus, Neptune and Pluto. Venus also enters a new sign, Libra, on the 13th. All of these transits centre around whether the groups and organizations you're a part of support you in the ways you need in this present moment. These transits will ground you more deeply in the communities that uplift who you are now, as well as encouraging you to reconsider how much you immerse yourself among those who may subtly try to change who you are. The litmus test from these transits is whether you can be authentically yourself within these groups.

Scorpio's season begins on the 22nd, bringing your mental wellness centre-stage. A major theme of this month is striking more of a balance between work and play. The Sun transiting Scorpio also asks you how supportive the balance between solo time and social time is. Both are necessary for robust mental health, but only when in the proper ratio. Be open to being shown whether you need to make room for one more than the other this month.

November

Best Days Overall: 23-27
Most Stressful Days Overall: 8-12
Best Days for Love: 3-7
Best Days for Money: 20-24
Best Days for Career: 16-20
Power Word: Align

It's almost time, Sagittarius! November's astrology kicks off while we're still in Scorpio season, so you have a few more weeks to wait before your turn. Mars gets a running start, though, and enters Sagittarius on the 4th. Mars is the planet associated with all things kinetic, so get ready to gallop, centaur. This transit provides additional support around physical pursuits of all varieties. Be mindful that you typically lose your filter with this transit – even more than normal – and it's important to be aware of how you express yourself. The full Moon in Taurus shines brightly one day later. This lunation builds on the themes of Mars in Sagittarius, in that it centres around the physical body for you. This full Moon prompts you to pause and ask your body what it needs. Adjustments to diet, exercise and routine that nourish or support your body are particularly encouraged by the cosmic weather.

Mercury turns retrograde in your sign on the 9th. This transit absolutely has miscommunication and misinterpretation written all over it. With Mars being in your sign as well, it's super-important that you're intentionally and actively listening. Furthermore, if you're presented with a contract of any sort, it's vital that you read it carefully with the help of a third party. On the 17th the Sun, Jupiter and Saturn all harmoniously align in a beautiful grand water trine. This transit supports heartfelt connection for you, centaur, and also can make you feel a little more sentimental than normal.

The new Moon in Scorpio occurs on the 20th, centring around mental health for you. Specifically, this new Moon emphasizes the theme of Scorpio season for Sagittarius, which is about maintaining a balance between socializing and alone time. This lunation works with you if you're putting in an effort to prioritize this equilibrium in your schedule. Sagittarius' season officially begins on the 21st. Happy Birthday! It's time to dream big and set your sights on your goals for this solar revolution. Identify three words that you seek to embody this coming year and integrate them into spiritual routines or reflective time. Who do you want to evolve into over the coming year?

December

Best Days Overall: 16–20
Most Stressful Days Overall: 10–14
Best Days for Love: 1–5
Best Days for Money: 25–29
Best Days for Career: 15–19
Power Word: Abundance

Happy December, centaur! Are you having a good Sagittarius season? The cosmic weather for this month kicks off with a full Moon in Gemini, your polar sign. This lunation illuminates relationships and collaboration for you. More specifically, it's the culmination of an emotional cycle within an existing partnership or regarding your attitude towards partnership. Gemini is the communicator, and, if you've got a partner, this full Moon promotes having vulnerable conversations with your special someone. If you're single, this lunation actually reinforces marketing yourself if you're ready to mingle.

The next piece of astro-weather is a slowdown that occurs around the 9th, given Mars and Saturn finding tension with one another. This transit is especially restless for a kinetic centaur such as yourself. The purpose of this transit is to force you to tie up existing loose ends before galloping towards a horizon of new possibility. There will be plenty of time for galloping later this month! Speaking of which, the metaphorical traffic jam begins to dissipate when Mars enters Capricorn on the 15th. This transit has a light and a shadow side for Sagittarius. On one hand, this transit supports the hustle and grind to accrue wealth. However, this transit is also associated with flagrant expenditure. While being mindful not to be hyper-vigilant, definitely apply some frugality to your spending for the next six weeks.

The new Moon in your sign occurs on the 19th. This lunation supports you being your greatest cheerleader as you round out the month and plan your goals for the coming year. Knowing you, you've already got a list of goals you're seeking to accomplish. This lunation occurs two days before the start of Capricorn's season, during which you're spurred to take your ideas and actualize your first steps. Whether that's in journaling, strategizing, confiding in a close friend or something else altogether, taking these dreams from the internal to the external world is the first step towards materializing them. Venus enters Capricorn on the 24th, which further compounds the financial themes of Mars in the sign. Wishing you abundance in 2026, dear centaur!

Capricorn

♑

THE GOAT

Birthdays from
December 21
to January 19

Personality Profile

CAPRICORN AT A GLANCE

Element – Earth

Ruling Planet – Saturn
  Career Planet – Venus
  Love Planet – Moon
  Money Planet – Uranus
  Planet of Communications – Neptune
  Planet of Health and Work – Mercury
  Planet of Home and Family Life – Mars
  Planet of Spirituality and Mental Health – Jupiter

Totem – the Orator

Colours – black, indigo

Colours that promote love, romance and social harmony – puce, silver

Colour that promotes earning power – ultramarine blue

Gem – black onyx

Metal – lead

Scents – magnolia, pine, sweet pea, wintergreen

Quality – cardinal (= activity)

Qualities most needed for balance – warmth, spontaneity, a sense of fun

Strongest virtues – sense of duty, organization, perseverance, patience, ability to take the long-term view

Deepest needs – to manage, take charge and administrate

Characteristics to avoid – pessimism, depression, undue materialism and undue conservatism

Signs of greatest overall compatibility – Taurus, Virgo

Signs of greatest overall incompatibility – Aries, Cancer, Libra

Sign most helpful to career – Libra

Sign most helpful for emotional support – Aries

Sign most helpful financially – Aquarius

Sign best for marriage and/or partnerships – Cancer

Sign most helpful for creative projects – Taurus

Best Sign to have fun with – Taurus

Signs most helpful in spiritual matters – Virgo, Sagittarius

Best day of the week – Saturday

Understanding a Capricorn

The virtues of Capricorns are such that there will always be people for and against them. Many admire them, many dislike them. Why? It seems to be because of Capricorn's power urges. A well-developed Capricorn has his or her eyes set on the heights of power, prestige and authority. In the sign of Capricorn, ambition is not a fatal flaw, but rather the highest virtue.

Capricorns are not frightened by the resentment their authority may sometimes breed. In Capricorn's cool, calculated, organized mind all the dangers are already factored into the equation – the unpopularity, the animosity, the misunderstandings, even the outright slander – and a plan is always in place for dealing with these things in the most efficient way. To the Capricorn, situations that would terrify an ordinary mind are merely problems to be managed, bumps on the road to ever-growing power, effectiveness and prestige.

Some people attribute pessimism to the Capricorn sign, but this is a bit deceptive. It is true that Capricorns like to take into account the negative side of things. It is also true that they love to imagine the worst possible scenario in every undertaking. Other people might find such analyses depressing, but Capricorns only do these things so that they can formulate a way out – an escape route.

Capricorns will argue with success. They will show you that you are not doing as well as you think you are. Capricorns do this to themselves as well as to others. They do not mean to discourage you but rather to root out any impediments to your greater success. A Capricorn boss or supervisor feels that no matter how good the performance there is always room for improvement. This explains why Capricorn supervisors are difficult to handle and even infuri-ating at times. Their actions are, however, quite often effective – they can get their subordinates to improve and become better at their jobs.

Capricorn is a born manager and administrator. Leo is better at being king or queen, but Capricorn is better at being prime minister – the person actually wielding power.

Capricorn is interested in the virtues that last, in the things that will stand the test of time and trials of circumstance. Temporary fads and fashions mean little to a Capricorn – except as things to be used for profit or power. Capricorns apply this attitude to business, love, to their thinking and even to their philosophy and religion.

Finance

Capricorns generally attain wealth and they usually earn it. They are willing to work long and hard for what they want. They are quite amenable to foregoing a short-term gain in favour of long-term benefits. Financially, they come into their own later in life.

However, if Capricorns are to attain their financial goals they must shed some of their strong conservatism. Perhaps this is the least desirable trait of the Capricorn. They can resist anything new merely because it is new and untried. They are afraid of experimentation. Capricorns need to be willing to take a few risks. They should be more eager to market new products or explore different managerial techniques. Otherwise, progress will leave them behind. If necessary, Capricorns must be ready to change with the times, to discard old methods that no longer work.

Very often this experimentation will mean that Capricorns have to break with existing authority. They might even consider changing their present position or starting their own ventures. If so, they should be willing to accept all the risks and just get on with it. Only then will a Capricorn be on the road to highest financial gains.

Career and Public Image

A Capricorn's ambition and quest for power are evident. It is perhaps the most ambitious sign of the zodiac – and usually the most successful in a worldly sense. However, there are lessons Capricorns need to learn in order to fulfil their highest aspirations.

Intelligence, hard work, cool efficiency and organization will take them a certain distance, but will not carry them to the very top.

Capricorns need to cultivate their social graces, to develop a social style, along with charm and an ability to get along with people. They need to bring beauty into their lives and to cultivate the right social contacts. They must learn to wield power gracefully, so that people love them for it – a very delicate art. They also need to learn how to bring people together in order to fulfil certain objectives. In short, Capricorns require some of the gifts – the social graces – of Libra to get to the top.

Once they have learned this, Capricorns will be successful in their careers. They are ambitious hard workers who are not afraid of putting in the required time and effort. Capricorns take their time in getting the job done – in order to do it well – and they like moving up the corporate ladder slowly but surely. Being so driven by success, Capricorns are generally liked by their bosses, who respect and trust them.

Love and Relationships

Like Scorpio and Pisces, Capricorn is a difficult sign to get to know. They are deep, introverted and like to keep their own counsel. Capricorns do not like to reveal their innermost thoughts. If you are in love with a Capricorn, be patient and take your time. Little by little you will get to understand him or her.

Capricorns have a deep romantic nature, but they do not show it straightaway. They are cool, matter of fact and not especially emotional. They will often show their love in practical ways.

It takes time for a Capricorn – male or female – to fall in love. They are not the love-at-first-sight kind. If a Capricorn is involved with a Leo or Aries, these fire types will be totally mystified – to them the Capricorn will seem cold, unfeeling, unaffectionate and not very spontaneous. Of course none of this is true; it is just that Capricorn likes to take things slowly. They like to be sure of their ground before making any demonstrations of love or commitment.

Even in love affairs Capricorns are deliberate. They need more time to make decisions than is true of the other signs of the zodiac, but given this time they become just as passionate. Capricorns like a relationship to be structured, committed, well regulated, well defined, predictable and even routine. They prefer partners who are nurturers, and they in turn like to nurture their partners. This is their basic psychology. Whether such a relationship is good for them is another issue altogether. Capricorns have enough routine in their lives as it is. They might be better off in relationships that are a bit more stimulating, changeable and fluctuating.

Home and Domestic Life

The home of a Capricorn – as with a Virgo – is going to be tidy and well organized. Capricorns tend to manage their families in the same way they manage their businesses. Capricorns are often so career-driven that they find little time for the home and family. They should try to get more actively involved in their family and domestic life. Capricorns do, however, take their children very seriously and are very proud parents – particularly should their children grow up to become respected members of society.

Horoscope for 2025

Get ready to speak your truth in 2025, Capricorn. The year starts off with the north node moving into Pisces for the first time since leaving the sign in 2007. The north node brings increase and the eclipses to the communication sector of your chart. As a result, this year your totem to embody is 'the Orator'. Based on the cosmic weather of 2025, there will be potency and power behind your words. Ground yourself in what you seek to achieve and speak it into existence. Your message must be grounded in your beliefs and convictions, which will undergo a restructuring this year as well.

This year is noteworthy because it features numerous planets shifting signs for the first time in several years. One such planet is Saturn, your planetary ruler. Saturn moves into Aries for the first time in almost 29 years. Saturn in Aries brings scrutiny and discipline to home and domestic life for you. You can anticipate your responsibilities within the home to noticeably increase this year, while your physical home is also being scrutinized by this transit as well. Moving should not be a spur-of-the-moment decision this year. More on this in the home and domestic life section below.

Partnership and relationships are another area of focus with Capricorn's astrology this year. Jupiter, the planet of growth and expansion, enters Cancer, your polar sign, mid-year. In doing so, Jupiter begins to transit the relationship sector of your chart for the first time in 12 years. Although no eclipses occur in the sign of Cancer or Capricorn, your relationship sector is ruled by the Moon, so there will be additional kinetic (or frenetic) energy around relationships during the spring and autumn/fall eclipse cycles, as will be further discussed in the love and relationship section.

There are four planetary retrograde periods occurring this year between the signs of Aries and Pisces. For you, Capricorn, this links the communication sector to the home and domestic life sector of your chart. These transits will in their own way pose the question, 'How does your upbringing and current domestic life influence the ways you approach communication?' March is a kinetic month astrologically and includes two of these planetary retrogrades, in addition to two eclipses, as will be referred to throughout the sections of this horoscope and in its own monthly horoscope.

For a quarterly view of the year, the first quarter features a focus on communication and scrutiny around relationships for you, Capricorn, and the second features the energy starting to shift towards home and domestic life. The third compounds the focus on home and domestic life, and also centres around love or relationships. The final quarter of the year returns to a focus on communication, while keeping love and relationships centre-stage.

Health

(Please note that this is an astrological perspective on health and not a medical one. Any health-related symptoms should be evaluated by a qualified healthcare professional.)

The physical health sector of your chart undergoes two distinct transits this year. For the first six months of 2025 Jupiter will be completing its already ongoing transit centred around physical wellness and routines, bringing growth and expansion to this area. It's important to note that its effect equates to a 'more is more' energy. Essentially, if you have your physical wellness routines in place, Jupiter will only increase your productivity, efficiency and output. However, if you don't have such routines in place, Jupiter will only augment those behaviours that are not yielding the desired results. Thankfully, Jupiter is a planet that's easier to work with than others. Making a concerted effort to cement these routines is of great importance prior to the summer, in preparation for Uranus to begin its transit in this region of your chart.

Uranus rules instability, innovation and individuality, among many other significations. The planet takes 84 years to go around the zodiac, so its ingress into Gemini this year, moving into the physical health and routines sector of your chart, is likely a first for you in your lifetime. Uranus in this section of your chart is a wild card and promotes an 'expect the unexpected' mentality. That means it's vital to already have your exercise and dietary routines up and running in anticipation for the turbulence the planet can create. Uranus in this section of your chart also encourages the use of technology as a means of supporting your physical wellness and routines. Downloading, using or even devising your own apps that track nutrition or health data, or that provide exercise coaching, are examples of how to work with transiting Uranus.

Your health planet is Mercury, which undergoes three retrograde periods this year. Mercury's first retrograde occurs amid the spring eclipse cycle from March 15 to April 7. The second period takes place during Cancer's and Leo's seasons, from July 18 to August 11. The final retrograde period is from November 9 to November 29. These retrograde periods function like audits, and force you to rethink and re-evaluate how you approach physical wellness. The March retrograde occurs in tandem with a Venus retrograde and the eclipses, meaning that you can anticipate a toll on your body. It's critical to properly strike a balance between work, rest and play in March, given the month's frenetic cosmic weather.

Here are the specific areas of the body to focus on this year:

- Bones and joints: these are a perennial area of focus for Capricorn as it rules these parts of the body in medical astrology. Making a concerted effort to include mobility work into your routine exercise regime is strongly recommended. Consult a doctor if there are concerns around bone density issues.
- Heart: both Mercury, your health planet, and Mars undergo retrograde periods in Leo (which rules the heart) this year. Avoiding behaviours especially harmful to the heart is particularly recommended during these retrogrades. Mars will be retrograde in Leo at the start of January, and Mercury will be retrograde in Leo in July and August.
- Hips: Mars spends the majority of its retrograde in Capricorn's 7th house, which rules this part of the body in medical astrology. Being mindful to prevent tight hips, so yoga, breathwork and other forms of activation exercises are encouraged.

Love and Social Life

There's a fair amount of astrological activity centred around relationships for Capricorn in 2025. The year starts off with Mars already retrograde in Leo. On January 6 Mars dips back into Cancer, where it stays retrograde until February 23. This transit occurs in Capricorn's 7th house of partnership. Mars rules conflict and assertion, so if you've got a partner, expect this retrograde to audit how you both approach and navigate conflict. If you're single, this applies to friends and close one-on-one relationships as well. The purpose of this transit is to promote sustainability in your relationships through aligning more clearly on expressive and receptive forms of confrontation. Remember, conflict has the potential to brew intimacy if navigated properly. After Mars turns direct in February, it will stay in your relationship sector until mid-April.

Your relationship planet is the Moon, which is very busy in March with a lunar eclipse in Virgo on the 14th and a solar eclipse in Aries on the 29th. Eclipses are evolutionary transits that catalyse growth through scrutiny and shake-ups. These eclipses occur in tandem with Venus also turning retrograde. This combination of transits definitely puts your relationship's proverbial feet to the fire. Reciprocity and mutual support are the key to successfully navigating these transits, which will only exacerbate a power imbalance in the relationship dynamic. In addition, Venus retrograde is an invitation to begin to explore how you communicate. Do you censor yourself for the sake of a partner? Do you feel comfortable discussing things authentically with your partner? You will explore these questions with this retrograde and the other planetary retrogrades occurring in Pisces.

Abundant Jupiter shifts into your relationship sector in June and stays there for a year. This planet in your relationship sector reinforces the priority of attaining a feeling of 'home' within partnerships. There's an element of safety and security that 'home' affords that's highlighted while Jupiter transits this sector. Partnerships reflecting this virtue will grow abundantly during this transit. If you're single, striving to find emotional or sentimental compatibility is more heavily weighted than physical compatibility over the next 12 months. If you've got a partner, Jupiter in Cancer in your relationship sector is an ideal transit in which to live together if you don't already. Readjusting the feng shui of your home is also strongly encouraged.

Career and Finances

On the heels of two years of eclipses in your career sector, 2025 is more neutral and has no major transits occurring in this area of Capricorn's chart. Capricorn's career planet is Venus, which will be retrograde from the start of March until April 11. This occurs in tandem with the first eclipse cycle, so expect some turbulence or instability within this sphere of life during the spring. The career focus of Venus retrograde is centred for you around identifying whether or not your current career trajectory is aligned to your values. Both Capricorn and Cancer, its polar sign, are tasked this year with leveraging their value system as a barometer for the long-lasting sustainability in this area of life. For you, Capricorn, this also connects to your totem of the Orator. If you were prompted to do so, could you speak proudly about your current career? If not, what adjustments need to be made in order for this to be possible? If you're not working right now, Venus retrograde also applies to your legacy, posing the question, 'Can you articulate what your legacy will be?' Venus is the planet of values and spurs you to ensure the legacy you leave is aligned with your value system.

Capricorn's finance planet is Saturn, which oscillates to and from your home and domestic life sector. Buying or selling real estate is highlighted this summer during Saturn's transit in Aries. While not a dealbreaker, be aware that Mercury will be retrograde from July 18 to August 11, a notorious time for miscommunications and glossing over fine details. Aside from Saturn, the only planetary interaction with your finance sector comes from Pluto. Be mindful to understand what risks you are to exposed to in joint finances or investments with others. This is a year centred around communication for you, Capricorn. Proper vetting of joint ventures is always expected, but it's important to note how there's serious cosmic emphasis around doing your due diligence. Avoid joint ventures during March and September, given that the eclipse cycles are occurring in those months.

Home and Domestic Life

Home and domestic life is a prominent area of focus as a result of the number of transits occurring in this sector of Capricorn's chart, as well as the activity of Mars, this sector's planetary ruler. The year starts with Mars retrograde, which absolutely stokes the flames at home. This transit's home and domestic life themes are directly linked to those for partnership, so living with a partner only compounds them. How you approach conflict within the home is definitely up for review, and this now extends beyond partners and especially applies to parents or family members. The cornerstone piece of Mars retrograde advice when provoked is 'Respond instead of react'. Responding requires a split second of thought before coming up with a reply. This retrograde can also affect the physical home, because Mars rules this sector of your chart. New renovations should not be made during this retrograde (January 1 to February 23), but it's fine to continue with or return to projects that are already underway.

Of the planets entering this sector of your chart, Saturn and Neptune will spend the most time here and have the greatest influence. Saturn rules discipline, restriction and structure, entering this sector on May 24 and remaining until September 1, while Neptune rules compassion and rose-coloured glasses. Saturn's transit is a time when new renovation projects should take place. Neptune's influence in relation to your physical home is in carving out a sanctuary space within the home to which you can retreat when you need to recharge. This space should preferably be one that others need permission to enter. With regard to family dynamics, Saturn and Neptune scrutinize whether your emotional needs are being met by those whom you consider family. Asserting your emotional needs within the context of family is yet another way you're being tasked to embody the Orator. Both Saturn and Neptune will retrograde back into your communication sector by October, which is an ideal time to address your needs. Saturn and Neptune will more formally move – and stay – in your home and domestic life sector in 2026.

Self-improvement

This is your year to embody the Orator, so a main area of focus for self-improvement is improving how you approach communication, specifically to better assert your needs and articulate your goals. Saturn, your planetary ruler, is wrapping up its 2½-year stay in the communication sector of your chart, bringing restriction to the sector that it transits, and stimulating hard work and mastery. With Saturn oscillating in and out of this region of your chart, this is the year when you step into your power through your voice. Jupiter is your communication planet, supporting you to speak with conviction and self-assurance.

September is an especially noteworthy month for communication as there's a lunar eclipse in Pisces that strikes this sector of your chart in tandem with Saturn re-entering it on September 1. This eclipse is paired with a solar eclipse in Virgo that lights up your higher education and spirituality sector. If you don't know where to start when analysing how you approach communication, identify how its style is influenced by your spiritual philosophy. Educate yourself on how to assert yourself by reading or listening to experts in the field. This eclipse will also illuminate limiting patterns in your way of communicating with yourself. Negative self-talk should not be ignored, and analysing its root causes is vital to unlocking the potent astrological energy around embodying the Orator.

Month-by-month Forecasts

January

Best Days Overall: 8-12
Most Stressful Days Overall: 3-6, 21-22
Best Days for Love: 12-15
Best Days for Money: 17-20
Best Days for Career: 10-13
Power Word: Audit

Happy Birthday, sea goat! This year starts off in the wake of a new Moon in your sign. New Moon, new year, new sea goat. New Moons usher in new emotional cycles and your new Moon is always in line with the vibe of the new year – 'Out with the old, in with the new'. More specifically, this lunation encourages you to take time analysing what still serves you in your life and what doesn't. This month is especially relationship-oriented because Mars enters Cancer, your polar sign, on January 6. Mars has been retrograde for a bit, and its ingress into Cancer sharpens your focus on re-evaluating and redefining the dynamics of your relationships. No need to fear; relationships built on reciprocity only shine during this time.

The full Moon in Cancer on the 13th compounds this cosmic weather, serving as a spotlight on existing relationships. Given the

Moon's association with the regulation of feelings, definitely book-mark this week to experience more emotions. As mentioned above, these transits absolutely will illuminate relationships predicated on mutual support. On the flip side of the coin, these transits will also highlight where you might be pouring more into someone else's cup than they are pouring into yours. Mars' retrogrades require the most methodical communication. If you do happen to get into a confrontation, approach any necessary conversations with compassion and a heavy dose of active listening as well. A good day to have these conversations could be the 19th, when Venus is conjunct to Saturn, your planetary ruler.

The 19th is also the start of Aquarius' season, your annual solici-tation to fix a keen eye on your budget and streams of income. To be honest it's perfect timing, given that it's the first month of the year. This Aquarius season features the Sun meeting up with Pluto just two days later in your house of finances. Pluto is all about shedding, burying and unearthing. This transit therefore spurs you to really excavate all the places from which your money comes and goes. Pluto also rules buried treasure, so you may be surprised by what you find, with the new Moon in Aquarius on the 29th supporting your metaphorical archaeology. This lunation is a perfect time to create new streams of income if you've been intend-ing to do so.

February

Best Days Overall: 6-10
Most Stressful Days Overall: 13-17
Best Days for Love: 23-26
Best Days for Money: 24-27
Best Days for Career: 1-3
Power Word: Inspect

Happy February, Capricorn! The first few days of this month feature two sets of planets in harmonious alignment with one another. First up on February 1 is Venus' meeting with Neptune. This tran-sit calls upon you to take action towards nourishing your spirit.

Give yourself the opportunity to be immersed in nature or spend time in your local community this weekend. Mercury and Jupiter work well with each other when they align on the 3rd in a transit that is heavily communication-oriented. Public speaking and writing are two examples of activities that get powered up by this transit. The Sun follows suit on the 9th, meeting up with Mercury and further supporting any conversations you need to have.

February 12 features a significant full Moon in Leo. This lunation is at odds with Uranus, the planet of destabilization and liberation. For everyone, this transit galvanizes roaring your truth, but for you, sea goat, this is also a financial transit. The theme of financial independence is especially highlighted by this full Moon. Full Moons are emotional, so if you've been striving towards financial independence, this lunation will tug on those heart strings a bit. Last month had a financial focus to it and this full Moon is a check-in on how carefully you've been following your budget.

On February 23 Mars finally turns direct and its retrograde is over. This is especially harmonious for Capricorn, as Mars is currently in your polar sign, Cancer. The magnifying glass on relationship dynamics that were being heavily scrutinized during the retrograde dulls in intensity over the next several weeks. That doesn't mean it disappears, but rather it clears the pathway for the next dynamic steps to be made. Mars rules drive, ambition and assertion, so turning direct puts some wind in your sails towards achieving your 2025 goals.

Pisces' season begins on the 18th and shines a spotlight on how directly you communicate. Do you censor yourself for the sake of others or confidently speak your truth? Spend time over this solar season taking a good look at your pattern of behaviour in this regard. The new Moon in Pisces on the 27th centres around this question and offers you the opportunity to usher in a new approach to how you communicate.

March

Best Days Overall: 9-14
Most Stressful Days Overall: 25-30
Best Days for Love: 22-26
Best Days for Money: 3-8
Best Days for Career: 12-14
Power Word: Familial

There is so much astrology to discuss, Capricorn, so let's jump right into it! The first day of the month starts off with Venus turning retrograde in Aries. Venus' retrogrades are always inventories of our relationships. For you, this retrograde revolves around relationships within your home and with family. Venus rules self-worth and our values, so expect this retrograde to highlight how home life or family dynamics influence these things. This Venus retrograde is an ideal time to prioritize quality time at home and with loved ones.

On March 14 the first eclipse of 2025 occurs in Virgo. Eclipses are evolutionary transits that promote growth through tension and shake-ups. This eclipse has all the bearings of a transit that could precipitate a much-needed trip for the purpose of reflection. For Capricorn, there's a heavy spiritual component to this lunation. Connected to this theme is the idea that sometimes we need to remove ourselves from our daily routine and travel in order to gain important insights we wouldn't be able to ascertain otherwise. Mercury mimics Venus the following day by turning retrograde in Aries. This transit compounds the influence of Venus retrograde and adds additional scrutiny around how communication - or the lack thereof - affects family or home dynamics. It's important both to not leave things unsaid at this time and also - equally imperative - to approach conversations with loved ones as methodically as possible. This eclipse season with two retrogrades will have everyone activated.

Aries' season begins on March 20, with the second eclipse of the month occurring on the 29th in Aries and Neptune entering the sign for the first time in your lifetime on the 30th. So much Aries energy! Aries' season reminds you of your importance within the structure of your household and family. Whether you realize it or not, you *are* influential. This power is heightened by the solar eclipse in Aries on the 29th. The phrase 'With great power comes great responsibility' comes to mind. Whether it's with family, other loved ones or those you live with, the astrology of March centres around how you impact others in these spaces. The beginning of this Neptune transit demands that you evaluate how your spirituality is influenced by home and family.

April

Best Days Overall: 2–6
Most Stressful Days Overall: 23–27
Best Days for Love: 11–15
Best Days for Money: 7–10
Best Days for Career: 11–15
Power Word: Productivity

Happy April, sea goat! The first week of April's astrology features multiple soft and supportive transits. Saturn, your planetary ruler, forms harmonious aspects with Uranus on the 4th and Mars on the 5th. This is super-productive energy to lean into. Saturn rules structure, so when it aligns with the planet that rules breakthroughs (Uranus) and the planet that rules momentum (Mars), you can get a lot done! If you're looking for an ideal day to sign contracts and really get the proverbial ball rolling, wait until after the 7th if possible because Mercury will end its retrograde on that date.

On April 12 there's a full Moon in Libra, your fellow cardinal sign. The full Moon in Libra always has a career focus for Capricorn. That being said, this full Moon is special because Venus ends its retrograde on this day as well. The day of the full Moon itself is not an ideal day for making career moves, considering that Venus is essentially not moving. If you're motivated to make such moves, plan for a day over the next week since you'll still be in the wake of the lunation and only then will Venus start moving faster. Libra is a heavily relational sign, and this full Moon revolves around the relationships you've cultivated and currently navigate within your career. Take it upon yourself to express gratitude to those co-workers or business collaborators who support you day in, day out.

On April 19 the Sun enters Taurus. Taurus season is a romantic and creative time of year for Capricorn, so make sure to carve out time for these two areas of your life. Taurus is a security-oriented sign, so lean into creative self-expression as a form of grounding. Remember, periods of rest or play are as equally important to productivity as work time. The last week of the month gets a little bumpy, with Mars opposing Pluto on the 27th. Mars opposite Pluto can unearth buried frustrations. This transit's goal is to promote growth in relationships through resolving long-standing issues. If you find yourself caught up in the heat of this transit, do your best to temper the flames through responding instead of reacting. Fortunately, the 27th features a new Moon in Taurus, which is a lovely lunation centred around cultivating security and abundance. The 28th or 29th are ideal days to schedule something romantic or to take the day off from excessive working to recharge.

May

Best Days Overall: 20–25
Most Stressful Days Overall: 13–18
Best Days for Love: 2–6
Best Days for Money: 7–10
Best Days for Career: 8–12
Power Word: Structure

It's May, Capricorn! May's astrology begins on the 2nd when Venus conjoins with Neptune in Aries for the first time in your lifetime. This transit is light and dreamy, and for Capricorn it centres on home and family dynamics. It's an ideal transit to nest at home with loved ones or take advantage of this energy by doing some belated spring cleaning. Venus harmoniously aligns with Pluto on the 6th, a transit that promotes physical transformation for you, Capricorn. This simple transit reminds us that sometimes all it takes to change our outlook on life is switching things up. Get a new haircut, put on a fun outfit or take a unique exercise class.

On May 12 the full Moon in Scorpio occurs on the same day that Mercury squares off with Pluto. This full Moon centres on culminations within groups of friends, communities and organizations for Capricorn. If you've become involved in a new organization or group in the last six months, this full Moon is a turning point in your acceptance within the community. As mentioned, this full Moon is accompanied by a tense connection between Mercury and Pluto. This transit is investigative in nature, so a productive way to channel this energy is through really getting to know friends by discussing topics you haven't explored together. Mercury–Pluto aspects put everyone on edge, so be mindful not to overstep the mark.

Saturn enters Aries on May 24 for the first time since leaving the sign in 1999. Saturn in Aries scrutinizes the health and sustainability of your home and of the dynamics at play there. If you know you need to make any form of repairs to your physical home, or the layout of your living spaces are due for some much-needed feng shui, now is the time. Saturn bolsters sustainable structures, whether they be actual physical structures or the integrity of a relationship. Gemini's season begins on May 20 and the new Moon follows suit on the 26. The new Moon in Gemini is an analytical new Moon that's centred around physical wellness for Capricorn. Take a moment to check in with your body and ask what it needs. This is the time to ensure you're consistently hydrating, nourishing yourself and moving your body when possible.

June

Best Days Overall: 5–6, 27–30
Most Stressful Days Overall: 20–25
Best Days for Love: 6–9
Best Days for Money: 5–8
Best Days for Career: 10–14
Power Word: Relational

Hi, Capricorn! June's astrology features not one, not two, but three planets entering new signs at the start of the month. First up is Venus entering Taurus on the 6th. Venus adores being in Taurus, and brings a glow to your creative and romantic life. This is a genial transit, encouraging you to lean in to creative self-expression when you're feeling stifled. Put a pin in that recommendation for later. On the 8th and 9th, Mercury and Jupiter enter Cancer, and Jupiter spends close to 12 months in this sign, the first time in 12 years that the gas giant has entered your polar sign.

This transit represents the beginning of a new cycle around partnership. How has partnership in your life grown and evolved over the last 12 years? What have you learned from this cycle? Now is a turning-of-the-chapter moment for you with relationships. If you're in a happy relationship, don't worry, as Jupiter will only work to improve it. Basically, Jupiter makes things bigger, so aspects of the dynamic you want to address in order to promote growth will rise to the surface to address.

The full Moon in Sagittarius is on the 11th. Sagittarius is a kinetic fire sign associated with truth and freedom, and this full Moon is financial for you, illuminating your spending habits and budget practices over the last six months. Don't shy away from really examining what you see. This full Moon supports diversifying your financial portfolio, if you have one. Sagittarius is highly spontaneous, so watch out for excessive sudden spending around this date.

On June 20 the Sun joins Mercury and Jupiter by entering Cancer. There's a confluence of energy building around relationships now. It's important to note that this Cancer season does start off a little turbulently, given that the Sun quickly squares off with Saturn and Neptune on the 22nd and 23rd. This combination of transits plays on conflating productivity with worth, and you might feel overwhelmed in the face of accomplishing tasks or managing responsibilities. As recommended above, focus on what you can control and lean in to grounding practices, such as your favourite form of creative self-expression. Moreover, break up large tasks into smaller ones and celebrate each victory, regardless of how seemingly insubstantial it is.

July

Best Days Overall: 24–28
Most Stressful Days Overall: 13–17
Best Days for Love: 20–24
Best Days for Money: 8–12
Best Days for Career: 3–7
Power Word: Empower

Happy July, Capricorn! July's cosmic weather begins with several harmonious Venus transits as Venus wraps up its time in Taurus and enters Gemini. A big focus of this first week is on physical fitness and holistic wellness. Be more intentional this week about what you eat and how you nurture your body. Venus in Gemini is a social transit, so find fun ways to exercise or support your body with others. Uranus makes a major shift into Gemini after staying continuously in Taurus since 2019. Uranus in Gemini is a game-changing transit for society that will lead to major technological innovations that change how we communicate with and relate to one another. Uranus will be in Gemini until November, before concretely entering Gemini next year.

Howl! It's your full Moon, sea goat, on the 10th. This full Moon in Capricorn centres around how you communicate with and generally treat yourself. This full Moon forces you to confront the ways you're your own biggest critic. Make an effort to uplift yourself and give yourself some much-deserved TLC. This is especially important because Mercury turns retrograde in Leo on the 18th.

Mercury will be transiting the anxiety sector of Capricorn's chart, forcing you to identify the root causes of any long-standing fears or anxieties. The purpose of this transit is to remedy these root causes for long-lasting emotional regulation. Given that Mercury is in Leo, owning and taking pride in your individuality and authenticity are strongly recommended.

Leo's season begins on the 22nd, with the new Moon following a couple of days later. This new Moon has several aspects built into the lunation chart, meaning there's a ton of kinetic energy. This lunation builds on the sentiment to self-empower around what makes you uniquely you, so take time to honour your authenticity this week. The month ends with Venus entering Cancer, your polar sign. Venus in Cancer supports quiet time at home with a special someone. This is a cuddly transit for you, Capricorn, which prompts you to soften up. If you're single, this transit also supports re-decorating to make your home feel more welcoming.

August

Best Days Overall: 12–16
Most Stressful Days Overall: 5–9
Best Days for Love: 23–26
Best Days for Money: 29–31
Best Days for Career: 11–15
Power Word: Human

Hi, sea goat! August's astrology centres around confronting a perfectionist mindset and becoming more comfortable with human error. On the 1st Venus tensely aspects both Saturn and Neptune. This transit is the first of several transits this month encouraging you to cut yourself some slack, as it can often heighten your inner critic in order to force you to confront this voice with love. Mars enters Libra on the 6th, a transit that typically revs Capricorn's engine around making career moves, although these are delayed by a couple of weeks thanks once again to Saturn and Neptune.

Coupled with the full Moon in Aquarius on the 9th, Mars finds tension with both Saturn and Neptune. This transit actually has road rage vibes or the feeling of being stuck in traffic. For Capricorn, a sense of restlessness also revolves around career and finances. This full Moon will illuminate precisely where frustration abounds for you with finances and how you make money, a feeling that will likely spill over into how you regard your career. The good news is that Mercury ends its retrograde on the 11th, opening the door for productive conversations after this date. And in more good news, Venus harmoniously conjoins with Jupiter on the 12th. This transit brings a boost to partnership for Capricorn. Plan on spending the day with your special someone, or put yourself out there if you're single. This transit also applies to collaborations as well.

On the 22nd it's officially Virgo season, which begins with a potent new Moon on the 23rd. This new Moon spurs you to break away from belief systems that no longer serve you. Specifically, this lunation will strongly promote ushering in a new cycle focused on an organic and authentic form of spirituality. Furthermore, don't be surprised if coupled with this is a surprise trip or sudden plans for a far-flung voyage. Sometimes the best way to gain a new perspective is through uprooting ourselves from our daily hustle and bustle. The month ends with one last transit confronting you with your inner critic. Venus plays tug of war with Pluto on the 27th, a transit that can inspire hyper-vigilance, especially around finances for Capricorn. Allow this transit to reveal how your relationship with money influences how you approach your interpersonal relationships.

September

Best Days Overall: 2-3, 13-16
Most Stressful Days Overall: 6-9, 24-25
Best Days for Love: 19-23
Best Days for Money: 15-19
Best Days for Career: 17-21
Power Word: Watershed

It's eclipse season, sea goat! As a reminder, eclipses are evolutionary transits that promote growth through destabilization and scrutiny. The first eclipse of the month occurs on the 7th and is a full
Moon lunar eclipse in Pisces, comprising an examination around
your relationship to communication. More specifically, this lunation spotlights whether you censor yourself and don't feel comfortable communicating 100 per cent authentically in all of your
interpersonal relationships. Are there specific people or specific
environments with whom or in which you find yourself especially
censoring yourself? This eclipse will likely create some tension in
order to catalyse long-lasting sustainable change. Another aspect
of communication this eclipse will highlight is how you communicate during conflict and whether this serves your highest good.
Conflict is messy, of course, but when handled sensitively it can
actually brew profound intimacy with the other person in the
dynamic. Allow this lunation to show you in what ways you can
mature when it comes to handling conflict.

The second eclipse of September occurs on the 21st and is a new
Moon solar eclipse in Virgo. This is the second new Moon in Virgo
and builds off the theme of last month's new Moon. It's a watershed transit revolving around liberating yourself from outdated
belief system that no longer serve you, while also centring around
teaching and learning. If you've been meaning to get involved in
some form of education from either the teacher/coach or student
perspective, this eclipse will spur you to do so.

Libra's season begins on the 22nd, with the Sun aspecting
several planets over the next three days. Libra season is all about
confronting the ways in which you might limit your ability to reach

the next level in your career or pursue what you're really passionate about. More will be illuminated in this regard with the new Moon in Libra next month. In the meantime be open to being shown the root causes for any unconscious blockers you may be putting in your own path. The cosmic weather for September ends with Mars squaring off with Pluto on the 24th, making everyone a little extra crabby. Navigate the first week of Libra season with compassion for yourself and those around you.

October

Best Days Overall: 25-30
Most Stressful Days Overall: 11-16
Best Days for Love: 20-23
Best Days for Money: 2-6
Best Days for Career: 28-31
Power Word: Long-term

Happy October, sea goat! This month's cosmic weather begins on the 6th with the full Moon in Aries. This lunation is meaningful because it functions as a noteworthy part in the emotional cycle ushered in by the new Moon lunar eclipse in Aries at the end of March. 'With great power comes great responsibility' was the phrase used to describe that lunation for you, and it's echoed this month. This full Moon spotlights your familial relationships, home life and real estate. More specifically, this transit prompts you to advocate for your emotional needs at home and with family.

The cosmic weather then starts to shift towards public life, career and legacy. Between the 11th and the 15th Venus will aspect every planet from Saturn to Pluto, and enter Libra on the 13th. The astrology of this week concerns how your self-esteem or value systems influence your long-term career goals. What do you want to be remembered for, Capricorn? The new Moon in Libra on the 21st is a great transit in which to take actionable steps in the direction of your answer to this question. This new Moon forces you to confront any limiting thoughts or mindsets you have around what you think is possible to achieve. The first step towards seeing it is believing it, dear sea goat!

Scorpio's season takes off on the 22nd, with the Sun immediately aspecting Uranus and Pluto over the following two days. This transit encourages enmeshing yourself in your social circles, which allow you to be 100 per cent authentically yourself. If you feel as though you have to put up a front or don a mask in certain groups, this solar season calls for you to re-evaluate how deeply you should be immersing yourself in such an environment. The month ends with a productive Mars–Jupiter connection. Capricorn is represented as a sea goat who can look to the summit of a mountain or the bottom of the ocean knowing that it might take many years of hard work, but it'll get there. This transit is a great boost in motivation towards reaching the top of one of the many mountains you're climbing.

November

Best Days Overall: 22–26
Most Stressful Days Overall: 7–11
Best Days for Love: 17–21
Best Days for Money: 20–24
Best Days for Career: 25–29
Power Word: Redefine

Happy November, Capricorn! Mental health and wellness are the decisive features for November. November's cosmic weather begins on the 4th with Mars moving into fiery Sagittarius, where it stays for the entire month. The two sides of a Mars transit are an influx of kinetic energy and the potential for irritation. For you, this transit revolves around mental health and wellness. As a result, it's hyper-important you keep your schedule balanced. This transit will push you to strike more of an equilibrium between solo time and social time. The full Moon in Taurus follows the next day, illuminating creativity and romance in your life. This is a great transit for you to ground yourself in your favourite form of creative self-expression or even work on monetizing this passion. Moreover, this lunation pushes you to carve out time around this date for play or pleasure.

For the last time in 2025 Mercury turns retrograde on the 9th, in Sagittarius. Mercury is co-present with Mars in Sagittarius and only compounds the focus on your mental wellness. As a result, it's paramount to not overcommit or exert yourself this month. Mercury retrogrades motivate us to embody 're-' words such as 'reflect' and 'redefine'. For you, sea goat, this retrograde spurs you to redefine your relationship with your mind, either through confronting your tendency to overthink or your propensity to be hyper-critical. It could also be helpful for you to address these habits through calming behaviours like breathwork and mindfulness.

The new Moon in Scorpio occurs on the 20th and is a social transit for Capricorn. If you've been meaning to get involved with a new organization or community, this is the ideal transit in which to do so. This lunation encourages new beginnings within your existing social circles as well, so be open to how you may deepen your involvement in these groups over the next few weeks. Sagittarius' season begins on the 21st. This solar season is visionary and inspires you to contemplate your goals for 2026. For you, Capricorn, you'd especially benefit from carving out alone time so you can reflect on all you've accomplished this year and consider where you want to go from here.

December

Best Days Overall: 1-2, 24-30
Most Stressful Days Overall: 5-10, 15-16
Best Days for Love: 19-22
Best Days for Money: 2-6
Best Days for Career: 20-24
Power Word: Consistency

It's almost your season, Capricorn, but first there's some cosmic weather we must discuss. The full Moon in Gemini is bright and full on the 4th. This lunation illuminates your relationship with your physical body, especially how it's evolved over the last six months. One of the lessons of Gemini is that we all embody duality. This full Moon isn't promoting hyper-vigilance in moderating what you eat or how you work out. Rather, it's supporting a healthy mix of discipline and pleasure in your routines. This full Moon pairs with the new Moon in Gemini in asking your body what it needs. Sagittarius season is a time associated with indulgence, so make sure to enjoy it, while also striving to achieve balance through your routines.

Saturn, your planetary ruler, contributes to a bit of a slowdown around the 9th when Mars squares off with it. This transit is frustrating and typically comes with a hefty dose of restlessness. The purpose of this transit is to force you to internalize the idea that your worth isn't determined by your productivity. Cut yourself some slack, sea goat! Thankfully, after this transit fades, Mars enters your sign, which really revs your engine. The next six weeks kick into high gear, especially with your solar return (your birthday) right around the corner. Do more than just have good intentions to make the most of this energy. For example, identify three words you seek to embody this coming year. Integrate these words into your spiritual routines, journal about them or compose a mantra based on them that you can repeat to yourself next year. Also explore why you've chosen these words and how this relates to your overarching goals for 2026.

The Sagittarius new Moon occurs on the 19th and centres around mental wellness for you, sea goat. This lunation reminds you that establishing homeostasis within your body is actually key to calming the mind. Remember that this month is all about striking a balance. Capricorn's season begins on the 21st and Venus enters your sign three days later. Capricorn is the sea goat, so step into 2026 knowing that it may take consistency, routine and grit, but you'll get to the top of any mountain or the bottom of any ocean in your own time.

Aquarius

~~~

THE WATER-BEARER

Birthdays from
January 20
to February 18

Personality Profile

AQUARIUS AT A GLANCE

Element – Air

Ruling Planet – Uranus
  Career Planet – Pluto
  Love Planet – Sun
  Money Planet – Neptune
  Planet of Health and Work – Moon
  Planet of Home and Family Life – Venus
  Planet of Spirituality and Mental Health – Saturn

Totem – the Seeker

Colours – electric blue, grey, ultramarine blue

Colours that promote love, romance and social harmony – gold, orange

Colour that promotes earning power – aqua

Gems – black pearl, obsidian, opal, sapphire

Metal – lead

Scents – azalea, gardenia

Quality – fixed (= stability)

Qualities most needed for balance – warmth, feeling and emotion

Strongest virtues – great intellectual power, the ability to communicate and to form and understand abstract concepts, love for the new and avant-garde

Deepest needs – to know and to bring in the new

Characteristics to avoid – coldness, rebelliousness for its own sake, fixed ideas

Signs of greatest overall compatibility – Gemini, Libra

Signs of greatest overall incompatibility – Taurus, Leo, Scorpio

Sign most helpful to career – Scorpio

Sign most helpful for emotional support – Taurus

Sign most helpful financially – Pisces

Sign best for marriage and/or partnerships – Leo

Sign most helpful for creative projects – Gemini

Best Sign to have fun with – Gemini

Signs most helpful in spiritual matters – Libra, Capricorn

Best day of the week – Saturday

Understanding an Aquarius

In the Aquarius-born, intellectual faculties are perhaps the most highly developed of any sign in the zodiac. Aquarians are clear, scientific thinkers. They have the ability to think abstractly and to formulate laws, theories and clear concepts from masses of observed facts. Geminis might be very good at gathering information, but Aquarians take this a step further, excelling at interpreting the information gathered.

Practical people – men and women of the world – mistakenly consider abstract thinking as impractical. It is true that the realm of abstract thought takes us out of the physical world, but the discoveries made in this realm generally end up having tremendous practical consequences. All real scientific inventions and breakthroughs come from this abstract realm.

Aquarians, more so than most, are ideally suited to explore these abstract dimensions. Those who have explored these regions know that there is little feeling or emotion there. In fact, emotions are a hindrance to functioning in these dimensions; thus Aquarians seem – at times – cold and emotionless to others. It is not that Aquarians haven't got feelings and deep emotions, it is just that too much feeling clouds their ability to think and invent. The concept of 'too much feeling' cannot be tolerated or even understood by some of the other signs. Nevertheless, this Aquarian objectivity is ideal for science, communication and friendship.

Aquarians are very friendly people, but they do not make a big show about it. They do the right thing by their friends, even if sometimes they do it without passion or excitement.

Aquarians have a deep passion for clear thinking. Second in importance, but related, is their passion for breaking with the establishment and traditional authority. Aquarians delight in this, because for them rebellion is like a great game or challenge. Very often they will rebel strictly for the fun of rebelling, regardless of whether the authority they defy is right or wrong. Right or wrong has little to do with the rebellious actions of an Aquarian, because to a true Aquarian authority and power must be challenged as a matter of principle.

Where Capricorn or Taurus will err on the side of tradition and the status quo, an Aquarian will err on the side of the new. Without this virtue it is doubtful whether any progress would be made in the world. The conservative-minded would obstruct progress. Originality and invention imply an ability to break barriers; every new discovery represents the toppling of an impediment to thought. Aquarians are very interested in breaking barriers and making walls tumble – scientifically, socially and politically. Other zodiac signs, such as Capricorn, also have scientific talents. But Aquarians are particularly excellent in the social sciences and humanities.

Finance

In financial matters Aquarians tend to be idealistic and humanitarian – to the point of self-sacrifice. They are usually generous contributors to social and political causes. When they contribute it differs from when a Capricorn or Taurus contributes. A Capricorn or Taurus may expect some favour or return for a gift; an Aquarian contributes selflessly.

Aquarians tend to be as cool and rational about money as they are about most things in life. Money is something they need and they set about acquiring it scientifically. No need for fuss; they get on with it in the most rational and scientific ways available.

Money to the Aquarian is especially nice for what it can do, not for the status it may bring (as is the case for other signs). Aquarians are neither big spenders nor penny-pinchers and use their finances in practical ways, for example to facilitate progress for themselves, their families, or even for strangers.

However, if Aquarians want to reach their fullest financial potential they will have to explore their intuitive nature. If they follow only their financial theories – or what they believe to be theoretically correct – they may suffer some losses and disappointments. Instead, Aquarians should call on their intuition, which knows without thinking. For Aquarians, intuition is the short-cut to financial success.

Career and Public Image

Aquarians like to be perceived not only as the breakers of barriers but also as the transformers of society and the world. They long to be seen in this light and to play this role. They also look up to and respect other people in this position and even expect their superiors to act this way.

Aquarians prefer jobs that have a bit of idealism attached to them – careers with a philosophical basis. Aquarians need to be creative at work, to have access to new techniques and methods. They like to keep busy and enjoy getting down to business straightaway, without wasting any time. They are often the quickest workers and usually have suggestions for improvements that will benefit their employers. Aquarians are also very helpful with their co-workers and welcome responsibility, preferring this to having to take orders from others.

If Aquarians want to reach their highest career goals they have to develop more emotional sensitivity, depth of feeling and passion. They need to learn to narrow their focus on the essentials and concentrate more on the job in hand. Aquarians need 'a fire in the belly' – a consuming passion and desire – in order to rise to the very top. Once this passion exists they will succeed easily in whatever they attempt.

Love and Relationships

Aquarians are good at friendships, but a bit weak when it comes to love. Of course they fall in love, but their lovers always get the impression that they are more best friends than paramours.

Like Capricorns, they are cool customers. They are not prone to displays of passion or to outward demonstrations of their affections. In fact, they feel uncomfortable when their other half hugs and touches them too much. This does not mean that they do not love their partners. They do, only they show it in other ways. Curiously enough, in relationships they tend to attract the very things that they feel uncomfortable with. They seem to attract hot, passionate, romantic, demonstrative people. Perhaps they know instinctively that these people have qualities they lack and so seek them out. In any event, these relationships do seem to work, Aquarian coolness calming the more passionate partner while the fires of passion warm the cold-blooded Aquarius.

The qualities Aquarians need to develop in their love life are warmth, generosity, passion and fun. Aquarians love relationships of the mind. Here they excel. If the intellectual factor is missing in a relationship an Aquarian will soon become bored or feel unfulfilled.

Home and Domestic Life

In family and domestic matters Aquarians can have a tendency to be too non-conformist, changeable and unstable. They are as willing to break the barriers of family constraints as they are those of other areas of life.

Even so, Aquarians are very sociable people. They like to have a nice home where they can entertain family and friends. Their house is usually decorated in a modern style and full of state-of-the-art appliances and gadgets – an environment Aquarians find absolutely necessary.

If their home life is to be healthy and fulfilling Aquarians need to inject it with a quality of stability – yes, even some conservatism. They need at least one area of life to be enduring and steady; this area is usually their home and family life.

Venus, the generic planet of love, rules the Aquarian's 4th solar house of home and family, which means that when it comes to the family and child-rearing, theories, cool thinking and intellect are not always enough. Aquarians need to bring love into the equation in order to have a great domestic life.

Horoscope for 2025

What do you seek, water-bearer? The astrology of 2025 continually prompts you to explore the various areas of your life with a mindset fixed on growth. In January the north and south nodes move into your finance sectors. Seeking financial abundance is top of your mind this year as the nodes bring the eclipses to this area of life. Eclipses are evolutionary transits that stimulate growth through scrutiny and shake-ups, and they will be further discussed in subsequent sections of this horoscope.

This is an important year astrologically, as Saturn, Uranus and Neptune will all be changing signs. When slow-moving planets like these change signs, societal shifts take place. One such example is Uranus, which moves into Gemini for the first time since leaving the sign 76 years ago. Uranus entering Gemini ushers in the creation of technological innovations that will greatly impact the ways we communicate with and learn from one another. From a modern astrological perspective, Uranus is your planetary ruler, so anticipate this shift to greatly influence how you approach embodying 'the Seeker'.

Embodying the Seeker means being open to learning, and 2025 features four planetary retrograde periods starting in your communication and learning sector. These periods will confront you with re-evaluating how you approach communication with yourself and others, and they will be discussed in detail later in this horoscope. Mars rules all things related to conflict, and although it won't begin its retrograde in your communication sector, it will impact this area of life for you.

Aside from finances and communication, exploring long-standing anxieties or fears is another way the astrology of 2025 prompts you to embody the Seeker. Health and wellness also get put under the proverbial magnifying glass mid-year when Jupiter, the planet of growth and expansion, enters Aquarius' physical health sector in June. Mars' retrograde at the start of the year in this sector also contributes to this being an important topic, which will be elaborated upon in the health section below.

For a quarterly view of this year, the first quarter features a focus on finances and health, while in the second the cosmic focus moves towards communication, with finances remaining highly relevant. The third quarter concentrates particularly on communication and learning, with some focus on mental health as well, and the final quarter of the year returns the primary spotlight to finances, while also maintaining an inventory of physical wellness routines.

Health

(Please note that this is an astrological perspective on health and not a medical one. Any health-related symptoms should be evaluated by a qualified healthcare professional.)

This area of life is heavily emphasized by the astrology of this year. Starting with physical health, the year begins with Mars already retrograde in Leo, your polar sign. On January 6, Mars dips back into the physical health sector of your chart. Mars stays retrograde in this sector until February 23 and occupies the sector until April 18. Any existing health concerns you may have must be addressed by a medical professional, given Mars' inflammatory properties. After Mars turns direct, the red planet in this sector of your chart means it will be well worthwhile to establish routines around exercise and movement, while adopting newfound hobbies related to sports is also a signification of Mars occupying this area of your chart.

Growing and expanding healthy routines is a major component of this year once Jupiter enters your physical health sector in June. Jupiter takes 12 years to go around the zodiac, and this therefore serves as the beginning of a new 12-year cycle around how you actively support your physical health. Jupiter magnifies existing behaviours and outcomes, so you are greatly encouraged to already have your routines in place prior to its ingress into this sector in June. Jupiter in Cancer also supports making adjustments to your home that support your holistic health. Examples of this include installing exercise equipment, organizing your kitchen to accommodate a healthier diet and making adjustments to your bedroom to better support a good night's sleep.

In addition to physical health, the astrology of this year also focuses on your mental health and wellness. More specifically, both eclipse seasons include themes of addressing and combating fears or anxieties. March's eclipse season is noteworthy as Mercury, the planet that rules the anxiety sector for Aquarius, turns retrograde in tandem with the spring eclipses. This eclipse season spurs you to unearth the root causes of long-standing fears or anxieties – only by doing so can you maintain consistent long-term emotional regulation. Overarchingly, the south node transits the anxiety sector of your chart all year, promoting the shedding of fears or mindsets that no longer serve you.

Here are the specific areas of the body to focus on this year:

- Shins, calves and ankles: these parts of the body are a perennial area of focus as Aquarius rules them in medical astrology. Given the confluence of transits in your physical health sector, consistently doing your mobility exercises and stretching is strongly suggested.
- Belly and liver: Mars will be retrograde in Aquarius' 6th house, which rules these parts of the body. Mars occupies this area for Aquarius for over six months this year. Be mindful around carrying tension in your abdomen.
- Brain: regulating your nervous system is a primary area of focus for health as a result of how the eclipses fall this year. Addressing dissociative behaviours or harmful coping behaviours is vital if you are to leverage the transformational astrology of this year.

Love and Social Life

Social life and partnership are not as emphasized as other areas of life this year. That being said, there are some relevant transits that impact them. Jupiter begins the year by transiting Aquarius' pleasure sector, broadening the ways you creatively self-express and approach recreation. Jupiter is your social life planet and will still be in Gemini during this period, supporting you through utilizing your passions as a means of networking with others. The arts and entertainment are also supported by this transit, and because Jupiter rules beliefs and convictions, activity in these areas will be more sustainable if aligned with core spiritual values.

Your love planet is technically a luminary, the Sun, and it has an interesting year navigating its aspects with the slower-moving planets. Typically, these slower-moving planets are spread out across various degrees of various signs, but this year they will be occupying similar or the same degrees of their signs for extended periods of time. This means that the Sun undergoes spurts of heavy activity followed by periods of very limited activity. As a result you should anticipate noticeable peaks and troughs in your relationships this year. Every planet that can turn retrograde will do so at some point in 2025, so it's especially important to align with partners on communication. Embodying the Seeker means getting curious about the most conducive ways to approach partnership.

Career and Finances

As mentioned at the start of this horoscope, financial matters are a major theme for Aquarius this year. Of the four planetary retrogrades that occur in your finance sector in 2025, two of them occur in March with the eclipses. Mercury and Venus both turn retrograde in March, entering your finance sector during the last week of the month. Mercury is traditionally associated with commerce, making this a time to review the value of your investments and possibly even reallocate resources accordingly. The spring and autumn/fall are both times where debts, taxes and inheritances are being scrutinized. The lunar eclipse in Virgo on March 14 and the solar eclipse in Virgo on September 21 are two transits in particular that precisely correlate with this realm of financial matters. Be mindful around anything in the legal sphere involving taxes and inheritances. It's ill-advised to borrow money or acquire debts that are unnecessary during both eclipse seasons.

Buoyant Jupiter is your finance planet and at the start of June it enters Cancer, one of its favourite signs to be in. Jupiter in Cancer indicates there's wealth to be accrued in real estate or within family concerns. If you're pursuing real estate as a source of income, an ideal time to do so would be after Jupiter enters Cancer. More specifically, Saturn leaves your finance sector from May 24 to September 1, so sometime over the summer between June and the end of August. Jupiter in Cancer also supports building streams of income aligned with the family business or in collaboration with family members.

Saturn and Neptune both wrap up extended stays in your finance sector. Saturn has been occupying your finance sector since March 2023 and exits for the summer before its retrograde period has the planet returning one more time. Saturn rules restriction, discipline and hard work, making this period feel restricted financially. This summer is an exciting time financially as Saturn loosens its grip around finances, so ensure that you have a sustainable budget in place as you'll be tempted to spend extravagantly. Neptune rules illusion, spirituality and rose-coloured glasses; it has occupied your finance sector continuously since 2012, and exits this space from March 30 to October 22. Neptune leaving your financial sector will provide you with a profound sense of clarity around financial matters. One way to embody the Seeker would be to work with a financial forecaster at this time to fully understand the scope of money entering and exiting your accounts.

Your career planet is Mars, which begins the year retrograde. It's primarily retrograde in your physical health and routine sector, which means this transit functions as an audit of how your career affects your ability to maintain good, healthy habits. Mars spends a considerable amount of time in your partnership sector as well, so there's some additional strain on maintaining a work/life balance. November is also a noteworthy month for readjusting career goals as Mercury will be retrograde in your career sector.

Home and Domestic Life

This area of life is moderately impacted this year with only a few relevant transits to discuss. Aside from the following transits, this area of life should be considered as in a period of status quo. Your home and domestic life planet is Venus, which undergoes its retrograde period from March 1 to April 12, so re-evaluating your living situation will be further towards the front of your mind in the spring. As mentioned in the finances section of this horoscope, there's money to be made in real estate this year. The temptation to move or rent out property is considerable in the spring. Wait until Venus' retrograde period is over before making any massive changes, if possible. Venus retrograde also impacts interpersonal dynamics within the home, where communication will be scrutinized as Venus enters its retrograde period within this sector of your chart. Avoid making assumptions and clarify all your communications with those you live with.

Uranus, the planet of innovation, instability and individuality, has been transiting this sector of your chart continuously since 2019. Uranus moves out of it from July 7 to November 7, these four months providing you with the opportunity to really plant roots where you live. Taking active steps towards turning your house into a home will pay valuable emotional dividends for you and those you live with. Retrogrades encourage you to embody 're-' verbs, so work with Venus' retrograde by reviewing what aspects of where you live can be revitalized to make you feel more at home. Uranus moving into Gemini also encourages turning your home into a space that's more conducive to allowing you to explore your creativity. Whether you creatively self-express through singing, dancing, painting or something else, there's a strong invitation to set up your living space in a way that enables you to lean more into these passions.

Self-improvement

Curiosity is an important virtue for Aquarius to adopt as a means of self-improvement this year. The astrology of 2025 promotes embodying the Seeker totem. Communication is a theme under the umbrella of becoming the Seeker that is emphasized by this year's cosmic weather. Mercury undergoes three relevant retrograde periods this year, the first occurring from March 15 to April 7. This retrograde period spurs you to re-evaluate your patterns of communication and any communication quirks you may have. The second occurs from July 18 to August 12, forcing you to reflect on how you can improve your communication within the context of a partnership. Are you comfortable asserting your needs with a partner? Do you struggle with direct communication? The last retrograde period occurs from November 9 to November 29, taking what you learned from the second retrograde and shifting it to a re-evaluation of your communication patterns in social and professional circles. This year's astrology strongly encourages you to not fear retrogrades but rather view them as an invitation to embody the Seeker.

After two years of eclipses in your higher education and spirituality sector, there's very little activity in this area of life this year, which means that the way forward is maintaining the status quo when it comes to routines around spirituality and higher education pursuits. With curiosity being the overarching theme for the year, get curious about these areas of life and see where they take you. Venus' retrograde (March 1 to April 12) is an explicit invitation to do so.

Lastly, with the north node moving into the finance sector of your chart, your relationship to materialism and consumerism is heavily scrutinized this year. Recognizing that intangible qualities like self-esteem or self-worth are not determined by material assets will be an ongoing reality to explore in 2025. Mercury's first and third retrograde periods are two transits that will disturb this way of thinking. Saturn's stay in your finance sector (January 1 to May 24; September 1 to December 31) is also a time in which actively addressing your relationship to materialism will be present.

Month-by-month Forecasts

January

Best Days Overall: 19-21, 29-31
Most Stressful Days Overall: 2-3, 13-16
Best Days for Love: 17-20
Best Days for Money: 28-31
Best Days for Career: 8-12
Power Word: Apple

Happy New Year, Aquarius! The start of another year means it's almost time for your season. The cosmic weather for this month revolves around the expression 'An apple a day keeps the doctor away'. Basically, the big theme for January is all about the importance of maintaining physical wellness routines. This is especially pertinent because 2025 begins with Mars already retrograde. Mars has been retrograde in Leo, your polar sign, forcing a hard look at your relationships and whether or not there's any reciprocity in them.

On January 6 Mars retrograde re-enters Cancer, which means the focus shifts to physical health and wellness. Are there behaviours or practices that you've been meaning to adopt at the beginning of this new year, water-bearer? Treat this transit as a form of audit around how attentive you are to your bodily needs, including diet, exercise and any other form of physical regulation. Moreover, if you've been avoiding going to a doctor or specialist and have the means to do so, this transit is an overt invitation to do this.

Mars rules drive, ambition and assertion, while Mars retrograde can make you feel stuck or like things are extra-chaotic. As a result, it's super-important to be grounded in your body during this time. This energy is only compounded by the full Moon in Cancer on January 13. Remember, while your mind may not be a trustworthy narrator, your body never lies. Devote some time during the full Moon to quieten your mind in order to tune into your body and its needs.

It's your solar season – Aquarius season – on January 19. Happy Birthday! Aquarius season is your time to shine, quite literally. Take some time around your solar return (your birthday) to pick three words you seek to embody this coming year. They could be anything – balanced, courageous, tender, self-compassionate, the list goes on. Focus on these words when meditating or grounding yourself for the rest of the year. Allow these words to guide the new wellness routines you create as well. The new Moon on the 29th is an ideal day to begin this practice.

February

Best Days Overall: 3–7
Most Stressful Days Overall: 10–14
Best Days for Love: 23–27
Best Days for Money: 14–18
Best Days for Career: 7–10
Power Word: Methodical

Happy February, Aquarius! This month's cosmic weather begins in the middle of your solar season. I hope you have the best year yet! The first few days of the month begin sweet enough, with a dreamy Venus–Neptune transit on the 1st and a cerebral Mercury–Jupiter transit on the 3rd. The Venus–Neptune transit encourages whatever activity uplifts your spirit, whether that be play or rest. Fortunately, this transit falls on a Saturday, so block time off on your calendar so you can be focused on working with this energy. The first week of the month also features a build-up to Mercury and Jupiter's harmonious alignment. When Mercury and Jupiter work together they provide incredible support for any form of communication or analysis. If writing is an important part of your life, leverage the energy this weekend. This is also a good weekend on which to have pragmatic and overdue conversations with loved ones, given the upcoming cosmic weather.

This turns spicy come February 12, with a loud full Moon in Leo, your polar sign. This full Moon has a chaotic aspect between the Sun (your outward identity) and Uranus (the planet of turbulence and liberation). Full Moons represent culminations of emotional cycles, with this full Moon revolving around one-on-one partnerships and relationships for you, likely providing a watershed moment for either existing relationships or your point of view on how you approach relationships. Uranus doesn't walk on eggshells, so it's extra important to navigate any tension methodically. Remember, communication is a two-way street, with active listening being just as important as speaking. Fortunately, this lunation can also highlight strength, resilience and grit in reciprocal relationships.

The Sun leaves Aquarius and enters Pisces on the 18th, with the new Moon in Pisces following on the 27th. Both of these transits are financial in nature for you. After an exciting birthday season it's imperative to start your year with a clear forecast of what your budget is. Treat the new Moon as an invitation to begin new financial ventures you've been planning or begin dreaming up new ways to increase your net worth.

March

Best Days Overall: 20–24
Most Stressful Days Overall: 13–17
Best Days for Love: 8–12
Best Days for Money: 21–25
Best Days for Career: 5–9
Power Word: Speak

March is a super-busy month astrologically, Aquarius, so we have a lot to discuss! On March 1 Venus turns retrograde in Aries. Venus' retrogrades always revolve around re-evaluating or reflecting on our relationships. For Aquarius, this retrograde specifically focuses on communication within relationships. Situations that highlight dysfunction in communication both from you and the other person in your dynamic are likely to abound. The goal of the retrograde is to bolster your existing and future relationships through confronting limiting patterns of communication or confronting non-negotiables you insist on for partners around communication.

The first eclipse of 2025 occurs as a full Moon lunar eclipse in Virgo on the 14th. Eclipses are evolutionary transits that promote growth or change through shake-ups and tension. This eclipse is financial in nature for you but specifically focuses on how your money grows or shrinks as a result of other people. If debts are owed to you or you have unpaid debts you owe, expect this eclipse to turn up the heat to get them rectified. Financial abundance is the end goal here, so make moves to set yourself up for success, even if it's something as simple as keeping to the budget you created last month.

On the 15th Mercury mimics Venus by turning retrograde in Aries. Mercury retrograde compounds the focus on communication in relationships, given that the planet rules all things communication. Remember, communication is a two-way street, with listening being just as important as actively expressing yourself. On the 20th the Sun also enters Aries. In addition to communication, this is your annual invitation to get to know your neighbourhood or local community better. Explore local events, local nature trails or new places of business you've never visited before. The second eclipse of the year occurs on the 29th in, you guessed it, Aries. So much Aries energy! This eclipse centres on whether your needs are being met in all domains of your life. If there is imbalance and you don't feel fulfilled or accomplished, that's where the tension will arise from this transit. Neptune leaves Pisces and enters Aries for the first time in your lifetime on the 30th. This transit spurs you to examine how your spirituality currently informs or can inform how you approach communication.

April

Best Days Overall: 5–9
Most Stressful Days Overall: 26–30
Best Days for Love: 16–19
Best Days for Money: 6–9
Best Days for Career: 20–24
Power Word: Clarity

Happy April, water-bearer! April's astrology starts off with a confluence of soft and sweet transits during the first week. Saturn finds harmony with Mars on the 5th, the same day that Venus also levels with Mars. This is an enriching transit for cultivating abundance in your personal relationships. Quality time is the name of the game for the first week of this month. On April 7 Mercury ends its retrograde and goes direct. This means the wonkiness you're likely experiencing around communication, transportation and technology will begin to dissipate. Remember, astrological transits don't function like light switches, so there will be a gradual improvement around the efficacy of these Mercury-ruled matters.

On April 12 the full Moon in Libra occurs just as Venus ends its retrograde and goes direct. The full Moon in Libra is a spiritual and educational full Moon for Aquarius. Full Moons tend to be emotional, and this one encourages you to make a concerted effort to be consistent with your spiritual routine and practices. If you've been seeking guidance, this full Moon is the ideal time to seek counsel from a practitioner you trust. Venus direct in Pisces not only supports seeking spiritual clarity, but falls in Aquarius' 2nd house of finance, clearing the way for you to take action to grow your streams of income.

Taurus' season begins on April 19. Taurus is the fixed earth sign centred around security. This solar season revolves around home and family dynamics for Aquarius, and is the ideal time to be doing home-improvement or organization projects. The new Moon in Taurus occurs on the 27th but is paired with a tense face-off between Mars and Pluto. Mars-Pluto transits tend to be inflammatory in nature. Be mindful that one signification of this transit is buried anger rising to the surface. If you find this transit particularly resonates with your chart, recognize that the end goal is to shed the rage you've held onto for too long. The end of the month's energy encourages you to only concern yourself with what's in your locus of control and not fret about variables beyond it.

May

Best Days Overall: 4–9
Most Stressful Days Overall: 13–18
Best Days for Love: 26–30
Best Days for Money: 3–7
Best Days for Career: 22–27
Power Word: Creative

It's May, Aquarius! The cosmic weather for this month begins on the 2nd, when Venus meets up with Neptune in Aries for the first time in your lifetime. Venus and Neptune together facilitate a chill vibe. Venus–Neptune energy is best used to fuel more existential or big-picture thinking. While this transit does promote rest, it can also elicit dissociative behaviour, so do your best to make sure the ways you recharge are holistically supportive. Venus then aligns with Pluto on the 6th. This transit is more creative in essence, promoting transformation around creative self-expression and romance. Aquarius is known for being innovative and different, so dare to lean into creativity in new or unique ways at this time.

On May 12 there's a full Moon in Scorpio on the same day that Mercury squares off with Pluto. This full Moon centres around career for you, Aquarius. Specifically, it represents a culmination of the last six months. Have you been satisfied in your career or are there changes you seek to make? This lunation features a harsher Mercury–Pluto aspect. While these aspects can make everyone feel on edge, they're great for investigation. Use the potent energy of this lunation for some much-needed self-discovery around your satisfaction with where you're at in your career journey. Have your ultimate career goals shifted in the last six months?

Saturn enters Aries for the first time since 1999 on May 24. This ingress ushers in a 2½-year period of maturation around how you communicate, revisiting themes around your patterns of communication that came to light in March with the eclipse in Aries and the two retrogrades. The Sun enters Gemini on May 20, followed by Mercury entering Gemini on the 25th and the new Moon following suit on the 26th. That's a lot of Gemini energy! Gemini transits are creative and romantic for Aquarius. This new Moon is an excellent lunation in which to tackle a new creative endeavour or doing something spontaneously romantic with a special someone.

June

Best Days Overall: 1-6
Most Stressful Days Overall: 18-23
Best Days for Love: 10-13
Best Days for Money: 25-29
Best Days for Career: 3-6
Power Word: Body

Happy June, Aquarius! The start of this month features multiple planets shifting signs, which creates a noticeable change in the cosmic weather. Venus loves being in Taurus and, for Aquarius, brings its warmth to themes of home and family. Now is the time to make moves towards cultivating a living space that serves as a beacon to attract the energy you wish to work with. Studying and implementing the fundamentals of feng shui could be just the thing to revitalize the energetic flow in your home. On the 8th and 9th Mercury and Jupiter enter Cancer. Jupiter spends about a year in each sign, so this is the first time in 12 years Jupiter is entering Cancer. Jupiter in Cancer ushers in a new 12-year cycle centred around physical fitness and how you care for your body. In what ways has your relationship with your body changed over the last 12 years? Bring with you what you've learned into this new chapter. If you're seeking to improve your physical fitness, nutrition or just your overall wellness, Jupiter will work with you over the coming year to help you do so.

On June 11 the full Moon is bright and in fiery Sagittarius. This is a highly social transit for Aquarius, encouraging you to immerse yourself in communities, groups or organizations that get you energized. Sagittarius rules worldliness, so this is also an opportune time to immerse yourself in and support communities who share different identity markers from your own. Believe it or not, Sagittarius is the sign associated with wisdom. There's so much to be learned from spending time in diverse environments.

On June 20 the Sun joins Mercury and Jupiter by entering Cancer. This Cancer season does start off tensely, with the Sun squaring off with Saturn and Neptune on the 22nd and 23rd. For Aquarius especially, this transit will likely trigger feelings of being overwhelmed or exasperation around staying within your typical routine. If you fall off your routine this first week of Cancer season, treat yourself with as much self-compassion as possible, as productivity does not equal worth, Aquarius! The new Moon in Cancer on the 25th will support you in resetting your rhythm and getting back into the swing of things.

July

Best Days Overall: 20-23
Most Stressful Days Overall: 25-28
Best Days for Love: 5-9
Best Days for Money: 9-12
Best Days for Career: 2-6
Power Word: Recharge

Hi, Aquarius! July's cosmic weather begins on the 4th with Venus meeting up with Uranus in Taurus just before entering Gemini. Venus in Gemini is a social transit that's particularly flirty and creative for Aquarius, and Uranus' involvement adds additional spontaneity and surprises to the mix. This transit is a great time to put yourself out there romantically, go on spur-of-the-moment dates or lean into your unique form of creativity. Modern astrologers attribute a ruling connection between Uranus and Aquarius. This is important because on July 7 Uranus enters Gemini for the first time since leaving the sign in 1949. That's quite the vibe shift! For the collective, this transit unequivocally will revolutionize the ways we communicate and approach learning, specifically as a result of technological innovations. For you, this transit ushers in a seven-year period of enhanced creative self-expression.

On July 10 the full Moon in Capricorn is bright and exact. This lunation illuminates how much structure you've implemented around your mental health and wellness routines. Furthermore, this full Moon spotlights how balanced you are in carving out time when you're social as well as solo time in which to recharge. Allow this lunation to shine light on these themes so you can adjust your routines accordingly. On July 18 Mercury turns retrograde in Leo, your polar sign. This retrograde has considerable potency to facilitate communication breakdowns and misinterpretation. For Aquarius, this is especially true within the dynamics of partnership. Make extra efforts to actively listen with partners, and communicate concisely and directly.

Leo's season begins on July 22 with a big roar as the Sun aspects five planets in its first three days navigating the sign. On the 24th the new Moon in Leo is exact and contains all these aspects within it. Aquarius is known for being the innovator and as a bit of a maverick, and this new Moon urges you to lean into your individuality in all facets of your life. New Moons represent the start of emotional cycles, with this one centring on embracing your authenticity and what makes you uniquely you.

August

Best Days Overall: 12–16
Most Stressful Days Overall: 5–9
Best Days for Love: 14–18
Best Days for Money: 22–26
Best Days for Career: 15–19
Power Word: Gratitude

Hi, water-bearer! This August is all about regulating the mind. Fun! The cosmic weather for the month begins promptly on the 1st as Venus finds tension with both Saturn and Neptune. These tussles normally provoke your inner saboteur to rear its not-so-nice head. The purpose of these transits is not to shy away from or ignore this voice, but actually to take a stand in choosing self-compassion or becoming your own biggest cheerleader.

It's your full Moon on the 9th. This full Moon is loud for you, given the fact that in addition to its being in your sign, Mars is facing off with both Saturn and Neptune. The big theme of this lunation is becoming comfortable with stillness. The full Moon in your sign is a culmination moment of all the ways you've grown since your birthday this year. Given that you're halfway through your solar return, there's typically some restlessness you experience about accomplishing the goals you set out this new year. Allow yourself the time and space to pause and not pursue. Take stock of how much you've already evolved and ground yourself in gratitude for that. Mercury ends its retrograde two days later, clearing the path for you to resume chasing the Sun. Venus and Jupiter lovingly meet up on the 6th in Cancer. For Aquarius, this transit promotes nourishing, supporting or finding equilibrium with your body.

On the 22nd the Sun enters Virgo, and one day later the Moon meets up with it to form the first of two new Moons in this sign. This new Moon revolves around breaking free of limiting patterns of spending or of any type of relationship with money that keeps you stifled. This especially applies if there are debts involved. This lunation strongly encourages you to create an action plan to ameliorate your relationship with finances, which could also mean taking steps towards allowing your money to grow whether through investments or developing new streams of income. The month ends with one last transit centred on achieving more mental clarity. Venus squares off with Pluto on the 27th, a transit that can elicit hyper-vigilant tendencies, especially in relationships. The goal of this transit is to remind you that when it comes to any interpersonal relationship, you can only control your actions and reactions, not the other person's.

September

Best Days Overall: 26–30
Most Stressful Days Overall: 6–8, 20–22
Best Days for Love: 24–28
Best Days for Money: 1–5
Best Days for Career: 23–27
Power Word: Endeavour

It's September, water-bearer! This month is a noteworthy month in the grand scheme of this year because it's our second and final eclipse season. Eclipses are evolutionary transits that promote growth through shaking things up and creating a little bit of tension. The first eclipse of the month occurs in Pisces on the 7th. This month's eclipses revolve around one of your big 2025 themes – your relationship to your finances. This eclipse occurs on the heels of the new Moon two weeks ago and augments the audit around your spending habits. The goal of this eclipse season is for you to not only gain the clearest picture possible about how you spend and save in the short term, but also what behaviours you can adopt that create a pathway for long-lasting financial abundance. It's hard to emphasize enough that ignorance around your personal finances, or general ignorance around how economic systems such as taxes work, is deleterious at this time. There's no need to become a financial whizz kid; even something as simple as watching some informational videos or taking a free online course around fiscal responsibility would pay significant dividends in the long term for you.

The second eclipse of September occurs on the 21st and is a second new Moon in Virgo. This eclipse is also financial but focuses more on how your finances are intertwined with others'. If you're signing any form of contract that involves sharing payment or splits up fees, make sure you dot your i's and cross your t's by reading every word twice. This is a new Moon solar eclipse, so the potential that other people might want to launch new financial endeavours is considerable. Once again, do your due diligence around this eclipse by ironing out the fine details of any sort of partnership.

Libra's season begins on the 22nd. Libra season for you centres around confronting limiting patterns of thought and behaviour around spirituality and spiritual beliefs. This Libra season, dear water-bearer, is about seeking out spiritual routines that welcome more balance into your life. Spirituality is not meant to be clung to, so don't allow astrology, Tarot or any other form of beliefs to incite fear or panic. Organic spirituality is only supposed to imbue you with empowerment and a feeling of agency.

October

Best Days Overall: 1–5
Most Stressful Days Overall: 10–14
Best Days for Love: 4–8
Best Days for Money: 26–29
Best Days for Career: 28–31
Power Word: Informative

Happy October, Aquarius! How are you feeling after an action-packed eclipse season? This month's astro-weather begins with the full Moon in Aries occurring on the 6th. This lunation functions as a universal check-in with all the themes surrounding the new Moon solar eclipse in Aries at the end of March. For you, the end of March eclipse centred around communication and your local community. This October full Moon poses the question whether your relationship to communication has changed? Do you feel as though you still censor yourself as much as you did in March in your various relationships? Have you adopted more active listening? This lunation brings to your attention the changes you could make to ensure your approach to communication better meets your emotional needs. Furthermore, this lunation spotlights your relationship to your local community and encourages you to immerse yourself in it. Go on an adventure and explore parts of your neighbourhood or city that you haven't yet visited.

The astro-weather then begins to centre around Venus as the planet forms aspects with Saturn, Uranus, Neptune and Pluto between the 11th and the 15th, and also moves into Libra on the 13th. This confluence of transits centres around higher education for you, water-bearer. Specifically, in what ways has a lack of any sort of education felt limiting to you? These transits prompt you to consider whether it's time to embark upon some learning, even if that means independent research or watching informative lectures in your free time. The new Moon in Libra on the 21st is an ideal time to usher in a new emotional cycle around educating yourself.

The Sun enters Scorpio on the 22nd, and then forms aspects with Uranus and Pluto over the next two days. Scorpio season will bring the cosmic magnifying glass to your career and legacy. This time of year is crucial for Aquarius to think about what they want to accomplish in 2026 when it comes to their career. In addition, are there steps you can take during this solar season to start building momentum towards achieving next year's goals?

November

Best Days Overall: 17–21
Most Stressful Days Overall: 8–12
Best Days for Love: 27–30
Best Days for Money: 13–17
Best Days for Career: 2–6
Power Word: Connection

Happy November, water-bearer! This month's astrology kicks off on the 4th with fiery Mars moving into visionary Sagittarius. This transit injects a heavy helping of kinetic energy into your social life. Sagittarius is spontaneous and adventurous, so don't be surprised if you get up to some spur-of-the-moment excitement. Sagittarius is also the sign associated with wisdom, so be open to learning from your social circles during this transit as well. The full Moon in Taurus spotlights your emotional security at home and within the dynamics of your family. If you've been needing to get something off your chest with family members or specific loved ones, this lunation will spur you to do so. It also promotes nesting, which is beneficial given how social the next six weeks will likely be with Mars in Sagittarius.

Mars isn't the only planet in Sagittarius. On the 9th Mercury in Sagittarius turns retrograde one last time in 2025. This transit can absolutely make you ripe for misinterpretation or misunderstanding, especially within friend groups. Do your due diligence with active listening and realize that there's no shame in asking for clarification if you think there's miscommunication. Assumptions are the enemy with this transit. On the 17th the Sun teams up with Jupiter and Saturn to form one of the most harmonious aspects, a grand water trine, which invites us to get in touch with our emotions. Cultivating intimacy and heartfelt connections are a major component of this transit.

Scorpio season concludes with its new Moon on the 20th. This new Moon welcomes new beginnings when it comes to career or legacy. This is an especially potent lunation if you're seeking to make a change at work. Whether it's switching careers, industries or even role responsibilities, this new Moon supports propelling yourself in the direction of what you want your legacy to be. Sagittarius' season begins on the 21st. This is really where socialization begins! Venus, the planet of splendour and love, follows suit on the 30th by entering Sagittarius. Looking ahead, it's a good idea to start striving to balance social time with some necessary alone time over the next few weeks.

December

Best Days Overall: 19-23
Most Stressful Days Overall: 6-10
Best Days for Love: 1-4
Best Days for Money: 14-18
Best Days for Career: 16-20
Power Word: Duality

It's almost 2026, water-bearer! Before we ring in a new year, let's chat about December's astrology. The cosmic weather begins on the 4th with the full Moon in Gemini. This lunation urges you to carve out more time for play and pleasure, and to balance these with work. Gemini is the sign that reminds us we all embody duality. Moreover, this lunation spurs you to lean into creative self-expression as a means of getting in touch with your emotions. Create and feel, Aquarius!

You'll feel a bit of a slowdown around the 9th, when Mars squares off with Saturn. This transit typically elicits frustration as productivity tends to be halted. This is an ideal time in which to take a cue from the full Moon and lean into creativity. Moreover, the goal of this transit is for you to focus on completing existing deliverables before generating new ones. Don't worry, there's plenty of cosmic weather this month for goal-setting later. Speaking of which, after this transit Mars enters Capricorn on the 15th, a transit that imbues a 'build your empire brick by brick' mentality. For you, water-bearer, it gives the green light to really start planning out what you seek to accomplish in 2026, as well as encouraging you to seek some solitude as a means of getting in touch with yourself and reflecting.

Sagittarius' season ends with the new Moon in Sagittarius on the 19th. As mentioned above, the theme of this month is striking a balance between work and play. On the work side of things, there's the prompt to find some solo time to get in touch with your 2026 goals and all you've accomplished this year. On the play side, there's this lunation, which encourages spontaneity within your social circles. This transit also encourages you to identify who your cheerleaders are within your friend groups and express your gratitude to them for their support. Capricorn's season begins on the 21st, spurring you to wrap up this year with small actionable steps to step into 2026 with momentum.

Pisces

THE FISH

Birthdays from
February 19
to March 20

Personality Profile

PISCES AT A GLANCE

Element – Water

Ruling Planet – Neptune
  Career Planet – Jupiter
  Love Planet – Mercury
  Money Planet – Mars
  Planet of Health and Work – Sun
  Planet of Home and Family Life – Mercury
  Planet of Fun, Entertainment, Creativity and Pleasure – Moon

Totem – the Protagonist

Colours – aqua, violet

Colours that promote love, romance and social harmony – earth
  tones, yellow, yellow-orange

Colours that promote earning power – red, scarlet

Gem – selenite

Metal – tin

Scent – lotus, petrichor

Quality – mutable (= flexibility)

Qualities most needed for balance – structure and the ability to handle form

Strongest virtues – psychic power, sensitivity, self-sacrifice, altruism

Deepest needs – spiritual illumination, liberation

Characteristics to avoid – escapism, keeping bad company, negative moods

Signs of greatest overall compatibility – Cancer, Scorpio

Signs of greatest overall incompatibility – Gemini, Virgo, Sagittarius

Sign most helpful to career – Sagittarius

Sign most helpful for emotional support – Gemini

Sign most helpful financially – Aries

Sign best for marriage and/or partnerships – Virgo

Sign most helpful for creative projects – Cancer

Best Sign to have fun with – Cancer

Signs most helpful in spiritual matters – Scorpio, Aquarius

Best day of the week – Thursday

Understanding a Pisces

If Pisces have one outstanding quality it is their belief in the invisible, spiritual and psychic side of things. This side of things is as real to them as the hard earth beneath their feet – so real, in fact, that they will often ignore the visible, tangible aspects of reality in order to focus on the invisible and so-called intangible ones.

Of all the signs of the zodiac, the intuitive and emotional faculties of the Pisces are the most highly developed. They are committed to living by their intuition and this can at times be infuriating to other people – especially those who are materially, scientifically or technically orientated. If you think that money, status and worldly success are the only goals in life, then you will never understand a Pisces.

Pisces have intellect, but to them intellect is only a means by which they can rationalize what they know intuitively. To an Aquarius or a Gemini the intellect is a tool with which to gain knowledge. To a well-developed Pisces it is a tool by which to express knowledge.

Pisces feel like fish in an infinite ocean of thought and feeling. This ocean has many depths, currents and undercurrents. They long for purer waters where the denizens are good, true and beautiful, but they are sometimes pulled to the lower, murkier depths. Pisces know that they do not generate thoughts but only tune in to thoughts that already exist; this is why they seek the purer waters. This ability to tune in to higher thoughts inspires them artistically and musically.

Since Pisces is so spiritually orientated – though many Pisces in the corporate world may hide this fact – we will deal with this aspect in greater detail, for otherwise it is difficult to understand the true Pisces personality.

There are four basic attitudes of the spirit. One is outright scepticism – the attitude of secular humanists. The second is an intellectual or emotional belief, where one worships a far-distant God-figure – the attitude of most modern church-going people. The third is not only belief but direct personal spiritual experience – this is the attitude of some 'born-again' religious people. The fourth is actual unity with the divinity, an intermingling with the spiritual world – this is the attitude of yoga. This fourth attitude is the deepest urge of a Pisces, and a Pisces is uniquely qualified to pursue and perform this work.

Consciously or unconsciously, Pisces seek this union with the spiritual world. The belief in a greater reality makes Pisces very tolerant and understanding of others – perhaps even too tolerant. There are instances in their lives when they should say 'enough is enough' and be ready to defend their position and put up a fight. However, because of their qualities it takes a good deal to get them into that frame of mind.

Pisces basically want and aspire to be 'saints'. They do so in their own way and according to their own rules. Others should not try to impose their concept of saintliness on a Pisces, because he or she always tries to find it for him- or herself.

Finance

Money is generally not that important to Pisces. Of course they need it as much as anyone else, and many of them attain great wealth. But money is not generally a primary objective. Doing good, feeling good about oneself, peace of mind, the relief of pain and suffering – these are the things that matter most to a Pisces.

Pisces earn money intuitively and instinctively. They follow their hunches rather than their logic. They tend to be generous and perhaps overly charitable. Almost any kind of misfortune is enough to move a Pisces to give. Although this is one of their greatest virtues, Pisces should be more careful with their finances. They should try to be more choosy about the people to whom they lend money, so that they are not being taken advantage of. If they give money to charities they should follow it up to see that their contributions are put to good use. Even when Pisces are not rich, they still like to spend money on helping others. In this case they should really be careful, however: they must learn to say no sometimes and help themselves first.

Perhaps the biggest financial stumbling block for the Pisces is general passivity – a *laissez faire* attitude. In general Pisces like to go with the flow of events. When it comes to financial matters, especially, they need to be more aggressive. They need to make things happen, to create their own wealth. A passive attitude will only cause loss and missed opportunity. Worrying about financial security will not provide that security. Pisces need to go after what they want tenaciously.

Career and Public Image

Pisces like to be perceived by the public as people of spiritual or material wealth, of generosity and philanthropy. They look up to big-hearted, philanthropic types. They admire people engaged in large-scale undertakings and eventually would like to head up these big enterprises themselves. In short, they like to be connected with big organizations that are doing things in a big way.

If Pisces are to realize their full career and professional potential they need to travel more, educate themselves more and learn more about the actual world. In other words, they need some of the unflagging optimism of Sagittarius in order to reach the top.

Because of all their caring and generous characteristics, Pisces often choose professions through which they can help and touch the lives of other people. That is why many Pisces become doctors, nurses, social workers or teachers. Sometimes it takes a while before Pisces realize what they really want to do in their professional lives, but once they find a career that lets them manifest their interests and virtues they will excel at it.

Love and Relationships

It is not surprising that someone as 'otherworldly' as the Pisces would like a partner who is practical and down to earth. Pisces prefer a partner who is on top of all the details of life, because they dislike details. Pisces seek this quality in both their romantic and professional partners. More than anything else this gives Pisces a feeling of being grounded, of being in touch with reality.

As expected, these kinds of relationships – though necessary – are sure to have many ups and downs. Misunderstandings will take place because the two attitudes are poles apart. If you are in love with a Pisces you will experience these fluctuations and will need a lot of patience to see things stabilize. Pisces are moody, intuitive, affectionate and difficult to get to know. Only time and the right attitude will yield Pisces' deepest secrets. However, when in love with a Pisces you will find that riding the waves is worth it because they are good, sensitive people who need and like to give love and affection.

When in love, Pisces like to fantasize. For them fantasy is 90 per cent of the fun of a relationship. They tend to idealize their partner, which can be good and bad at the same time. It is bad in that it is difficult for anyone to live up to the high ideals their Pisces lover sets.

Home and Domestic Life

In their family and domestic life Pisces have to resist the tendency to relate only by feelings and moods. It is unrealistic to expect that your partner and other family members will be as intuitive as you are. There is a need for more verbal communication between a Pisces and his or her family. A cool, unemotional exchange of ideas and opinions will benefit everyone.

Some Pisces tend to like mobility and moving around. For them too much stability feels like a restriction on their freedom. They hate to be locked in one location for ever.

The sign of Gemini sits on the cusp of Pisces' 4th solar house of home and family. This shows that Pisces likes and needs a home environment that promotes intellectual and mental interests. They tend to treat their neighbours as family – or extended family. Some Pisceans can have a dual attitude towards the home and family – on the one hand they like the emotional support of the family, but on the other they dislike the obligations, restrictions and duties involved with it. For Pisces, finding a balance is the key to a happy family life.

Horoscope for 2025

It's hard to overemphasize how important this year is for you, Pisces. For the first time since 2007 the north node enters your sign at the top of the year, bringing with it the eclipses for the next 18 months. Eclipses are evolutionary transits that stimulate growth through scrutiny and shake-ups. This is one big levelling-up year for you and your totem 'the Protagonist', because frankly your sign is the protagonist of 2025. This year also features several planets with periods of retrograde motion oscillating to and from your sign. This means they spend an extended period of time in your sign, only further compounding the astrological focus on Pisces this year.

This is a noteworthy year because slow-moving Saturn, Uranus and Neptune all switch signs, stimulating societal shifts. For you, Pisces, this is an especially big deal because both Saturn and Neptune leave your sign for part of the year, before fully moving into Aries next year. Saturn has occupied your sign since March 2023 and brought with it a ton of responsibility and the demand to be disciplined. Neptune takes 160 years to go around the zodiac and has consistently stayed in Pisces since 2012. Neptune's spiritual influence and dissociative tendencies finally leave Pisces for half the year, which will be further discussed in the self-improvement section.

Jupiter, Pisces' career-sector ruler, also changes signs mid-year, from Gemini to fellow water sign Cancer. Jupiter is the planet of growth and expansion, and this transit brings with it an abundance of splendour and creativity that should be leveraged in this ascension-filled year. Jupiter leaves your home and domestic life sector in June and, come July, Uranus shifts into this part of your chart. Instability and innovation in this area of life will be discussed in detail in the home and domestic life section of this horoscope.

Mercury, Venus and Mars all have periods of retrograde motion this year. Most noteworthy is the fact that Venus' sole retrograde period and Mercury's first retrograde period occur between Aries and Pisces, just like those of Saturn and Neptune. There's a heavy emphasis on financial matters as the planets move between your self-improvement and finance sectors all year. Mars is your finance planet, and its retrograde period will be described in detail in the career and finances section below.

For a quarterly view of this year, the first quarter features significant focus on self-improvement and relationships, while the second features a shift in focus towards finances. Finances and relationships are the prime area of focus in the third quarter, with the year ending as the planets move back into Pisces and the focus returns to self-improvement.

Health

(Please note that this is an astrological perspective on health and not a medical one. Any health-related symptoms should be evaluated by a qualified healthcare professional.)

The cosmic weather for this year asks you, 'Given that the astrology for this year centres around stepping into your power, do you have wellness routines in place to support this ascension?' Astrologically speaking, physical health and wellness routines are scrutinized at the start of 2025, with Mars starting the year already in retrograde motion in Pisces' 6th house of physical wellness. Mars is inflammatory in nature, so it's important to be mindful around diet and overexertion. Mars quickly moves out of this sector of your chart early in 2025, but nonetheless is still retrograde until February 23. It's especially important to be vigilant around physical health and wellness in the first week of January, with Mars retrograde facing off Pluto. January is an ideal month in which to schedule any necessary appointments with your doctor or wellness practitioner.

Your health planet is the Sun, which has a busy year given that its aspects with the outer planets tend to happen all together throughout the year. With Neptune and Saturn hanging out at roughly the same degree of the same sign for a significant part of the year, and Uranus and Pluto being in low degrees of signs for part or all of the year, there are some months when the Sun will aspect all four planets in the course of a week, which is unusual.

This means that health is an area of life with peaks and troughs this year. It also strongly reinforces the importance of maintaining the utmost consistency with physical wellness routines.

Here are the specific areas of the body to focus on this year:

- The feet: Pisces rules the feet in medical astrology, so this is an area of perennial focus for Pisces. With Saturn oscillating in and out of your sign, it's important to regularly decompress your feet through reflexology, massage and/or acupuncture.
- The heart: the Sun is your health planet and rules the heart. Maintaining heart-healthy practices is especially important during Mars' retrograde period and its transit through Leo (January 1 to January 6; April 19 to June 17).
- The digestive system: half of the eclipses in 2025 occur in Virgo, which rules the gut in medical astrology. Maintaining a diet supportive of gut flora and health is vital, especially around the eclipses in March and September.

Love and Social Life

Relationships are a significant area of focus for you this year, Pisces. The south node enters Virgo on January 11 and moves into your 7th house of partnership. The south node brings with it two eclipses this year, so expect major revelations about partnerships. As a reminder, eclipses catalyse evolution, typically through tension. The March 14 eclipse in Virgo occurs in tandem with the period of Venus' retrograde, which creates a potent reflection period around relationships. If you've got a partner, March is a month in which you'll be evaluating whether your needs are being met in the relationship and if there's equality in its power dynamic. If you're single, March is a good time to analyse your point of view on approaching relationships and your emotional availability for a relationship.

Two weeks after this eclipse Venus re-enters your sign and remains retrograde until mid-April. Venus retrograde overlaps with Mercury retrograde, which will also be in Pisces from the end of March to the start of April. The spring functions as a period in which you can audit your existing relationships – ones where you have concerns that are necessary to address but that have been long ignored will now likely face a watershed moment, as these retrogrades spur reflection and revisiting long-standing issues. Both retrograde periods finish in mid-April, and the planets move directly at full speed by mid-May.

September also features an important eclipse cycle around relationships, with the September 7 eclipse occurring in your sign and the one on September 21 occurring in Virgo, your polar sign. These eclipses focus on the two individuals in the phrase 'I with another', with the first eclipse embodying the 'I' and the second eclipse embodying 'another'. When in a relationship, people tend not only to navigate the relationship with the other person, but also the relationship with their own self. Themes around individuating within a partnership, or the general need for autonomy regardless of partnership status, need your urgent attention in this eclipse, Pisces. The second eclipse functions as a repetition and check-in on the themes active in the spring eclipse cycle.

Your ruling planet for your social life and social standing is Saturn, and these get a boost this summer when Saturn finally leaves your sign and enters Aries. Saturn will be in Aries from May 24 to September 1. This transit is noteworthy enough to mark on your calendar, and it encourages expanding your friend circles as Saturn's restrictive gaze shifts away from Pisces during this period. November features one of the harmonious aspects of the year involving Saturn – a grand water trine with the Sun and Jupiter. If you're seeking to move up in the ranks of a community organization or put together some sort of celebratory gathering, leveraging the energy of this magnificent transit is recommended. See your November horoscope for more information on this grand water trine.

Career and Finances

This section of life is complicated for you, Pisces, as your career sector is strongly uplifted by this year's astrology, but your finance sector is equally scrutinized. Buoyant Jupiter is your career planet and undergoes one of its favourite shifts, moving into the sign of its 'exaltation', Cancer. Jupiter wraps up its stay in Gemini, which it's been occupying since May last year. Gemini is the sign of the marketeer, so this period is an ideal time to network, and joining professional organizations is strongly advised prior to Jupiter's harmonious ingress into Cancer. Jupiter moves into Cancer on June 9 and stays there for approximately 12 months. Jupiter in Cancer is less focused on zeroes and ones than on feeling spiritually and emotionally fulfilled in a career. If possible, incorporate some form of philanthropy or volunteering into your job. Jupiter in Cancer is an abundant transit for you, Pisces. Outside of Jupiter, it's important to note that Mercury does turn retrograde in your career sector on November 9 and stays in this part of your chart until the 18th. November will be a month featuring a re-evaluation of your career goals and overall trajectory.

Your finance planet is Mars, which starts the year retrograde. When your finance planet is not moving directly, it's vital to adopt a more conservative stance around money, so focusing on saving instead of spending and investing is advised at this time. Mars turns direct on February 23 and will be moving directly at full speed come May 2.

There are four planets whose periods of retrograde motion include extended periods in Aries, Pisces' 2nd house of finances. Mercury and Venus are both retrograde this spring, just after Mars turns direct. Mercury rules commerce from a traditional astrological perspective, while Venus rules personal finances from the modern perspective, which both suggest that March in particular is a month in which to continue this frugal outlook around your wealth. March also features Neptune entering this sector of your chart and staying there until October. Neptune in your financial sector creates an air of nebulousness around finances, so before this date it would be wise to do an in-depth audit of all the ways money enters and exits your account. Lastly, Saturn enters Aries in May and remains until September 1. Saturn brings with it restriction and discipline, so the best way to work with this transit is to level up in your understanding around how finances and economics work. Examples include taking a course on financial literacy, hiring a finance advisor or doing your own independent research on topics in which you have knowledge gaps. While finances are not seemingly free-flowing this year, the cosmic weather is supporting you through this scrutiny by catalysing behavioural changes that will yield long-lasting dividends.

Home and Domestic Life

There are unexpected changes starting mid-year given Uranus' foray into Pisces' 4th house of home and domestic life in July. Uranus is the planet that rules breakthroughs and innovation, and is represented by the Tower card in Tarot because of its associations with sudden reversals or changes in direction. Uranus in your 4th house from July to December is a wild card for this area of life, as when it transits the 4th house it often puts pressure on those who are already struggling to keep their personal and professional lives in balance. Because Uranus is so closely associated with instability, it requires the individual going through the Uranus transit to manage only what's within their locus of control and to surrender to what's not. If there are any outstanding structural home-improvement projects you should be doing, plan to fix them before July.

Mercury is the planet ruling home and domestic life for you, and it undergoes three retrograde periods: March 15 to April 7, July 18 to August 11 and November 9 to November 29. These are periods in which to avoid starting any new refurbishments to your home, although it's fine to continue with projects already underway.

Self-improvement

After a 2½-year period of accountability and discipline, Saturn begins its exit from Pisces. Saturn has been in your sign since March 2023, and its summer vacation out of Pisces takes place from May 24 to September 1. Saturn returning to your sign come the beginning of September is noteworthy because once it leaves Pisces for good in 2026, it won't return to your sign for over 28 years. Its 2½-year period in Pisces ushered in an extended cycle around assuming responsibility and shedding relationships or identity markers that no longer served you. Allow this summer's respite from Saturn to give you the breathing room you need to identify what you seek to leave behind when the planet officially parts ways with your sign.

Saturn isn't the only planet planning on turning a new leaf away from Pisces. Neptune leaves Pisces this year from March 30 to October 22. Neptune rules literal and figurative fog, so Neptune leaving Pisces is like fog beginning to dissipate. Neptune has been in Pisces continually since 2012, so its exit from your sign is a significant milestone. Neptune brings with it spiritual enlightenment and ego-shedding. Thirteen years is a long time, and a good exercise to understand the impact of this transit would be to journal about who you were prior to this transit and who you are now. Anticipate your sense of perception to increase during Neptune's transit out of Pisces, and to improve with its official parting next year. Neptune will never again be in your sign during your lifetime after it formally leaves.

The north node entering your sign is perfect timing with these planets exiting Pisces. With this transit is the cosmic invitation to truly envision what's possible this year. Vision board, journal and schedule in active check-ins on your progress towards achieving your goals. Anticipate the eclipse seasons this spring and autumn/fall to be especially potent for you, given this year's astrology. After all, this is the year you embody the Protagonist.

Month-by-month Forecasts

January

Best Days Overall: 11–14, 30–31
Most Stressful Days Overall: 15–19
Best Days for Love: 27–31
Best Days for Money: 19–23
Best Days for Career: 8–11
Power Word: Evolve

Happy 2025, Pisces! The astro-weather this year begins on the 2nd with lovely Venus moving into your sign. Venus transiting your natal Sun is a dreamy transit, empowering you to take action around self-love. This is a softer transit, so it's mostly up to you to take advantage of the self-compassion energy that's readily available. Venus will stay in Pisces all month, so this can also be a monthly goal to work on. Schedule time to take yourself on dates this month.

We enter 2025 with Mars still retrograde, and on the 6th it re-enters Cancer. Mars will now be retrograde in Pisces' 5th house of creativity and romance, a transit that unequivocally makes itself known and felt. Mars is all about forward momentum, so a Mars retrograde is often met with a 'stuck feeling' and frustration, likely around 5th house matters of creativity and romance. Additionally, given that Mars is in the sign of Cancer, there's an added layer of how family or home dynamics affect your ability to creatively self-express and/or approach romance. The full Moon on the 13th illuminates these themes, as it will be applying to conjoin with Mars. Full Moons can be emotional times, so be disciplined with your grounding practices. Given the 5th house's association with children, this is also an ideal time to actively heal your inner child.

Aquarius' season begins on January 19, with the Sun meeting up with Pluto two days later on the 21st. This transit is about shedding aspects of your identity that no longer serve you, or claiming aspects of your identity that will serve who you want to be, and it's a great few days for therapy or life coaching. As mentioned in your yearly horoscope, 2025 is a noteworthy year for Pisces. This transit marks the beginning of the exciting evolution you're embarking on this year. Be gentle with yourself as you grow.

February

Best Days Overall: 1-3, 27-28
Most Stressful Days Overall: 10-15
Best Days for Love: 14-18
Best Days for Money: 24-27
Best Days for Career: 5-9
Power Word: New

Happy February, Pisces! February's astrology starts off with a couple of softer, harmonious transits. On the 1st Venus conjoins with Neptune in your sign just before it leaves to enter Aries. Venus-Neptune vibes are dreamy, idealistic and spiritual. The first weekend of February would be an ideal time to immerse yourself in nature or do something that uplifts your soul. Two days later Mercury and Jupiter align, supporting your communication. This is especially the case within the home and with family for you, Pisces.

The most noteworthy event of the month is the loud full Moon in Leo occurring on February 12. The full Moon in Leo is normally an expressive lunation, but this one is a little spicier given it's at odds with Uranus. Uranus rules instability, innovation and liberation, so this transit is likely going to set off some sort of relational fireworks around you, given that everyone - regardless of sign - will be feeling it. Full Moons represent culminations of emotional cycles, and for you, Pisces, this full Moon has a physical wellness component to it, combined with two primary motivations for catalysing action. First, it encourages getting out of your head and listening to your body. The mind may not be a trustworthy narrator, but the body doesn't lie. If you're able to develop a practice of quietening your mind more routinely, you'll be more present in your daily life, and in turn more open to growth and abundance. Second, this full Moon absolutely will highlight what aspects of your daily routine may not be supportive of your heart and/or heart chakra. Audit your routines and evaluate them both physically and spiritually to see if there are changes that need to be made.

Happy Birthday! Your solar season begins on the 18th, with the new Moon following on the 27th. New year, new you! The new Moon is all about ushering in new beginnings with regard to how you navigate life and talk to yourself. Identify three words you seek to embody this year and integrate them into meditation, journal prompts or affirmation routines. Allow yourself to explore why you seek to embody these words and be open to delving into what is blocking you presently from this embodiment.

March

Best Days Overall: 27–30
Most Stressful Days Overall: 1–3, 13–16
Best Days for Love: 4–8
Best Days for Money: 7–12
Best Days for Career: 21–25
Power Word: Expense

March has some of the most noteworthy astrology of the year, Pisces, so let's dive right in! On March 1 Venus turns retrograde in Aries. Venus rules personal finances, values and self-worth. When Venus is retrograde, we embody 're-' words around Venus-ruled concepts. For you, Pisces, this is a financial transit. Aries is a sign focused on assertion and getting its needs met. This retrograde will spur you to reflect on whether you're being as financially compensated as you should be. Also, this retrograde will encourage you to take a look at your budget and make sure you really understand all the ways money enters and exits your accounts.

Boom! The first eclipse of 2025 occurs on March 14 in Virgo, your polar sign, so transits in Virgo typically have a relationship orientation to them for Pisces. Eclipses are evolutionary transits that typically promote growth through tension or shake-ups, and this one will catalyse much-needed conversations with those you're closest to. This is because Mercury also turns retrograde in Aries the day after the eclipse. There's a service orientation to

Virgo, so the eclipse will spotlight reciprocity in your relationships. Pisces isn't known for being innately adept at enforcing necessary boundaries with others, so as a result you should expect this eclipse to highlight whether it's appropriate for you to do so.

Aries' season begins on the 20th, the second eclipse of the month occurs in Aries on the 29th and Neptune moves into the sign for the first time in your lifetime on the 30th. So much Aries energy! Aries season is the annual transit where you're motivated to buy, buy, buy. The transit not only falls in Pisces' 2nd house, but occurs right after your birthday. Normally, there isn't much scrutiny around this transit, but with the Sun in Aries being joined by two retrogrades and now an eclipse, it's super-important you avoid gratuitous spending. There's no need to be hyper-frugal, just recognize that sustainability around finances is the name of the game. Neptune moving into your 2nd house encourages you to take stock of all the possessions you do have and lean into gratitude instead of just focusing on what you don't have.

April

Best Days Overall: 4-6, 10-12
Most Stressful Days Overall: 25-29
Best Days for Love: 16-20
Best Days for Money: 19-22
Best Days for Career: 8-11
Power Word: Communicate

Happy April, Pisces! The cosmic weather for the first week of this month features Venus in your sign forming a harmonious alignment with Mars in Cancer on the 5th. This transit is super-romantic and creative for you. Venus and Mars are working together, hyping you up right now. On April 7 Mercury ends its retrograde and turns direct, doing so in your sign, which is significant. This retrograde featured some serious communication and technology breakdowns, but expect these to clear up soon. Mercury traditionally rules commerce, so the fact that it turns direct is exceedingly important, given the full Moon occurring in a few days' time.

On April 12 there's a full Moon in Libra. This is financial for Pisces and centred around how other people influence your financial well-being. Matters such as investments and debts are very much under the spotlight at this time, particularly as Venus turns direct on this day, complementing the fiscal nature of this lunation. Given that Venus is especially slow-moving this week, it's a good idea for any Pisces to embrace frugality for a few more weeks. Venus turning direct does give the green light for bold investment moves later in the month.

On April 19 Taurus' season begins. The Sun in Taurus is always a time in which your patterns of communication are spotlit. Did the Mercury retrograde bring to your attention how your typical methods of communication limit you? This Taurus season spurs you to take what you learned from the Mercury retrograde and make supportive changes. The last week of the month features the new Moon in Taurus on the 27th, an ideal time to take these steps forward. However, Mars will be opposing Pluto, which can absolutely ruffle people's feathers, so be mindful around confrontation on this day. Venus enters Aries on the 30th, a transit that while financial in nature for Pisces, is more focused on your spending habits. Venus in Aries functions like an invitation to start taking action on matters related to your stream of income.

May

Best Days Overall: 1–5, 22–24
Most Stressful Days Overall: 12–18
Best Days for Love: 2–7
Best Days for Money: 21–25
Best Days for Career: 5–10
Power Word: Haven

It's May, Pisces! The astrology for this month begins with Venus and Neptune conjoining on the 2nd in Aries. This transit is soft and ethereal, but not grounded. In fact, it especially can facilitate rose-coloured glasses for you, Pisces. Be mindful around your spending on this date because this transit falls in Pisces' 2nd house of money, an ideal time to create! Do some painting, drawing, sculpting, gardening, whatever takes your fancy. On May 6 Venus and Pluto support one another in a transit that encourages you to carve out some time to recharge and reflect. Although creative energy is still very much in the air, it may be best to take a break as a means of grounding.

The full Moon in Scorpio occurs on May 12 just as Mercury and Neptune tensely aspect one another. This full Moon is spiritual and educational for Pisces. One powerful way to honour this lunation is through carving out a sanctuary space you can retreat to when you feel overwhelmed, or use as the place where you enjoy your routine spiritual practice. Pisces is a mutable water sign that's heavily affected by its environment. This sanctuary space would function as a detox room and a haven of sorts.

Gemini's season begins on May 20, followed by Mercury entering Gemini on the 25th and the new Moon in the sign on the 26th. That's a lot of Gemini energy! Gemini is Pisces' 4th house of home and family dynamics. This new Moon is the ideal lunation for home-improvement projects, redecoration or feng shui work. Moreover, this new Moon is a perfect time to communicate with family and get anything that needs to be released off your chest. In the midst of this confluence of Gemini energy, Saturn enters Aries on May 24, ushering in a 2½-year period for you to audit how you make money and ensure your money grows, as well as providing a great opportunity for you to consult a licensed professional or take a course on fiscal responsibility. Saturn rules consequences and rewards, so by evolving in your relationship to your finances, you could see a payout from Saturn after this audit is finished.

June

Best Days Overall: 2-6
Most Stressful Days Overall: 17-23
Best Days for Love: 4-8
Best Days for Money: 25-28
Best Days for Career: 7-11
Power Word: Culmination

Hi, Pisces! On June 6 Venus first moves into its home sign of Taurus. Venus in Taurus supports Pisces' communication through allowing you to get more in touch with the values that inform your patterns of communication. On June 9 Jupiter enters Cancer. This is significant because your career planet spends about a full year in each sign, so there's a noticeable change in energy. Jupiter in Cancer is centred around pleasure and splendour for Pisces, it will demand you make room for play in your weekly routine and it's also an ideal transit in which to work on developing creative pursuits. Once again, Jupiter will spend many months in Cancer, so there's no need to feel like you need to conquer all your creative goals immediately – you might well need to pace yourself until the end of this horoscope.

On June 11 the full Moon in Sagittarius represents a culmination of all the work you've been putting into your career for the last six months. This lunation shines its light on whether you're still on track to achieve those career goals you envisioned for yourself a year ago or if the vision itself needs to be amended. Mars enters Virgo, your polar sign, on the 17th, a transit that brings a boost of kinetic energy in the realm of relationships for Pisces. If you're single, this is the time there's energy for you to tap into dating and partnership. If you've got a partner, this transit can rev things up. It's important to note that Mars rules conflict, so be mindful around potential arguments being spurred by Mars' transit.

Cancer's season begins on the 20th. Remember when I said there might be a need to pace yourself? Well, the Sun immediately squares off with Saturn and Neptune on the 22nd and 23rd, possibly making you feel exasperated by all you're seeking to achieve or with managing all of your responsibilities. So really do pace your-self, Pisces. Don't allow yourself to equate your worth with how productive you are. If you're really feeling the slowdown around this date, allow yourself the time to pause and recharge. The new Moon in Cancer on the 25th will help you to refuel and reset.

July

Best Days Overall: 27–31
Most Stressful Days Overall: 18–22
Best Days for Love: 6–10
Best Days for Money: 24–28
Best Days for Career: 2–6
Power Word: Quality

Venus takes all the focus for the start of July, Pisces. Venus high fives Uranus on the 4th at the very last degree of Taurus and then proceeds to shift into Gemini on the same day. Venus in Gemini is a social transit, and with Uranus' influence there's an added element of spontaneity and surprise. For Pisces, this transit particularly encourages quality time with family members and those you live with. Venus then finds harmony with Saturn, Neptune and Pluto over the 6th and 7th. These soft aspects only reinforce the themes of Venus in Gemini. On the 7th there's a *big* transit. Uranus moves into Gemini for the first time since it left the sign in 1949. This transit will lead to society-changing techno-logical innovations around how we communicate and approach learning.

On July 10 the Moon is full and in Capricorn. This lunation spot-lights the structure of the groups, organizations and communities you're immersed in. For organizations, this full Moon scrutinizes the sustainability of the existing structures or hierarchies they have in place and how you fit into them holistically. Also, evaluate if you're receiving the same type of support you're providing the groups or communities you're involved in. On July 18 Mercury turns retrograde again, which has all the potential to create communication breakdowns, especially around listening. If you feel as though you have been misinterpreted, it's vital you are as clear as possible in what you're trying to get across. Furthermore, it's equally important not to operate on untested assumptions during this retrograde.

Leo's season begins with a loud roar on the 22nd. Within the first three days of this solar season, the Sun aspects five planets, all of which are included in the new Moon chart that occurs on the 24th. This lunation has a universal theme about owning our authenticity. For you, Pisces, there's an added element of how your physical wellness may suffer as a result of not living 100 per cent authentically. Scrutinize the correlation between whether aspects of your identity aren't true to you and if they affect you physically. New Moons bring new cycles, and this lunation promotes you embracing your individuality.

August

Best Days Overall: 11–15
Most Stressful Days Overall: 5–9
Best Days for Love: 29–31
Best Days for Money: 16–20
Best Days for Career: 1–4
Power Word: Embrace

Hi, Pisces! The theme for this month concerns mental health, spirituality and wellness, more specifically self-compassion and isolation. First up is self-compassion. On August 1 Venus squares off with both Saturn and Neptune. This cosmic weather typically causes your internal monologue to turn extra-harsh towards yourself. The key with this tough transit is to not ignore this uptick in negative self-talk or to dissociate, but rather to stay right in the present moment and meet that voice with a louder pitch of self-compassion. Neptune's influence can absolutely inspire dissociative behaviour, so definitely give yourself the necessary TLC this first week of the month without resorting to unsupportive coping behaviours.

On the 9th the full Moon in Aquarius highlights your relationship to isolation. Isolating is sometimes the best thing for a Pisces when it comes to getting much-needed rejuvenation after a hectic period. However, too much isolation isn't sustainable for the psyche either. Allow this lunation to spotlight how isolation plays a role in your mental wellness routines. Do you need to carve out more alone time? Do you need to put yourself out there socially a bit more? This full Moon contains Mars facing off with Saturn and Neptune. This transit can make you feel restless, but the key is to embrace moving slowly and surrendering to what isn't in your locus of control. Thankfully, Mercury ends its retrograde on the 11th and Venus harmoniously meets up with Jupiter on the 12th. This Venus–Jupiter transit is especially romantic and creative for Pisces. If you're choosing to lean into solo time, treat this as an opportunity to embrace one of your favourite forms of creativity. If you're choosing to lean into being more social, this transit will work with you to go on a fun date with someone special.

Virgo's season begins on the 22nd, and a relationship-oriented new Moon for Pisces follows the next day. The new Moon in Virgo spurs you to analyse the reciprocity in your closest relationships. New Moons usher in new beginnings, with this lunation encouraging a new chapter of equity in your dearest one-to-one relationships. Mercury is direct, supporting constructive conversations with others.

September

Best Days Overall: 16–20
Most Stressful Days Overall: 7–11
Best Days for Love: 19–23
Best Days for Money: 1–5
Best Days for Career: 27–30
Power Word: Roots

Hi, Pisces! Remember in your yearly horoscope when I said this is a very important year? Well, September is a super-influential month for you. First, Saturn retrogrades back into your sign one last time on the 1st. The last three years have featured a maturation of your sense of self, and this is the last phase of this transit for you. Even more notably, it's eclipse season this month. The first eclipse occurs on the 7th in your sign. This eclipse centres around liberating yourself from aspects of your identity that no longer serve you or even apply. The cosmic weather is tense, but in an effort to get you to embody who you truly desire to become. Heads up – eclipses in your sign tend to be especially stressful, so double up on self-compassion and don't overexert yourself this month.

The second eclipse of September occurs on the 21st and is a new Moon solar eclipse in Virgo. This is technically the second new Moon in Virgo, so it's the second new Moon to centre around partnership for Pisces. As a result, this eclipse amplifies the theme of last month's new Moon, which was all about identifying reciprocity in partnership. If you've got a partner, this eclipse can function as a make-or-break transit. By this I mean that if your relationship is built on a solid foundation of mutual support, this eclipse has the potency to substantially deepen its roots. On the other hand, if there are issues surrounding an imbalance of support that have long been ignored, this eclipse will bring them abruptly to the surface for you to deal with. If you're single, this eclipse could very well catalyse a new-found partnership or put you in situations that force you to confront your emotional availability around partnership.

Libra's season begins on the 22nd. This is a financial time of year for Pisces, with the focus being on how your money is merged with or supported by others. The first week of Libra season features the Sun aspecting every planet from Saturn to Pluto. These transits position you to enforce much-needed boundaries around finances with others. Moreover, if flagrant spending is a vice, these transits will spur you to identify sustainable ways to curtail this behaviour.

October

Best Days Overall: 27-31
Most Stressful Days Overall: 21-25
Best Days for Love: 3-7
Best Days for Money: 4-8
Best Days for Career: 15-19
Power Word: Dynamic

Happy October, Pisces! I hope you're doing well after the eclipse in your sign. This month's astrology begins on the 6th with the full Moon in Aries, a transit that serves as a financial check-in to the themes present in the wake of the March new Moon solar eclipse in Aries. The theme of the cosmic weather at that time was about striking a balance between spending and saving. How's that going, Pisces? Have you adopted a more well-considered budget in the last six months? Has your budget changed noticeably in that time? This full Moon functions as a stopping point to check in with yourself if you need to make any adjustments, as well as being a cosmic invitation to double-check the health of any parts of your finances that you may have lost sight of.

The theme around finances continues into the second week of the month, with Venus forming several aspects between the 11th and the 15th and changing signs into Libra on the 13th. The focus of the cosmic weather shifts from your relationship to your money to how other people influence or affect your financial well-being. This could involve changes in the dynamic with your financial dependants, or simply receiving money from others – or giving it to them – more frequently around this time. The new Moon in Libra on the 21st ushers in a new emotional cycle around how other people affect your income. This is an excellent time to start thinking of new business ventures or, if you've already come up with an idea, taking a big step towards turning it into a reality.

The Sun enters Scorpio, your fellow water sign, on the 22nd. Scorpio season is a spiritual solar season for Pisces, so allow for the Sun's foray to illuminate new teachers or philosophies you can integrate into your spiritual value system. Take the opportunity during Scorpio season to spend time in spaces that connect you with the universe or your personal spirit. The month ends with a productive aspect between Mars and Jupiter on the 28th. These planets find harmony and facilitate a get-stuff-done energy for you during this last week of October.

November

Best Days Overall: 14-18
Most Stressful Days Overall: 8-12
Best Days for Love: 21-25
Best Days for Money: 17-21
Best Days for Career: 3-7
Power Word: Learning

Happy November, Pisces! The theme for this month centres around career and legacy - no big deal! The astro-weather kicks off on the 4th with Mars moving into Sagittarius. This is the first of the career sector transits and it's noteworthy, as Mars only enters a sign every two years. This transit works to jump-start what you're meant to do in order to cement your legacy. Mars is also associated with breaking things apart, so don't be alarmed if certain aspects of your career or what you're striving for fall away over the next six weeks. Mars is all about kinetic energy and drive, so now is the time to really pound the pavement when it comes to achieving your goals. The full Moon in Taurus occurs one day later and spotlights how secure you feel about speaking your truth. Given the Sagittarian energy building, this is especially the case within career contexts. Allow this lunation to show you where you can be more assertive and maybe where you need to be more methodical with your speech.

Speaking of which, Mercury, the planet of communication, turns retrograde one last time on the 9th. This transit will prompt you to reflect on your 2025 career goals and what you've accomplished, as well as what is rolling over to next year. Are your career goals still the same as they were in January of this year? Sagittarius' energy is all about the big vision. As usual, this transit makes communication wonky, and this is especially the case for you at work. Make sure you clarify any misunderstandings, and don't express any opinions founded on unexamined assumptions! On the 17th the grand water trine between the Sun, Jupiter and Saturn is exact. This is a beautifully harmonious transit supporting self-improvement. The Sun rules creative self-expression and is receiving support from Jupiter, the planet of growth, and Saturn, the planet of structure. Work with this transit by identifying up to three action items you can execute before the end of the year that will help further your career development or contribute to cementing your legacy.

Scorpio's season ends with its new Moon on the 20th. This lunation especially supports you if you're seeking to go back to college, get a certification or embark on some independent research. This lunation also supports travel for the sake of gaining perspective if you're in the middle of making some big decisions. Sagittarius' season begins on the 21st, bringing even more focus to your career and legacy. Once again, now is the time to start formulating those 2026 goals. A great way to honour this transit is through creating a vision board for what you seek to accomplish next year.

December

Best Days Overall: 1–5
Most Stressful Days Overall: 10–14
Best Days for Love: 24–28
Best Days for Money: 16–20
Best Days for Career: 19–23
Power Word: Beginnings

It's December, Pisces! This year has been super-pivotal for Pisces, so congratulations on navigating all the cosmic weather. Now, let's jump into the last month of 2025! The full Moon in Gemini starts the astrology of December off on the 4th. This full Moon spotlights home and family dynamics for Pisces. Gemini is all about embodying duality, and this lunation illuminates whether you're able to strike a balance between your public and private lives. Gemini is the communicator, so it's vitally important that if you feel a little extra-emotional around this date, you talk about it with someone and don't bottle it up.

There's also a cosmic slowdown caused by Mars and Saturn experiencing tension with one another. This transit is notorious for making you feel like you're stuck in traffic. With Mars still in Sagittarius, this very likely revolves around what it's possible to achieve within your career, as this transit forces you to grapple with and surrender to what is and isn't within the bounds of your control. Thankfully, the slowdown fades and Mars enters methodical Capricorn on the 15th. This transit jump-starts your social life and encourages you to spend quality time with friends as a means of recharging your metaphorical batteries. Mars in Capricorn is also very much associated with strategizing and goal-making. Treat this transit as an invitation to ground yourself in your 2026 goals.

The new Moon in Sagittarius is a breath of fresh air after that Mars–Saturn transit. This lunation occurs on the 19th and invites you to usher in new beginnings around your career. Last month's Mercury retrograde had you reflecting on all things related to your legacy. This new Moon offers you the opportunity to pursue exciting new beginnings in order to make a big step towards embodying who you want to become. If you're happy on your current path, this new Moon has a sky's-the-limit energy that supports big-picture envisioning. Capricorn's season begins on the 21st and Venus enters the sign on the 24th. These transits join Mars in Capricorn and further emphasize the importance of being uplifted by your community. You've grown so much this year and have big goals to chase in 2026 – don't forget it takes a village, Pisces.

Acknowledgements

I firstly would like to express my profound gratitude to the people of STAR ★ DATA, who truly fathered this book and without whom it could not have been written.

Thank you to Rachel Lang, my dear friend and incredible colleague, for believing in me.

Thank you to my parents and brother for their unconditional support.

And thank you to Megan, the person who introduced me to astrology. I'm so grateful.